# MILITARY MASCULINITY AND POSTWAR RECOVERY IN THE SOVIET UNION

ERICA L. FRASER

# Military Masculinity and Postwar Recovery in the Soviet Union

UNIVERSITY OF TORONTO PRESS
Toronto Buffalo London

Toronto Buffalo London
utorontopress.com

ISBN 978-1-4426-3720-7

Publication cataloguing information is available from Library and Archives Canada.

This book has been published with the help of a grant from the Federation for the Humanities and Social Sciences, through the Awards to Scholarly Publications Program, using funds provided by the Social Sciences and Humanities Research Council of Canada.

University of Toronto Press acknowledges the financial assistance to its publishing program of the Canada Council for the Arts and the Ontario Arts Council, an agency of the Government of Ontario.

Canada Council for the Arts | Conseil des Arts du Canada

# Contents

# Illustrations

# Acknowledgments

I am grateful to have the opportunity to thank the many people who have helped make this book possible. This project has been with me a long time. It has travelled with me to four universities and at least that many different cities in Canada, the United States, and Russia. At each stop, I have had the great fortune to work with some incredible scholars, students, librarians, and archivists, all of whom helped me in numerous ways.

I began considering the question of historical masculinities at the University of British Columbia in the late 1990s, a time of exciting new research in the field. Anne Gorsuch was instrumental in directing my early research and encouraging my interest in cultural history and sources. At the University of Illinois at Urbana-Champaign, I was fortunate to have the opportunity to work among an extraordinary group of faculty and fellow students in Russian history. I am particularly indebted to Diane Koenker, who created an ideal intellectual environment that was both supportive and challenging. She always encouraged my ideas and the project as a whole while also asking all the tough questions, and this project has been much improved by my attempts to answer even a fraction of them. Mark Steinberg's support and mentorship has also meant a great deal to me. His critiques of several early drafts of this project helped shape its final form.

Also at the University of Illinois, John Randolph and Antoinette Burton helped me think about both Russian history and gender history in new ways. Mark Micale and Kristin Hoganson encouraged me to think broadly about the scope of this project within global masculinity studies. John Lynn aided my understanding of military history, from correcting my mistakes about command structures to engaging in broader conversations with me about the methods and sources particular to that field. The staff at the Slavic Library at the University of Illinois are, without question, the very best in the field and provided much needed assistance, both in Urbana and long after I left. My cherished writing circle read more drafts of my work than I can count. I am grateful for the friendship as well as the intellectual support of Danielle Kinsey, Amanda Brian, Randall Dills, and Nathan Clarke.

I would also like to thank my colleagues in Soviet and East European history who have offered input and asked questions about my research. The members of the *Russkii kruzhok* and participants in several workshops at the Russian, East European, and Eurasian Center at the University of Illinois engaged with my work at various stages. Portions of this research have been presented over several years at the American Association for the Advancement of Slavic Studies and the (renamed) Association for Slavic, East European, and Eurasian Studies; the Berkshire Conference for Women's History; and the Congress of the Humanities and Social Sciences, and I thank participants at my sessions for comments that helped shape my research. In particular, Mark Edele has discussed DOSAAF and the postwar army with me, Roshanna Sylvester has offered insight on the cosmonauts, and I have benefited from several conversations with Karen Petrone and Catherine Baker about Russian masculinities. Claire McCallum kindly shared her book manuscript with me while it was in press. Christine Varga-Harris has been a key friend and mentor who has provided welcome professional advice and encouragement. At Goucher College in Baltimore, I was privileged to join a formidable cohort of women who were hired at the same time as me in a variety of humanities and social sciences disciplines and helped to cultivate a wonderful working environment. Sabbatical leave from Goucher also allowed me to return to Moscow and to continue writing.

In Russia, I am grateful to the many librarians and archivists who helped make my research possible. Like many of my colleagues who have spent time at the Komsomol reading room of the Russian State Archive for Social-Political History (RGASPI), I had the good fortune to work with Galina Mikhailovna Tokareva. Her knowledge of the collection, her friendliness, and her famous midday tea parties made my time there not only productive but enjoyable. I am also thankful for her assistance in gaining entry to the Russian State Archive for Scientific and Technical Documentation (RGANTD), where the staff was tremendously helpful and facilitated my access to several personal fonds. My thanks as well to the staff at the State Archive of the Russian Federation (GARF), the Russian State Library, and the Institute of Scientific Information on the Social Sciences (INION, now sadly closed). Olga Skatchkova, Margaret Peacock, Sean Guillory, Maya Haber, and Greg Kveberg, among others in the foreign historians' community, provided welcome companionship and collegiality in Moscow. Research for this project was supported by grants from the Social Sciences and Humanities Research Council of Canada and the Graduate College and Department of History at the University of Illinois.

Most of this book was written and revised in Ottawa. Jeff Sahadeo and Achim Hurrelmann gave me a home at the Institute of European, Russian, and Eurasian Studies at Carleton University, where I have benefited from access to scholars and students from a variety of disciplines. In the Department of History, Dominique Marshall found space for me to teach Soviet cultural and Cold War history, through which I met some incredibly thoughtful students as I worked through many of the ideas in this book. Susanne Klausen supplied crucial support at the proposal stage, without which the rest of the book might never have gotten off the ground. Susan Whitney read through the final manuscript with a fierce red pen. Michel Hogue has provided friendship and encouragement as well as writing and publishing advice. At the Carleton Library, Christine Taylor has been a tremendous help in securing obscure Soviet sources and other materials from outside Ottawa, without which I would not have been able to finish the book. My thanks to my research assistants as well: Eva Rogaar helped me find high-quality versions of the *Krokodil* cartoons analysed throughout the book; Oleg Schindler read and offered translation assistance for some military fiction written in a mix of Russian and Ukrainian; and Kateryna Pashchenko watched several Soviet war films and helped me decipher some particular turns of phrase.

At the University of Toronto Press, I am grateful to Richard Ratzlaff for his advice and his confidence in the project overall from the proposal through the first draft. Stephen Shapiro shepherded the book through its subsequent drafts and final publication with patience and encouragement. I would also like to thank Marilyn McCormack, Breanna Muir, Suzanne Rancourt, and the many people behind the scenes who have worked on my book. The Awards to Scholarly Publishing Program helped to finance the book's publication. Finally, I owe a tremendous debt to the two anonymous reviewers who went above and beyond in providing me with detailed notes and challenging questions across multiple drafts. Their deep engagement with my work is much appreciated, and the final product is infinitely richer because of it. All remaining errors and limitations are, of course, entirely my own.

Some of the material in this book first appeared in the following: "Masculinity in the Personal Narratives of Soviet Nuclear Physicists," *Aspasia* 8 (2014), 45–63; and "Yuri Gagarin and Celebrity Masculinity in Soviet Culture," in *Gender, Sexuality, and the Cold War*, ed. Philip E. Muehlenbeck (Nashville, 2017), 270–89. My thanks to Berghahn Books and Vanderbilt University Press for permission to reprint materials from those publications.

Finally, I find it impossible to express how much my partner has meant to me throughout this process. Danielle has been with this project since the beginning, and absolutely none of it would have been possible without her. Monty, the T-Rex of the chihuahuas, joined us a bit later on but has also put his own stamp on my work, taking writing breaks with his parents for our long walks through the central Illinois cornfields, up to the shops on Charles Street, and along the Rideau River. This is for my family.

# A Note on Transliteration

Unless otherwise stated, the translations from Russian throughout this book are my own. Throughout I use the Library of Congress system of transliteration. Occasional deviations from the LOC system exist for one of three reasons: the name is particularly well known (i.e., Yuri Gagarin instead of Iurii); the spelling I chose represents an effort to minimize confusion when the LOC transliteration would result in a word with a different meaning in English (i.e., Gherman Titov instead of German); or the name comes from a published English translation of a Russian source (i.e., Yakov Zeldovich instead of Iakov Zel'dovich). In chapter 3, I have translated Russian versions of European and American names into (or back into) English as accurately as I could discern for each individual (i.e., Adenauer, Tsaldaris, Wiley).

MILITARY MASCULINITY AND POSTWAR RECOVERY IN THE SOVIET UNION

# Introduction

On the evening of 22 November 1955 a pivotal moment occurred in the life of physicist Andrei Sakharov. He had a full glass of brandy and was comfortably seated at a banquet to honour the scientists who had developed the hydrogen bomb, which had been successfully tested for the first time earlier that day. He was not yet the famous international figure he would become. (A decade later, his work in nuclear physics, which had earned him renown in the Soviet military, would matter less to Western observers than his pacifist, dissident role opposing nuclear weapons as well as government censorship and control of Soviet intellectuals.) That evening he attended the dinner proud of the work he and his colleagues had done to advance science. He was a physicist, an intellectual, a colleague, a mentor to some and student to others, a faithful husband and doting father – all respectable masculinized identities in postwar Soviet society. But he was never a soldier, never part of the official military establishment that would decide when and where his scientific achievement, the hydrogen bomb, would be used. He felt impotent, permitted to invent but not control the invention, to help a war effort but not direct the weapons. His host that evening, Marshal Mitrofan Nedelin, was quite the opposite. A Hero of the Soviet Union for his Second World War service, a veteran of the Civil War of 1918–21, and deputy minister of defence at the time of the banquet in late 1955, Nedelin was a career military man. Sakharov later described him as "a thickset, stocky man who spoke softly but with a confidence that brooked no objection."[1]

Increasingly concerned about the military implications of the hydrogen bomb, Sakharov chose the banquet that night to make a stand, however brief, on the matter. He offered a toast: "May all our devices explode as successfully as today's, but always over test sites and never over cities." Nedelin and the rest of the room fell silent; then he rose, grinning at Sakharov, and held up his glass. "Let me tell a parable," began Nedelin. "An old man wearing only a shirt was praying before an icon. 'Guide me, harden me. Guide me, harden me.' His wife, who was lying on the stove, said: 'Just pray to be hard, old man, I can guide it in myself.' Let's drink to getting hard." Sakharov interpreted the parable as a commentary on the traditional Soviet chain of command, on his readiness for the particular battles of the Cold War should they come, and on his masculinity. "My whole body tensed, and I think I turned pale," he later wrote. "Many years have passed, but I still feel as if I had been lashed by a whip. Not that my feelings were hurt; I am not easily offended, especially by a joke. But Nedelin's parable was not a joke. He wanted to squelch my pacifist sentiment, and to put me and anyone who might share these ideas in our place."[2]

Historians of Soviet science and the intelligentsia have noted this story before, but always as a metaphor for the Communist Party's confirmation of its hierarchical approach to science research. Yuri Slezkine cites it to demonstrate Sakharov's emerging awareness that "the Party claimed the right to make all decisions about everything."[3] Istvan Harggitai writes that Nedelin must have decided to tell this "lewd parable" to show that scientists "were expected to make discoveries and produce bombs, but there should not even be a pretense that they might have a word in decision making."[4] Gerard J. De Groot calls Nedelin's words simply "an off-colour joke" meant to show Sakharov that scientists, again, were "not supposed to concern themselves with how their discoveries might be used."[5] Alexei Kojevnikov goes furthest in addressing the meanings of employing such sexualized language for a parable, noting that Nedelin used a "sexual allegory" to get his point across because the idea that Sakharov could challenge the party on the uses of this new weapon was as "unmentionable in serious public discussion" as sex would have been.[6] None of these accounts, however, take seriously the idea that Nedelin's "joke" – and Sakharov's narration of it – was grounded in specific postwar understandings and performances of masculinity and martial authority.

Nedelin could have chosen different words to chastise Sakharov for his fear of the potential military uses of the hydrogen bomb but instead chose to compare pacifism to sexual impotence. The historian does not often find such overtly sexualized language in Soviet public discourse, which may help explain why there are not many historical studies of the postwar and Cold War Soviet gender order. This one example, however, offers more than just the use of colourful language to convey a point about a hierarchy long familiar in the Soviet power structure. It was more than a metaphor about power in the Soviet system. Rather, it illustrates the particularly gendered nature of Soviet culture after the Second World War, at a moment when the renewal of an ideal of military masculinity that had been damaged by the war was at stake. Nedelin was nineteen years Sakharov's senior and a veteran of several wars, whereas Sakharov had received a student deferment from service. On this occasion the seasoned veteran took the opportunity to correct the young idealist scientist in the ways of military masculinity by asserting that he, Nedelin, was the more virile man. (With a subtle rhetorical flourish, Sakharov followed this story in his memoirs by pointing out that Nedelin was killed, violently and senselessly, when a planned intercontinental ballistic missile [ICBM] test went awry in 1960.)[7]

Sakharov's anecdote anchors the themes of this book, which investigates the ways in which Soviet policymakers attempted to reinvigorate military masculinity in the first two decades after the destruction of the Second World War, and how Soviet boys and men interpreted, acted on, and even repackaged those prescriptions in their own narratives. Despite the Soviet Union's victory, the war cost the country 27 million combatants and civilians – more than the losses of all other participating countries combined. Twenty million Soviet men died in the war.[8] The first postwar census, delayed until nearly fifteen years after the war out of fear of publicizing these startling numbers both at home and to Cold War rivals, revealed that there were only 74 men for every 100 women in the Soviet Union, with the number even lower in some age groups.[9] Yet demographics alone do not signify that a society is, or should be, preoccupied with gender identities; the processes by which masculinities and femininities are constructed, performed, and renegotiated shift and circulate according to myriad cultural factors.

This book explores the ways in which these processes aimed to re-establish military masculinity as a dominant cultural form. Reaching this goal involved a commitment by those in power in the Soviet Union to reforge the links between service and manliness that had characterized the military before the war but had been disrupted and decoupled through the wartime service of women (as well as teenagers, the elderly, ordinary farmers armed with pitchforks – essentially anyone who could fight). By investigating masculinity and military culture, the book analyses how and why the Soviet government set about reclaiming postwar martial spaces for men. Half a million women served in the Soviet military between 1941 and 1945, at least 120,000 of them in combat roles.[10] As Anna Krylova has written, the necessities of this extraordinary mobilization involved a "regendering of the Soviet military – turning exclusively male spaces and identities into mixed and shared ones."[11] As women's contributions became better publicized in the press by 1943, writers even had to adjust their assumptions and specify, when using the word "soldier," whether the subject was a female soldier (*zhenshchina-soldat*) or a male soldier (*muzhshchina-soldat*).[12] Despite exemplary service in all fields, including combat, Soviet women were demobilized quickly at the end of 1945 and were not permitted to re-enlist.[13] Soviet history has seen this pattern of remasculinizing military roles after women's wartime service before: following the Civil War, which had included the military participation of women in Russia and its borderlands, Stalinist culture of the 1930s reemphasized soldiering among men.[14] The Second World War, however, which dwarfed the already brutal Civil War, required an even broader postwar recovery effort to recalibrate codes of martial masculinity. This effort would thoroughly rebuke the service of women to an even greater degree than had occurred in the 1920s and 1930s.

The themes examined in the following chapters include postwar conscription and evasion anxieties, military education and establishing appropriate role models for adolescent boys, misogyny in cartoons about foreign militaries, nuclear science research spaces, and cosmonaut publicity. In each of these areas, government agents sought to clarify and reinforce notions of masculinized Soviet fortitude that they feared were undermined by high male casualties and women's service in the war. Because women were no longer allowed to serve in the military – a restriction that also affected the perception of their qualifications to embark on militarized Cold War work such as nuclear physics research or space flight – conversations about martial identities required talking about masculinity. By talking about it, policymakers signalled deep unease with the postwar gender order in Soviet society, in which disproportionate numbers of male war deaths had led to the highly visible fact that, in the countryside and the cities, in private and public, the Soviet Union had become a country of women.[15] If that fact could not be corrected demographically, perhaps it could be done by reconnecting masculinity and military service.

Two postwar cartoons in the popular satirical journal *Krokodil* (The Crocodile) exemplify the shift in cultural narratives away from women's service. In a 1946 cartoon set at a planetarium, two elderly women sat together. "What are you looking at?" one asked, to which the other replied, "The stars." The second woman was gazing with fondness not above her, however, but at the row behind her. There sat a younger woman in uniform, with two stars displayed prominently on her coat (Fig. I.1).[16] Ten years later, *Krokodil* pointed out that women could only be seen to masquerade as soldiers: in a series

Figure I.1 At the Planetarium
"What are you looking at?"
"The stars."

*Krokodil*, 30 April 1946, 15.

of cartoons in 1957 showcasing the silliness of the carnival world, where nothing is what it seems on the surface, an old, hobbled man removed his mask to reveal that he was in fact young and strong. Meanwhile, a knight in shining armour removed its helmet to reveal an equally absurd sight: a beautiful young woman (Fig. I.2).[17] The mockery of women in military roles also took an uglier turn for many women veterans, as they faced accusations and assumptions in postwar society about their sexual availability, as a means of downplaying their combat achievements.[18] *Krokodil* will be discussed at length in chapter 3, and in moments throughout the other chapters, as a key vehicle for the transmission of martial masculine ideas in Soviet culture.

It is often taken for granted in writing about the Soviet Union's militarized society that the state's goal was the socialization of young men. Yet even among gender scholars, that assumption has not been routinely parsed. Ellen Jones' germinal 1985 study of Soviet military sociology asserts as a matter of course that military service was a "rite-of-passage for adolescent males" that played a key role in men's socialization.[19] Jones' observations are worth quoting extensively, because this book is premised on unpacking the sentiments she takes as a given. Writing in the 1980s, Jones noted:

> The predominance of women in the Soviet school system and the active participation of Soviet highschool [*sic*] girls in school leadership means that the typical Soviet male is socialized in an environment dominated, qualitatively and quantitatively, by females. The conscript tour is generally the first sustained contact of young men with an all-male environment; and Soviet officials stress its importance in providing male role models and instilling masculinity. From this perspective Soviet officials may feel that use of servicewomen on a large scale would undermine the all-male environment of the service experience, and weaken a key aspect of the armed forces' socialization role.[20]

Similarly, sociologist Marina Yusupova writes that "the post-war years were a time when military service, obligatory for all able-bodied men in the USSR, was promoted as a sacred duty of Soviet citizenship and the main school of masculinity."[21] She then moves on to analyse interview data about men and military identities during the Afghanistan war and in post-Soviet Russia. But what does it mean not only for a military command structure but for broader forces in society to raise men in

Figure I.2 At the Carnival

*Krokodil*, 10 August 1957, 11.

military masculinity? Militarism is not intrinsically linked to masculinity; that connection must be repeatedly forged by societies committed to building and maintaining it.

In that sense, Sakharov's tense relationship with Nedelin was much more than what it appears – a pacifist, civilian scientist, who had not served in the Second World War, frightened of the patriarchal power wielded by a decorated military man. Masculinized power dynamics interacted not as a tug-of-war between "soft" and "hard," as Sakharov characterized it, but as a network of identities whose advantages and disadvantages constantly shifted. Sakharov's concern about his "hardness," and that one point of contact between Sakharov's and Nedelin's masculinities at the banquet in 1955, is not the entire story. It only serves as the entry point into the broader story about military masculinities and Soviet postwar identities told in this book. Sakharov's voice is not necessarily unreliable, but his self-identification with wounded masculinity belongs on a spectrum. The "soft" scientist and "hard" marshal that Sakharov described were not the end result of postwar gender negotiations shaping Cold War–era military masculinities. Rather, they were part of continuing, dynamic conversations about masculine subjectivity and the resumed deployment of martial masculine identities to guide and protect postwar society taking place in Cold War military institutions and in Soviet culture more broadly between 1945 and the mid-1960s. Without reconstructing military masculinity and repudiating femininity in the armed forces, postwar recovery would remain fragile and incomplete.

**Soviet Masculinities**

After 1917, the Bolshevik revolutionaries built the new Soviet state according to particular scripts of masculinity. The foundational Civil War that cemented Bolshevik control of the government from 1918 to 1921 set the tone for the battle motifs and idealization of soldiering that followed in Soviet culture, and it influenced the valorization of healthy male bodies as national symbols in literature, art, and political posters. By the 1930s, Joseph Stalin successfully cultivated support for his dictatorship in part by playing up his paternal image as father-comrade of the state. Nationalism relied on the propaganda of masculinized heroes, from Vladimir Lenin and Leon Trotsky during the revolution and Civil War to the newly trained tractor drivers of the 1920s, the record-shattering coal miners of the 1930s, and the patriotic soldiers of the 1940s. Socialist iconography of the virile male worker thus combined with a pervasive patriarchy during the Stalin era to create a heavily masculinized – and militarized – political culture. Yet while scholars of imperial Russian and Soviet gender orders have contributed important research on masculinities since the field first rose to prominence in the 1990s, the topic has not become a regular or routine field of inquiry.[22] As Barbara Evans Clements argued in her introduction to the classic (and still the only) volume of essays on the subject in 2002, the imperial Russian and Soviet settings offer a unique view of the ways in which historical masculinities have been negotiated and performed. In particular, Clements notes that governments there had a firmer hand than their counterparts in the West in guiding masculine identity formations, as leaders were "intent on civilizing what they saw as the unruly masses of men by teaching them responsibility and self-discipline."[23] How these older patterns reasserted themselves after the Second World War, rebuilding military masculinity in new ways, have not yet been investigated.[24]

Any study of Soviet masculinities must take into account the unique place of women in socialism. Ideology regarding women's equality led to phenomena not widely seen in the West in the first half of the twentieth century, including the fact that most Soviet women worked outside the home and the state provided extensive social services for mothers. During the Second World War, moreover, Soviet women engaged in combat and maintained their communities on the home front in the absence of men. Othering, marginalizing, and excluding women from military service and its prescribed social identity was not a given in Soviet society, to be blamed, as was the case for the West, on systemic or capitalist inequality. Instead, as this book shows, that exclusion was a deliberate and ongoing process after 1945. Remarking the boundaries of gender categories that had become more fluid before and during the war was not confined to military institutions. Historians of the postwar era have begun to investigate ways that the Soviet government and society as a whole undertook the project of ensuring that women's extraordinary wartime roles did not go unchecked. For example, Philippa Hetherington has identified a "re-inscribing of traditional gender norms" and the "renewed pertinence of the gender binary" in postwar Soviet consumer culture.[25]

As historians of gender have argued, masculinity and war have no natural correlation; rather, the construction of one as contingent on the other is the result of specific historical processes.[26] In this book, I draw on Aaron Belkin's definition of martial masculinity as the "beliefs, practices and attributes that often have enabled individuals to claim a great deal of authority, perhaps more than any other form of masculinity, on the basis of their relationships with military institutions and ideas."[27] In the context of the Soviet Union after the Second World War, individual men claimed that authority far less than state institutions such as the Ministry of Defence and the Komsomol (Communist Youth League) wished they would. The degree to which individual actors had the opportunity to claim authority at all was also mediated by repression in Soviet society. Soviet military masculinity was shaped by both the needs of the state and the needs of the individual. War need not be on the horizon; martial identities are built not just for the future but in service to the past – in this case the Second World War. This connection played a decisive role in forming the policies and cultural agendas, pursued by those in power in military institutions after the war, that promoted men's – and abandoned women's – social and cultural conditioning for service.

Moreover, military masculinity need not be singular. As research in other contexts has shown, intersectional and diverse identities within general populations map themselves onto militaries as well.[28] As we will see throughout the book, many men – from conscripts to nuclear scientists – attempted to diversify the meanings of militarized masculinity in the Soviet Union after the war. However, state directives and cultural forces converged to undergird a singular vision of soldiering. The discrepancies between that hegemonic vision, and pluralities of masculine experiences and identities on the ground, will be explored throughout the following chapters. Policymakers' pursuit of an ideal Soviet military masculinity became a set of processes continually in motion, processes that created and included space for men's service but also shut down and excluded space for the participation of women. Soviet military authorities seeking to prescribe masculine behaviour after the war drew on deeply ingrained understandings of masculinized power dynamics not unfamiliar elsewhere in European history, particularly regarding the presumed hegemony of soldiering as a premier masculine identity. But in fashioning the meanings of service in the postwar world, the Soviet Union also had to work within its own specific context: the population's profound weariness of war, the deepening Cold War hostilities with the West, and the growing plurality in postwar society that increasingly offered young men the option of locating their identities, and authority, in nonmartial categories.

I hesitate to label these processes a "crisis" of masculinity or of the gender order. As Mary Louise Roberts has convincingly argued, the idea of masculinity in crisis has by now "been overworked to the point of semantic collapse."[29] Historiography on gender relations since the 1990s has focused in particular on gender instability in the wake of wars; for the twentieth century, this has meant highlighting the ways in which women taking on new roles in the public sphere, factory life, the corporate world, and even the military unsettled gender norms and displaced men serving at the front, leading to "crises" of masculinity when they returned. While this book is rooted in the adjustments military cultures undertook to correct the aberration of women's wartime service and to reclaim martial spaces for men, these processes are better characterized as transformation rather than crisis.[30]

No scholar of masculinities has done as much for the field, and generated as much provocative and crucial discussion, as Raewyn Connell. Her work shaped my introduction to gender studies and the history and sociology of masculinities as a graduate student and has influenced my thinking on the subject ever since; it thus maintains a firm footprint on this book.[31] While not importing it uncritically, I consider Connell's work on hegemonic masculinity in the 1990s a useful way to think about the persistence of Soviet tropes such as the New Soviet Man or, in military imagery, the Defender of the Motherland, and to examine how they reinforced and protected male power, even in a country like the Soviet Union with nominal gender equality. While dominant, those tropes were not simplistic; despite offering a clear model, these larger than life stereotypes for men were complex identities rife with contradictions and uncertainties, as we will see in the following chapters. Early Bolshevik attempts to distil permitted identities into categories like worker (and collective farm worker), soldier, party member, specialist, and so forth created for the historian a series of templates for analysing hegemonic masculinity. As Connell and James Messerschmidt wrote in clarifying the meaning of hegemonic masculinity in 2005, it "was understood as the pattern of practice (ie: things done, not just a set of role expectations or an identity) that allowed men's dominance over women to continue."[32] The dominant image of the Red Army serviceman in Soviet culture since the Civil War informs this book's focus on military masculinity rather than on other important gendered sites, such as masculinity and domesticity, consumerism, agriculture, sports, fatherhood, the performing arts, or on the shop floor, all of which still need far more research.[33]

Connell's critics have rightly pointed out that her concepts of hegemonic, subordinate, and complicit masculinity risk essentializing men, that they rely on heteronormative gender structures that privilege male–female difference and exclude other gender categories, and that they neglect to acknowledge the dynamic ways in which masculine practices borrow from each other to create "hybrid" forms "capable of reconfiguring [themselves] and adapting to the specificities of new historical conjectures."[34] This book explores the pursuit by military policymakers of a hegemonic martial masculinity. This exploration is not intended to define or endorse a particular static form of inquiry, but rather to provide a jumping off point for analysing how a society accustomed to prioritizing military masculinity dealt with the disruption to that ideal caused by a brutal war, and how that ideal was pursued anew – how hegemony as a relational form was reconfirmed and maintained – as part of postwar recovery narratives.

**The Soviet Union after the War**

In recent years, a number of excellent historical studies of postwar Soviet society and culture have emerged, many focusing on what has become known as the era of late Stalinism (from 1945 to the leader's death in 1953), others on the Khrushchev era after 1956, and all increasingly mindful that the years in between do not necessarily provide an easy periodization break. A particularly useful approach has been to study population groups on the margins of society – veterans, youth, prisoners, so-called hooligans, or gay men, for instance – in order to show, in part, that subcultures were not so far from the mainstream after all.[35] These studies show that, in a time when war had shaken up prewar Bolshevik social categories, Soviet society was in flux, with groups and individuals confronting major social shifts in their daily struggles to move forward and rebuild. The plight of Second World War veterans in particular has drawn important historical studies. Mark Edele has demonstrated the significance of veterans in successfully negotiating as an interest group for concessions from a government not accustomed to granting them. Robert Dale has focused on the reintegration of veterans in the city of Leningrad in the wake of the wartime blockade and postwar political purge there. Claire E. McCallum, one of the few postwar historians to discuss masculinity, has found that artistic representations of two particular Soviet archetypes, soldiers and fathers, shifted according to diverging needs in postwar culture.[36] Analysing the postwar re-establishment of military masculinity requires adjusting the timelines – late Stalinism, de-Stalinization, and the Thaw in postwar history – because the trajectory in which martial spaces were reclaimed for men after 1945 did not entirely fit these signposts. Distinct events, like Stalin's death in 1953, did result in obvious shifts. But at other times, continuity is more striking than change, as seen in *Krokodil*'s stunningly consistent reliance, over a period of twenty years, on cross-dressing as a symbol of masculine weakness (chapter 3), or in nuclear scientists' narratives of their encounters with state power (chapter 4).

Youth have provided another identity group attracting recent historical work. Young people were identified as markers of hope for rebuilding war-torn society but were simultaneously stigmatized for their lack of wartime service. Thus, they navigated a tense space in the late 1940s and 1950s. Authorities worried about stylishly dressed young men on the streets of Moscow – men whom Komsomol secretary A.N. Shelepin described in 1954 as "young people with Tarzan haircuts, dressed up like parrots, who molested girls and spent their nights in bars" – and enthusiasm for western dance crazes overtaking youth at factory clubs.[37] At the same time, the generation that came of age during and immediately after the war emerged from it eager to chart its own path. As Juliane Fürst has written, young people in late Stalinism "challenged the system's right to define what it meant to be young and Soviet."[38]

I join this conversation to examine masculinity not only through the lens of marginalized groups, but rather via the most dominant institution in Soviet society – the military. It is generally acknowledged in Soviet history that the armed forces were held in high esteem at home after the war. But this has led to the assumption that the elevation of Second World War soldiers in the Soviet imagination carried through the immediate postwar decades, with only the war in Afghanistan in the 1980s finally tarring that image, and looser state control under *glasnost'* leading to increased evasion and desertion beginning at that time.[39] However, this book argues that military authorities' concerns about men's postwar fitness for military participation and willingness to serve began much earlier, in the late 1940s. It also finds that any narrative promoting a hegemonic martial masculinity in Soviet culture after the war was largely a fantasy of policymakers, with Soviet society engaging in much more complex discourse about masculinity than the government might have wished, or could admit.

Part of this story involves youth, but the book also looks at men and images of masculinity in military institutions at several key points in the typical life cycle, including schooling, conscription call-ups, work, marriage, and fatherhood. Moreover, as we see in chapter 4, elderly men could be found reformulating their narratives about how their younger selves negotiated their identities in military-adjacent work. We also see generational cooperation and conflict involving students at military academies and their instructors, graduate students in physics and their laboratory mentors, a general and his cosmonaut charges, and, in cartoon form in chapter 3, the honourable young Soviet worker and the hunched, moustache-twirling old warmongers alleged to be running Western militaries.

Before introducing the specific subjects explored in the following chapters, one more important note is required. As an institution that built, maintained, and protected hegemonic masculine power structures, the Soviet military re-established postwar soldier masculinity in the aftermath of brutal war crimes: the widespread rape of German women by Red Army soldiers in Berlin in 1945, as well as the rape of women of other nationalities in Eastern Europe who were deemed to have been Nazi collaborators. Jeffrey Burds has characterized this violence as "grounded in hate, a white-hot-burning desire for vengeance against German atrocities."[40] The literature on this subject is still emerging. So far, it is more abundant in histories of Germany than of the Soviet Union.[41] Historians of sexual violence in war have asked whether such an act committed by soldiers is an aberration from military masculinity or its logical culmination. In other words, is rape to be framed as something the honourable, disciplined archetype of the soldier rejects, or as something implicitly supported by a toxic masculinity born in the barracks? For the Red Army at the end of the Second World War, it is possible that rape was an outcome consistent with the objectification of Soviet servicewomen throughout the war.[42] It was also about reforging power hierarchies among men by humiliating and emasculating German men, many of whom were forced to watch the assaults.[43] It should not come as a surprise that this horrific history within the postwar Soviet armed forces goes unmentioned in all the archival sources and literature this book examines, but it nonetheless haunts any discussion of military masculinity and postwar identity. Further research into specific outcomes of this history for masculinity in the Soviet Army would be very welcome.

## Sources and Narratives

The book combines textual analysis, visual analysis, and archival research in order to highlight the multiple narratives that contributed to rebuilding the military as a masculine space in the postwar period. The two chapters that make up Part I, Military Masculinity and the Postwar Armed Forces, explore institutional narratives. The first chapter examines discourses about conscription after the war to track the fears of service evasion that gripped policymakers in the Ministry of Defence and the Komsomol. Government concern over correct masculine behaviour and identity drove conscription discourses in the late 1940s and 1950s just as much as concern over actual army performance and preparation in this era of relative peace. This chapter introduces the theme of conscription and masculinity – or more broadly of choice and control – that runs throughout the book. While gender scholars have done important work in exploring how governments, including in the Soviet Union, attempted to control women's bodies, movements, and identities, similar work has not been done for men. As Tetyana Bureychak has written, the Soviet state engaged in "various approaches to control men's behaviour" throughout the century, including well-known campaigns against alcoholism, infidelity, and other affronts to communist morality[44] – to say nothing of state control of all citizens in housing, employment, access to goods, and even many leisure pursuits. One cannot understand Soviet masculinities without investigating the particular ways in which men encountered state power, and this interface with the state is one of the defining characteristics that separate Soviet and Euro-American masculinities in the twentieth century. But we will see in this chapter and those that follow that state efforts to control the narrative of men's enlistment and service in the military itself, or in military-adjacent institutions, did not go unchallenged or, in some cases, unsupported. Re-establishing military masculinity after the Second World War required not only a collection of directives from the centre, such as those that called for remobilizing troops in 1948 (chapter 1) or for *Krokodil* to publish assaults on martial femininity in the 1950s (chapter 3), but also the cooperation, negotiation, and participation of Soviet men who chose how to shape their encounters with military masculinity.

Chapter 2 explores how emerging brotherhoods among boys and young men before they reached the age of conscription were nurtured by military institutions in the late 1940s. With the state no longer willing to promote women's service or employ women veterans in military industries, it would fall to surviving male veterans to play the role of father or older brother in military families such as the Suvorov officer academies and the Voluntary Society for Cooperation with the Army, the Air Force and the Navy (DOSAAF), a civil defence organization. In these settings, policymakers attempted to prescribe a culture of soldiering to postwar youth, and in the process, to rebuild the postwar army exclusively for men. But the cadets and their instructors often had very different ideas than those of the administrators about how to build (or, conversely, to challenge) military authority. We see the frustrations of state actors in trying to define and enforce appropriate masculine behaviour for boys in these institutions, leading in part to authorities initiating a broader campaign to deliver martial masculine role models through postwar literature and film.

Institutional archives from the Komsomol and the Ministry of Defence can only take the story so far, however. As gender scholars know, the traditional archive has its limits. In Part II, Military Masculinity outside the Armed Forces during the Early Cold War, I consult narratives outside archival confines to engage in deep readings of published and visual sources such as cartoons, memoirs, newspapers, periodicals, and films. In doing so, I want to suggest that it is not only the choice of the historian to move the narrative into the realm of public culture, but it was in fact the choice of an array of policymakers in government and the military to do so. The archival conversations between the Komsomol and Ministry of Defence explored in Part I show that the conscription of soldiers and the education of future officers alone could not reinforce codes of military masculinity in postwar society. The three related case studies in Part II show that the cultural realm outside official military institutions contributed to that goal, with authorities implicitly admitting that broader cultural tools would need to be engaged beyond service training points in order to more fully recharge military masculinity in Soviet society. Its recreation and maintenance would gain far more visibility in *Krokodil* cartoons, the celebration of nuclear physicists, and – capping the postwar development of military masculinity – the flights of the inaugural cohort of cosmonauts than through the institutional directives examined in Part I.

Chapter 3 analyses the use of sexualized and misogynist imagery of European and American diplomats and military figures in the popular Soviet satirical journal, *Krokodil*, to link masculinity with Cold War military fortitude. In portraying foreign military authorities as feminized, queer, or sexually deviant in some way, *Krokodil* contributed to the establishment of norms for martial identities outside the regular forces – by drawing and enforcing visual boundaries in the popular press for what Soviet masculinity could *not* be. These cartoons created a particular way of seeing service and authority, demonstrating a patriarchal outlook more broadly in Soviet society that privileged heteronormative male dominance.

Chapter 4 returns to Sakharov and Nedelin. It discusses memoirs written by nuclear physicists in the 1970s through the 1990s about their Cold War work in the 1950s. The memoirs reveal several layers of narrative in building masculinized identities for these scientists who worked on the first Soviet nuclear project. Tales they tell as memoirists locate them as simultaneously powerless, constantly surveilled by the state and othered by men in the military institutions dictating their work; complicit, upholding patriarchal privilege in their laboratories and negotiating their own masculinity by reinforcing their workplaces as hostile to women; and nearly deified as superior beings, armed with the knowledge and technical expertise to design weapons that could destroy the world. In this chapter, the male narrator's process of emplotting himself into his own story reveals a variety of masculine identities at work. Although the physicists themselves experienced a fraught relationship with militarism, with many of them, like Sakharov, later becoming advocates for peace at great personal risk, their laboratories in the late 1940s and 1950s also served as cultural sites of masculinized rearmament outside the armed forces. The gendered coding of workplaces in these memoirs shows the male narrator's commitment to casting himself as the lead in his own story as a soldier of the Cold War – sometimes as a reluctant conscript or rank-and-file researcher, and sometimes as a deity empowered above the generals at test sites.

Chapter 5 moves into the early 1960s to examine the final stage in the re-establishment of military masculinity that had been undertaken in Soviet society since 1945: the public celebrity of the first six cosmonauts. While outwardly symbolizing the Soviet commitment to peace, the early cosmonauts became the most significant militarized brotherhood of all in the Cold War, commanding cultural prestige in Soviet society outside the regular armed forces. The cosmonaut program of the early 1960s became a site where the codes of military masculinity being rebuilt since the war came together in the body, face, and actions of air force officer Yuri Gagarin and his cohort. Routinely dressed for public appearances in their uniforms, the five male cosmonauts became leaders of Soviet efforts to prescribe Cold War masculinity and embody martial attributes missing in Soviet culture after the Second World War. As the sixth person in that first cohort and the only woman, Valentina Tereshkova, a civilian, was not granted access to the same levels of celebrity or military and technological authority as her colleagues in uniform. The creation of cosmonaut myths and the production of their post-flight images relied on a collaborative shaping of cultural understandings of manliness, building on a soldier archetype but also renewing its image for Cold War publicity at home and abroad. Historians of the space program have noted that Gagarin's launch and subsequent celebrity deliberately coincided with the new Communist Party program that the Twenty-Second Congress adopted in 1961, which emphasized the crafting of a New Soviet Man who would shepherd the country towards full communism by 1980.[45] In chapter 5, however, I reposition Gagarin and his colleagues not only as inspirations for a newfound drive to locate Soviet manhood in the communist future, but as the end result of a campaign begun in 1945 at the Suvorov academies, and in 1948 with (men's) remobilization, to rebuild masculinity. The first cosmonauts represented the final stage of the postwar project to reimagine and remasculinize military authority in Soviet culture.

Throughout, the book undertakes two main approaches. The first treats military masculinity as a process; its renewal and maintenance as a dominant form required constant tending. A society's anxieties about its gender norms do not necessarily reveal themselves in clear admissions, directives, or even in linear identifications of causes and effects. Gendered understandings of how and why martial identity came to be coveted after the war emerged as much less absolute and more of a continuing process. The second approach, in examining narratives from a variety of sources, asks how stories about masculinity are told, who tells them, and why those voices have been privileged. Some are here because I went looking for them (e.g., opinions in the Ministry of Defence about conscription), but others are here because they found me accidentally (e.g., Sakharov admitting to feeling impotent in one sentence and God-like in the next; Suvorov cadets ostracizing each other from their new military families). Others I never did find, such as draft dodgers confessing their motives or cartoonists explaining their visual choices. As strands of multiple narratives, these stories enrich historical understandings of the complexities of military masculinity at this particular peacetime moment in Soviet society.

The reader should be aware that each chapter visits major topics in Soviet history that have their own deep historiographies, including those of military service, the visual arts, science, and the space program. I am mindful of and refer to the work of other scholars in these fields throughout, but my goal is not to rehash the entire history of Soviet science, for instance, in chapter 4, nor to fully explain the social history of military education in chapter 2. Rather, this book ties those often disparate themes together by examining them through the lens of martial masculinity and arguing that, from 1945 to the mid-1960s, these sites worked together to create a deep process in which military authority was given back to men.

# PART ONE

# Military Masculinity and the Postwar Armed Forces

*Chapter One*

# Conscripting Soviet Manhood

In a cartoon from a May 1954 issue of the satirical magazine *Krokodil* (The Crocodile) called "Hypochondriac," a young, muscular man in work trousers and boots visited the doctor looking for a diagnosis. Observing his brawn, the doctor told him he "must be crazy" if he wanted a medical exemption. "Well," the man replied, "then give me *that* diagnosis" (Figure 1.1).[1] *Krokodil* was a state publication and subject to censorship, but it was also known for making problems in Soviet society visible, if under the guise of humour.[2] The Second World War had elevated the soldier to new heights in the Soviet popular imagination, but it also sparked anxiety for policymakers about whether the next generation of young men, a depleted population group since the war, would continue to value soldiering as a key masculine identity. Military service, after all, was not only a profession or duty but an imperative for (male) citizenship in the Bolshevik state. As Mark von Hagen has shown, a state founded through war and revolution came to rely in the 1920s and 1930s on the state-building expertise of Civil War commanders and veterans who reinforced that foundational vocabulary of battle motifs in politics, industry, and culture.[3] The Second World War increased that martial reverence exponentially.

This cartoon encapsulates Ministry of Defence anxieties after remobilization began in 1948: the army needed young men, not only for their fresh bodies and renewed vigour, but also to model a moral, disciplined, and appropriately masculine way of life to youth who were believed to be increasingly seduced by western consumerism and leisure pursuits. Less clear, however, was the degree to which these young men needed the army. This image indicates that at least by 1954, the ubiquity of evasion was common knowledge in Soviet society and had

Figure 1.1 Hypochondriac
"For you? A medical certificate? You must be crazy!"
"Well, then, give me *that* diagnosis."

*Krokodil*, 20 May 1954, 14.

earned a place on *Krokodil*'s short list of topics available to be mocked. In remobilizing, policymakers at the Ministry of Defence and the Komsomol (Communist Youth League) were informed not only by troop replenishment needs but also by a newfound alarm over the fact that the postwar generation of boys and young men were avoiding both the voluntary and compulsory components of Soviet military culture; as such, they were choosing not to engage with the most important shaper of masculine identity in Soviet society. Although evasion figures are notoriously difficult to pin down, postwar crime statistics have shown that desertion was the most common charge against conscripts coming into contact with the legal system, at least until Stalin's death.[4] Officials sought to catalogue the problem of military avoidance, make sense of it, and ultimately to resolve it. Doing so required extensive conversations about what these young men were missing if they did not serve, the kinds of men who would do such a thing, and who was to blame for their apparent failure to see the social and cultural benefits as well as the training provided by service.

At a time when able-bodied young men were needed more than ever in the labour force, the government nonetheless engaged in a remobilization campaign beginning in 1948 that aimed to conscript and train – if not necessarily to deploy – millions of young men for military service. Beginning with that remobilization period, this chapter discusses the complexities of reinforcing postwar military masculinity in two related areas of service: civilian training rubrics through mass defence work and the evasion strategies of conscripted men. In the first, the chapter examines the Voluntary Society for Cooperation with the Army, the Air Force and the Navy (*Dobrovol'noe obshchestvo sodeistviia armii, aviatsii, i flotu*, or DOSAAF), an early Bolshevik civil defence organization reconfigured in 1951 for the Cold War that linked military masculinity to the civilian population. Both men and women were active and welcome in DOSAAF, but as we will see here and in chapter 2, this civilian training institution also had a particular mandate to introduce teenage boys and young men outside the regular forces (including adolescents who had not yet reached conscription age) to the basic skills of service. DOSAAF worked in tandem with other institutions, like the officer academies that will be discussed in chapter 2, to ensure that young men's lives regularly intersected with martial categories in Soviet society.

DOSAAF's archival records as well as its official publications, the monthly journals *Voennye znaniia* (Military Knowledge) and *Kryl'ia rodiny* (Wings of the Motherland), reveal frustration, bewilderment, and an ill-defined mandate for the organization tasked with maintaining universal male service – and remobilizing without permitting women's participation – in a country no longer at war. Although postwar military archives remain unavailable to Western researchers, the Komsomol maintained detailed (if not comprehensive) records of conversations between regional Komsomol groups and central Ministry of Defence officials about service evasion among young men in many regions of the country. For both civilian defence and conscription discussions, though, a significant shift occurred in 1954 when previously internal concerns about young men's military preparation began to appear much more openly in the pages of the press, both nationally, as the above *Krokodil* cartoon demonstrates, and in the more specialized military periodicals like *Voennye znaniia*. This relative openness suggests that debates about men's militarized roles had broader purchase in postwar Soviet society and could not be contained. Discussions about service and evasion in these sources show the leadership grappling with changing ideas about masculinity and youth culture. As historians of youth have found, teenage boys might have been more interested in exploring other identities available to them in postwar society.[5] The effects of pre-conscription training on that age group and its gender identity development have not yet been explored, however. Thus, this chapter focuses on young men between about the age of sixteen in DOSAAF through to conscription at eighteen. Significantly and surprisingly, by looking at these conversations in DOSAAF, the Komsomol, and the Ministry of Defence, it becomes apparent that military service would turn out *not* to be the primary means of recalibrating codes of military masculinity in postwar society. As we will see in later chapters, that role would be picked up by the cultural realm that existed outside official military institutions.

The following discussion of institutional records is not intended to be a comprehensive history of conscription or a full social history of army service in the postwar years. Although the late 1940s and 1950s have been underserved in military historiography, many existing studies provide a social history of the Red Army and its successor after 1948, the Soviet Army.[6] Instead, this chapter offers a case study of selected moments, compiled from an incomplete set of records about a taboo topic, during which Defence and Komsomol authorities – speaking only to each other and silencing the voices of their subjects – called into question the military fitness of young men after 1945. This chapter also introduces Part I of the book, in which we will see that state archives do not in fact offer the clearest path to illuminating the processes by which military masculinity was constructed and reinforced in the first two decades after the war. Gender historians have used a variety of sources to locate and explicate the complexities of gender regimes at various points in history, and some have successfully found discussions of masculinity in state archives.[7] For this particular moment in the history of Soviet masculinities, however, as we will see in Part II, sources outside the official purview of Soviet authorities, including the popular press, memoirs, and diaries, make visible the remilitarization of masculine identity in ways official records do not. These institutional records are not without their uses, of course. They demonstrate the limits of Soviet archives but also the ways in which flawed and incomplete archives must be read in tandem with other types of sources to create a fuller picture of the directives, anxieties, and uncertainties that plagued attempts to demarcate martial identity after 1945.

**Conscription in War and Peace**

Conscription emerged in the late eighteenth century for several reasons. It provided defence for the new American and French republics; it contributed to building nation-states through the participation of a cadre of citizens in the defence of the homeland; and it became a tool of governments searching to harness the skill and energy of populations of young men. First introduced as a temporary measure during the American Revolution, conscription would emerge as a permanent feature of Euro-American liberal democracies during the French Revolutionary Wars. The 1793 announcement of the *levée en masse* introduced a new concept into military and political discourse as well as social history: the legal and permanent requirement that men of a certain age declare military allegiance to a nation-state rather than to a local political or aristocratic leader, and that they fight as citizens of that polity in an effort to defend it from outside attack.[8] As many scholars of the military and society have shown, conscription often entails goals beyond regularly gaining new bodies for service. For example, in nineteenth-century Prussia, a leader in military innovation, conscription not only helped define citizenship and enfranchisement for men but arguably helped democratize a rigid, class-based society.[9] Conscription has also moulded historical gender roles. In the wake of the French Revolution, the nominal equality of male citizenship vis-à-vis conscription required men to adjust their views of class-based masculinized authority.[10] In early twentieth-century Finland, fierce debates about conscription helped define masculinity and the Finnish nation-state as it emerged from Russian imperial control.[11]

Conscription first appeared in Russia under Peter I at the end of the seventeenth century, although the law governing its enforcement was selective and had limited effect. Universal service became law in the Russian empire under Alexander II in 1874. Exemptions based on social class were eliminated, at least on paper, although select categories such as clergymen, physicians, and members of certain groups in Central Asia, Siberia, and the Caucasus remained exempt.[12] Following renewed threats from the Prussian military, as well as the pressing domestic concern of reshaping Russian society in the wake of the emancipation of the serfs, conscription became as much a tool for controlling peasant populations and promoting Russian nation-building through the notion of the citizen-soldier as it did a military doctrine.[13]

The persistence of an autocratic government in Russia meant that conscription there took on a different character than in European democracies with citizenship-for-service ideologies. Indeed, one does not generally find in imperial Russian and Soviet history the cycles of public debate about conscription that characterized liberal democracies in the United States or Europe.[14] The history of the Red Army from the Civil War through the Second World War has been well documented by historians, including its mandate to serve as a tool of Bolshevik social transformation.[15] The military service law of 1925 required all citizens to participate in the defence of the Soviet Union, with workers singled out for service that included paramilitary training, active duty for five years, and reserve obligations after release until the age of 40. In 1939, spurred by militarization in Europe and Stalin's concern about loyalty in the armed forces, a new military service law was enacted. It remained in effect until 1967. This law was suspended during the Second World War to allow for extraordinary mobilization requirements, including reductions in education deferments, lower health requirements, and temporarily enlisting women. Apart from that suspension during the war, the 1939 law guided postwar service up to 1967 with the following major provisions: all male citizens had to serve; the age of conscription was eighteen or nineteen depending on the level of secondary school completed; new cohorts were called up once per year in the fall, and they served for two to three years for ground forces and four to five for the air force, navy, and border guards.[16]

Selling obligatory military service during peacetime to war-weary populations after the Second World War proved to be challenging in other countries as well. In Britain, for instance, the 1939 debate about conscription resumed after the war, as the government of Clement Attlee sought to justify extending mandatory service in a Cold War context and a rapidly decolonizing world.[17] For Attlee, Cold War fears of Soviet expansionism should Britain not retain sufficient troops for any new conflict superseded even his own Labour Party's usual ideological position against conscription as detrimental to industrial labour.[18] France also retained conscription after the war, assigning its forces primarily to fight independence movements in French colonies.[19] In the United States, selective service remained in effect from 1940 to 1973, although it was not universal and featured an increasing number of deferments over that period of time.[20] Postwar Germany, meanwhile, was the site of extensive and complex debates among occupation forces seeking to defang the Nazi military structure. In the newly created Federal Republic of Germany, the government quietly maintained its armed forces as a shield against communist expansion.[21]

In the Soviet Union, as in Western countries, Cold War geopolitics influenced the postwar remobilization drive. Hiding the extent of Soviet economic devastation, for example, was crucial to maintaining and expanding the country's reputation in the West as a military force to be reckoned with.[22] The Truman Doctrine and accompanying Marshall Plan in 1947, increasing tension over the occupation zones in Berlin, and whispers of a military alliance in the works between the United States and Western Europe led the Soviet government to re-evaluate its military preparation in the event of a new war and to reorganize its armed forces. It used the Red Army's thirtieth anniversary celebrations in February 1948 to announce that demobilization after the Second World War was complete, releasing millions of enlisted men from service. (Women had already been demobilized by a decree in September 1945).[23] It set the stage for a new round of recruitment under new guidelines, with new goals and a new generation of young men. From its peak strength of 12 million men in 1944, the army reduced its ranks to only 2.8 million by 1948.[24] After troop numbers climbed again to about 5.3 million men by Stalin's death in 1953, Nikita Khrushchev, increasingly convinced that a large standing army was unnecessary during the Cold War, again reduced the forces to 3.6 million by 1958. Khrushchev proposed cutting another 1.2 million men in 1960, but this plan was halted by the Berlin crisis in 1961.[25]

Soviet remobilization and the continuation of conscription in the late 1940s took place amid the powerful collective trauma that the war had wrought. Virtually every family, at least in the western half of the country, had lost loved ones (overwhelmingly fathers, brothers, and sons) and many had also lost their homes, jobs, neighbourhoods, and even entire cities. No Soviet citizen remained untouched by the extreme violence not only of war in general but this war in particular, in which the Nazis had openly and aggressively sought to destroy the Soviet people.[26] In her work, Catherine Merridale has tried to recapture a sense, often lost in the numbers, of just how devastating the violence was on a human level:

> The carnage was beyond imagination. Eyewitnesses described the battlefields as landscapes of charred steel and ash. The round shapes of

> lifeless heads caught the light like potatoes turned up from new-broken soil. The prisoners were marched off in their multitudes ... Almost the entire army of the prewar years, the troops that shared the panic of those first nights back in June, was dead or captured by the end of 1941. And this process would be repeated as another generation was called up, crammed into uniform, and killed, captured, or wounded beyond recovery. In all, the Red Army was destroyed and renewed at least twice in the course of this war ... American lend-lease was supplying the Soviets with razor blades by 1945, but large numbers of the Red Army's latest reserve of teenagers would hardly have needed them.[27]

The unique horrors of that war have affected our understandings of Soviet military service ever since. The extreme challenges of Soviet service date back to the Civil War and were exacerbated by the hardships of the Second World War, when everything from food and clothing to weapons and even basic training were in short supply, if not altogether non-existent.[28] The enactment of the new Law on Universal Military Service Obligation in 1967 was another turning point, lowering service requirements from three to two years, creating greater turnover but also increasing polarization between conscripts in the first year versus those in the second.[29] The latter group, known as *dedy*, or "grandfathers," gave rise to the now infamous hazing system of *dedovshchina*, or "rule by the grandfathers." By the 1980s and 1990s, the heart-wrenching stories emerging in Russia from veterans' and mothers' activist groups about the horrific physical abuse conscripts suffered at the hands of fellow servicemen began to influence longstanding perceptions of service.[30] Scholars of conscription during the war in Afghanistan in the 1980s and in post-Soviet Russia have been right to characterize service in those years as a persistently violent experience for young men. One analyst of the post-Soviet Russian military has written that "For several decades [after World War II], the young Russian male has had a very different military upbringing, one forged through hardship, revolution, and tumultuous change."[31] Another draws a straight line from 1939 to the 1967 law, implying that *dedovshchina* and extreme service hardships characterized the military throughout that timeframe, as well as after 1967.[32]

But the period from 1945 to 1967 did not see anywhere near the same horrors as the eras before and after. At least on paper, serving in the intervening years was a relatively benign experience. Moreover, it was increasingly sold as a benign experience by policymakers eager to convince young men that both DOSAAF's pre-conscription training and army service itself were places to play sports, read officially sanctioned magazines, and make friends. The next sections examine the confusion and irritation among policymakers, particularly from roughly 1948 to 1958, as they became convinced that young men were deliberately shunning training and service and in doing so, were avoiding contact with state-sponsored categories of military masculinity.

## DOSAAF and Young Men in Civilian Defence

Participation in DOSAAF offered a method for re-establishing morality, discipline, and social control of the country's young men, especially the generation coming of age in the late 1940s and early 1950s that had not fought in the war. DOSAAF's civil defence mission helped normalize the peacetime forces, providing a "pro-military value pattern" in Soviet civil society.[33] While in some ways continuing the work of its predecessor organizations, DOSAAF also faced different foreign policy concerns, youth issues, gender constructions, and, especially, different notions of what would be required in order to continue building socialism in a postwar world. DOSAAF helped to equalize the balance between civilian and military communities, and in the process, it helped define masculinized terrain in the Cold War.

Although DOSAAF itself was formed only in 1951, it belonged to a tradition of voluntary societies in the Soviet Union that dated back to the founding of its predecessor organization, Osoaviakhim, in 1927. Osoaviakhim (Society of Friends of Defence and Aviation-Chemical Construction), the largest voluntary association in the country before the Second World War, had grown out of a perceived need to integrate the Red Army into civilian society in the aftermath of the Civil War.[34] The Bolsheviks decreed in 1919 that universal military training would become a requirement in the new state, and that basic military training should be provided to citizens without interrupting their labour contributions. That principle laid the groundwork for the establishment of Osoaviakhim – and later, DOSAAF – cells in the country's schools and workplaces, in order to pursue civil defence training without detracting from education or production.[35] Stalin's intervention in Osoaviakhim might also have served as another means of keeping the military on a short leash in the 1930s. By separating military training duties between the Red Army and Osoaviakhim, Stalin effectively diffused the power of the military, and by locating basic training in a voluntary society, he created a counter to the perceived coercion of conscription.[36] As we will see, however, young men of conscription age did not necessarily appreciate this distinction.

The decree that established DOSAAF, part of the Ministry of Defence, in its new incarnation in 1951 described the society's goals as follows: "DOSAAF organizes military training, propaganda for military and military-technical knowledge, the development of military sport, the delivering of lectures, reports, and conversations on technology, aviation, naval, and historical themes, and publishes newspapers and journals."[37] DOSAAF's training was intended to be much more widespread than that offered in specialized military academies (to be discussed in chapter 2), and it was directed at the future rank and file, not officers. More specifically, DOSAAF had three declared aims. First, it focused on civil defence training in factories, collective and state farms, and educational institutions. Second, it engaged in basic military training for pre-conscription youth. This training nominally included both boys and girls, but permitted activities were differentiated by sex, and more emphasis was placed on preparing boys for military service. Third, the society emphasized training in "military-technical types of sports."[38] This category was dominated, at least in DOSAAF publications, by motorcycle racing and shooting.

DOSAAF was not only a youth-oriented organization; it sought to provide comprehensive basic defence training for all citizens and to this end, it opened chapters throughout the country in factories, housing cooperatives, and schools. But its paramilitary mandate also created conditions for the particular cultivation of young people, and especially young men, as members taking an active interest in defence work. This "preference for youth" dated back to Osoaviakhim's origins in the 1920s, precisely because the organization was responsible for providing basic training to pre-conscription aged young men.[39] DOSAAF's monthly journals, *Voennye znaniia* and *Kryl'ia rodiny*, regularly underscored this connection, which had the rhetorical effect of excluding women from the organization's self-professed most important work: "Youth, heading as reinforcements to the front lines of the Soviet Army," a *Kryl'ia rodiny* article stated in 1954, "must pass through our good [DOSAAF] schools, taking on physical education and conditioning through applied-military types of sport."[40]

Even after the Second World War, DOSAAF was charged with preparing the population for total mobilization, and girls and women were permitted and encouraged to participate in DOSAAF activities as part of that mandate. Ideally, according to scripts repeated in numerous DOSAAF publications, even "housewives" (a group assumed to be as remote from military identity or preparation as possible) could read DOSAAF brochures on defence topics and try to engage in discussions about "the life and activities of DOSAAF."[41] Young women with no other military training could learn to drive a car or operate a radio through DOSAAF, skills deemed valuable in the event of an attack. (In post-Soviet Russia, women have reported anecdotally that their main interaction with DOSAAF came when learning to drive.) In the immediate postwar years, however, its official magazine, *Voennye znaniia*, reflected the broader ambiguity in the government towards women's military service. Women rarely warranted mention in the journal. In one exception, in January 1947, an article underscored the ways in which gendered expectations continued to limit women's participation in martial culture. "Friday is Osoaviakhim day!" it declared, chronicling the activities at a Kiev factory, a practice echoed in the Osoaviakhim and DOSAAF chapters of workplaces across the country. Every Friday after their shift, the workers "take military lessons." For the men, lessons involved "assembling rifles and studying models of machine guns and grenades." The "girls" (*devushki*) who wanted to take part were given lessons in telephone and radio operation and Morse code signalling.[42] *Voennye znaniia* and its predecessor magazine, *Za oboronu* (For Defence),[43] were also silent about International Women's Day – unusual for a Soviet publication – until 1951, when its March issue featured a front-page article on "women patriots," but it still did not actually mention the holiday. The women featured, moreover, had contributed to the war effort by selflessly sending their husbands and brothers off to fight.[44]

The sex segregation of many paramilitary activities in DOSAAF led to the exclusion of women and girls from combat preparation such as rifle training. Even so, some in DOSAAF's leadership still felt that teaching women to drive or hang-glide were leisure pursuits that distracted the society from its more important mission of preparing young men for military service. In digesting the Council of Ministers' directive for the society in August 1951, DOSAAF administrators noted with frustration that

> the Soviet army and navy do not simply need parachutists who are able to land well, but parachutists who are able to get entrenched quickly and use firearms and cold steel; not simply riflemen who are able to use weapons,

> but soldiers who are able to overcome water boundaries, swim, and make a quality airborne or amphibious landing; not simply sailors who are able to swim and operate a boat, but sailors who know the fundamentals of infantry tactics and are able to wage war on land; not simply drivers and telephone operators, but *military* drivers and *military* telephone operators.[45]

Although DOSAAF claimed universality as a voluntary society, paramilitary training for young men was a priority. Some officials viewed the society's various sporting and educational pursuits, for both boys and girls, as a distraction from that goal.

## "No One Is Interested": Avoiding DOSAAF

If DOSAAF authorities did not particularly want to train civilians from outside the military community, many civilians, it seems, did not particularly want to join. Concerned with low membership numbers even as its predecessor organizations merged, DOSAAF leaders wondered in the late summer of 1951 about how to make the organization more attractive. The Soviet people were concerned with the reinforcement of the armed forces in an age of new hostilities with the West and they supported any endeavour devoted to strengthening it, administrators maintained. At the same time, officials could not account for the fact that only 12 per cent of the adult population of the Soviet Union had joined the organization.[46] By mid-1952, the situation had not changed. "For six months the ranks of DOSAAF have accepted three million people and withdrawn from the register more than one million," administrators complained. "It is natural that members of the society move from one enterprise to another; they leave in connection with finishing their education and such, but where exactly did one million people disappear to? We propose that a small portion of some kind from this number went into the ranks of the army, but where are the rest?"[47] Another report from a regional DOSAAF leader in Velikolukskaia *oblast'* near Leningrad told a meeting of administrators in August 1952 that workers in his area repeatedly said they just did not have time to participate in DOSAAF's paramilitary activities, because they "had more important things to do." Reportedly one coal miner there who had used that excuse spent his spare time starting up and playing in a brass band instead of doing defence work.[48] In a July 1954 letter to *Voennye znaniia* that the editors titled "A Painful Question," a DOSAAF administrator in Stalingrad bemoaned low membership numbers there. "No one is interested" in joining, he wrote, which was a particularly harsh blow for military authorities in the famed wartime city.[49]

Authorities also portrayed their ability to reach boys before conscription age as an ongoing struggle. Despite its presence in schools and its partnership with the Komsomol, DOSAAF did not seem to appeal to teenage boys. *Za oboronu* and (after the renaming in 1948) *Voennye znaniia* consistently drew a generational line between the men who had served in the war and the boys who had been too young, blaming young people's perceived indifference on a lack of battle experience. "Most of the adult population of our country received substantial military training during the Great Patriotic War," the lauded general and DOSAAF chairman V.I. Kuznetsov wrote in 1948. The contributions of veterans to the society remained important, he noted, but it was also crucial to focus on young men who had missed the war years.[50] An editorial the following month reiterated Kuznetsov's point: "The majority of the adult male population" of the country was schooled at the front, but "we must circulate military propaganda to young people." Linking specific military skills to the society's seemingly benign, sports-centric program, the editors added, "If a young man joins DOSAAF and learns to drive or ride a motorcycle, he will be one step closer to being ready as a soldier."[51] The generational divide regarding service could also be couched more subtly: in July 1950, an article entitled "Duty and Courage" opened by reminding readers that, as they relaxed in these happy summer days of 1950, they must not forget the horrors of the summer of 1941.[52] The postwar generation of boys did not have adequate "consciousness about their [military] duty." Even those who joined DOSAAF did not always attend their classes and could be "negligent in military studies." Education was crucial, Komsomol and DOSAAF leaders argued, to "convince young people of the need to study military affairs and carefully prepare themselves in their military attitudes."[53]

But even when young men did join DOSAAF training clubs to take advantage of their programs to learn martial discipline through sport, they could not always be counted on to become part of the honourable new generation of military men that authorities wanted. A particularly egregious case made headlines in *Kryl'ia rodiny* in early 1954 and served as a cautionary tale for DOSAAF's membership. The article opened dramatically, with parachuting champion E. Naumenko looking back on his courtship with his wife, Tamara, in happier times: "Give me your heart, I am prepared to do everything for you that you wish!" They married in 1949, but Naumenko quickly became more interested in "family scandal" than "family happiness." He demonstrated the "egoism of a husband" in neglecting their child, physically abusing Tamara, and finally, several months earlier, kicking her and their child out on the street – while she was pregnant – in order to free up room in their apartment for his new girlfriend. This was not his first such transgression; in recent years, we are told, Naumenko had been married three times.[54] Excellence in military sports like parachuting normally inspired athletes to work towards success in all aspects of life. But with Naumenko, "this did not happen." He let his sports glory "go to his head." And most egregiously, he lost sight of the military discipline in which he had been trained. Six months later, a follow-up story on the "amoral behaviour" of Naumenko noted that the chairman of the DOSAAF committee in Ukraine had informed *Kryl'ia rodiny* that Naumenko had been stripped of the title of Honoured Master of Sport.[55]

In betraying his wife and children, Naumenko had also failed to meet the high expectations for him as an aviator and sports hero and as a DOSAAF member involved in paramilitary training. He was meant to model, not undermine, state efforts to recalibrate military training and education for peacetime. Naumenko's success in parachuting competitions brought visibility to his role as a man of honour representing DOSAAF to young people who might be sceptical of participating in one of the USSR's many voluntary societies. His actions towards his wife and children needed to be highlighted and publicly corrected in order to maintain the image of healthy masculinity in military education. Naumenko's flogging in the press also forecast broader trends in post-Stalin society about private life and proper behaviour for communist citizens, to be formalized in an edict on communist morality issued at the Twenty-Second Party Congress in 1961.[56] As we will see in chapter 5 with respect to the most famous aviators in the country and the world in the early 1960s, healthy portraits of marriage and fatherhood among military men, such as cosmonaut Yuri Gagarin (and even as ordinary citizens like Naumenko), mattered to the rebuilding of military masculinity.

DOSAAF leaders seemed surprised that young men after the war might not share the Ministry of Defence's continued commitment to military training or, for men like Naumenko, to enacting DOSAAF's credo of martial discipline in their daily lives. Civil society in the Soviet Union was built on voluntary societies like DOSAAF, and problems persisted throughout the century in building participation numbers. Many people avoided these organizations for a variety of reasons, most likely having to do with surveillance and the creep of the state into too many aspects of their daily lives. DOSAAF leaders' anxieties about membership might not have been unique, but it is noteworthy that citizens' aversion to paramilitary training existed alongside their aversion to other voluntary societies, despite the primacy of the military in Soviet culture. Echoes of June 1941 were certainly audible in DOSAAF's records of its early membership drives in 1951 and 1952, with fears of being unprepared for another attack often cited as the rationale for DOSAAF's training. More frequently, however, authorities seemed confused that young men were opting out of DOSAAF's voluntary training, eschewing not only rifle skills but also every other part of DOSAAF's mandate, which included lectures on Soviet military history, particularly of the Second World War; team sports (if motocross was too specialized, surely volleyball was benign enough?);[57] discussion circles about military themes; and so on. Although conscription dated back to the Civil War, Soviet military service and even military interest relied on a spirit of voluntarism and an assumption that (male) citizens of the revolutionary state would continue to see the imperative of defending it – particularly since women were no longer welcome in the military.

## Cataloguing Evasion

It became apparent to administrators in the Komsomol, the Ministry of Defence, and DOSAAF by late 1951 that reluctance to participate in military training was not limited to DOSAAF and the civilian realm. All three institutions began to express concerns over service evasion among conscripted men, as they were faced with increasing evidence from around the country that young men did not seem to ascribe the same sense of virility, purpose, and honour to soldiering that officials did. Roger Reese has found that the preeminence of the army in society after 1945 exacerbated this generational divide, because officers and government agents increasingly distant from the original Bolshevik principles of the Red Army lost touch with enlisted men. Between 1945 and Stalin's death in 1953, the ratio of officers to enlisted men was 1.0 to 4.5, or about twice as many as necessary, owing to the fact that those who had survived, and achieved glory, in the Second World War would not leave.[58] Officials in the armed forces and the Komsomol were largely made up of this older cohort who routinely couched mobilization after 1948 in generational terms, describing the new groups of postwar servicemen as weak, amoral, illiterate, shameful, diseased, and as deserters. In these narratives, Second World War soldiers always did better, fought harder, and demonstrated greater patriotism when serving.

The conscription of new troops was one site where this generational dichotomy played out. By 1950, military authorities had already established the immediate postwar years as a distinct era in which training was particularly weak.[59] Conscripts needed to be willing to defend the country "as their fathers and older brothers" had – an expression of nostalgia invoking not only a mythical past of masculine heroism but also the very real experience of the war in many Soviet families.[60] Juliane Fürst has found that generational rhetoric was mobilized after the war in a way that indicted young people as conservative and complacent. In contrast to the dictates of early Soviet ideology, she writes, "suddenly it was the fathers, not the sons, who stood for revolutionary ideals and became the bearers of state identity."[61] (For the military, at least, mothers and daughters would be consigned to the sidelines.) The Komsomol often called on veterans to help instil the proper sense of patriotism and service duty in the new generation of conscripts, particularly in regions that were identified as vulnerable to evasion, "hooliganism," and poor training in basic weaponry skills.

One method of avoiding conscription was to subvert health expectations and manipulate acceptable disease categories. To be sure, physical maladies and medical deficits constituted a real barrier to recruiting service-ready soldiers. The military repeatedly claimed that the conscripts in any given year (from 1945 to about 1960) were too small, too weak, and too diseased to fulfil their service obligations. In 1948, for instance, the Ministry of Defence summarized for the Komsomol the severity of health problems among that year's group of conscripts across the country, stating that youth born in 1928, 1929, and 1930 were deficient in physical development and height for their age. Incredibly, many were listed at under 150 centimetres tall (about five feet) and had significant bone and muscle deficiencies.[62] Many men from this group came from areas that had seen heavy fighting in the war, and they were the most likely to have damaged bones, cartilage, and soft tissue, as well as organ problems, bone defects, and cramping of the joints in their fingers and toes.[63]

Another common ailment across the country was trachoma, a highly contagious eye infection. The Komsomol reported in 1953 that the condition affected one in five conscripts in Moldova, one in three in the

Krasnoiarsk and Irkutsk *oblasti*, and as high as one in two for conscripts from Iakutsk, Chuvashia, and Bashkiria.[64] Trachoma was reported as an ongoing problem in Tajikistan in 1953, Bashkiria in 1955, and Turkmenistan in 1958, when it continued to plague nearly one-third of the young men conscripted that year.[65] Such health concerns for men who would have been children during the war, likely missing crucial nutrition and exercise needs in many areas of the country, cast a grim reminder of the level of devastation the war had wrought, not only among the population that fought in it, but also for future generations charged with the task of rebuilding the country. Rectifying such discernible problems with young male bodies, according to officials, needed to become a greater priority for the Komsomol and DOSAAF.

An even greater concern was the number of conscripts who appeared to be deliberately delaying or refusing treatment in order to remain ineligible for service.[66] In 1956 in rural Bashkiria, the Komsomol noted that some conscripts with trachoma were avoiding treatment.[67] By 1958, statistics regarding continuing conscript health issues through the previous decade began to worry Komsomol officials, who suspected that feigning disease had become a common draft evasion tactic. "Many Komsomol activists are of the mistaken opinion that it is impossible to cure trachoma, and that is why they do not seek out treatment,"[68] the Komsomol Central Committee reported in 1958. But other documents contradict that optimism. As Komsomol Central Committee Chair V. Semichastnyi admitted as early as 1953, there were a significant number of youth "who considered trachoma a defence against conscription into the army."[69]

Several other methods of evasion were reported throughout the country during the 1950s. In Armenia, where individual allegiance to the church was still grudgingly tolerated, the Komsomol reported several cases in the late 1950s of conscription-age men enrolling in religious seminaries to evade service. In at least one case, the conscript in question admitted that he did not in fact have any strong religious beliefs and, before enrolling in the academy, had never been to church.[70] On the western borderlands, another method of evasion was to feign Polish nationality. Although the list of national groups exempt from service after the Second World War was quite long and included nationals of any country not part of the Soviet Union before the war, Polish seemed to have been the nationality of choice for Slavic men seeking to evade service.[71] "Knowing that citizens of Polish nationality in the Soviet army are not conscripted," one 1951 report observed, "a large segment of youth during periods of conscription conceal their nationality, calling themselves Polish."[72] The report went on to cite a conscription drive that year in one *raion* in which out of 294 eligible youth, 260 claimed exemptions based on Polish nationality.[73] The logistics of how such a ruse was possible are unclear, especially considering the complications of everything from internal passports to surnames and language fluency. Yet authorities seemed to recognize this method as successful, at least in the short term. Most offenders were identified as eligible Belarussian men.[74]

Lastly, military officials expressed particular concern about instances of community complicity in the concealment of conscription-age young men from local military commissariats. Many recorded cases of this evasion tactic occurred in the Central Asian republics, where the army was associated with violent contact between local communities and imperial Russian or, after 1917, Soviet state power.[75] Postwar evasion techniques reveal how state plans for the young men of those republics often clashed with local needs – and with the wishes of the men themselves. In 1953 in a village in Tajikistan, two local *kolkhoz* (collective farm) leaders ushered two teenage brothers away from the village to an unknown location, with the knowledge and support of many other community members. In a neighbouring village that same year, another *kolkhoz* leader presented teenage boys to military medical commissions with fabricated symptoms of illness. In one *raion* in Tajikistan, an elderly man was found to be hiding sixteen young men, including two of his relatives. Villagers and *kolkhoz* leaders denied knowing the whereabouts of conscription-age young men when questioned by conscription committees.[76] Overall, of 213 conscription-age young men called before the regional military committee in January 1953 to begin their two years of required service in the Soviet Armed Forces, only 81 showed up.[77] In other cases, local Tajik leaders were accused of altering identification documents to inaccurately reflect the conscript's year of birth in order to allow him to evade service.[78] Still others took measures to ensure that, when youth were presented to medical commissions prior to conscription, they would display "obvious symptoms of disability."[79] One Tajik *raion* was found to have concealed 500 young men from authorities in 1953.[80] The Komsomol committee in Uzbekistan blamed the "shameful" facts of service evasion and desertion on the low level of political education among conscripted Uzbek youth.[81] In March 1951, four conscripts simply ran away from a conscription office in the Bukhara *oblast'*.[82] In May, the Tashkent Komsomol found conscripts also deserting their posts after answering the call to military offices. Among the cited reasons for desertion and evasion in the area were low levels of Russian fluency among conscripts, insufficient political education in Leninist principles, and an overly sentimental attachment to their families and local communities.[83]

All of these examples come from general files in the Komsomol archive relating to conscription, not any specifically devoted to evasion among non-Russian groups. Yet none discuss the issue for Russian men. Concerns about good socialist citizenship, participation, and compliance by Soviet nationalities in society more broadly would certainly also have applied to military service and evasion, real or perceived. Further research would be welcome on the ways in which non-Russian men grappled with constructs of Soviet masculinity, including how these men shaped ideals and conversations outside of gender regimes enforced by the centre.[84]

The training anxieties, disciplinary infractions, and outright evasion that characterized the military after remobilization began in 1948 were not necessarily unique to this country or time period. They were, however, notable in the Soviet Union after the Second World War because they were unexpected. Many factors converged at that time to minimize the strain of serving: the country was technically at peace (at least compared to the trauma of 1941–45 and the *dedovshchina* crisis that would develop after 1967); there were more than enough men serving, both enlisted and in the officer corps, and in fact troops were regularly undergoing reductions, not new conscription drives; and labour shortages meant that men were needed elsewhere in the economy. Military service might also have appealed to men with lower education levels; with ten grades the norm in the Soviet education system, the military required only a sixth to seventh grade education for mechanics, at least fifth grade for drivers, and third or fourth grade for infantrymen.[85] The main evasion methods that Komsomol and Ministry of Defence sources recorded in the 1950s did not resemble earlier methods Joshua Sanborn has found in the late imperial period, such as cutting off one's trigger finger, pouring acid into one's eyes or ears, or inducing illness through self-starvation.[86] Compared to earlier generations of evaders who took these extreme actions, showing a desperation commensurate with the hardships of serving in the imperial or early Bolshevik armed forces, the ways in which conscripts sought to avoid service after 1948 were as benign as postwar service itself. Evaders presumably shunned not only combat possibilities but also desk jobs in the military. Deferments for physical reasons have always been rare in the Soviet military. As Harriet Fast Scott and William F. Scott have written, "if the individual can perform some useful function in civilian life he can also perform some task in the Armed Forces."[87] Why, then, did the Ministry of Defence, partnered with the Komsomol, place such emphasis on military service for young men during this time, and why should these men seek to avoid service? If one need not fear active combat duty or a decades-long term of service as in previous generations, the answer might be more cultural – to avoid contact with a certain type of military masculinity that the state sought to prescribe.

We need to know more about these young men who avoided contact with DOSAAF and the military. As Sanborn has pointed out, it is always difficult to ascertain the exact frequency and rationale for service evasion, "since the most effective methods were designed to leave no imprint upon the record-keepers of the state."[88] For those who did serve, memoirs abound for the Second World War and the war in Afghanistan in the 1980s, but not for the peacetime forces of 1948 to the 1960s. Were these young men influenced by Stalin's refusal after 1948 to commemorate the war, fearing the popularity of his generals?[89] Shelving war talk might have had the unintended consequence of lowering service expectations, or at least the appeal of military careers, in the eyes of teenage boys and young men. Even in a time of peace, did the shadows of the horrors their elders had suffered in the war against the Nazis influence their avoidance? Or perhaps they were the part of society that Juliane Fürst has recently described as "dropping out" of socialist life: these individuals and communities might not have openly aimed to resist or subvert the regime, but they nonetheless "wanted distance – spatial, mental, and ideological – from the regime ... and they wanted to achieve this aim by *not* doing rather than doing something."[90] Without further access to their stories, the reasons remain elusive. The state-directed narratives about these men's non-compliance, however, reveal that conscription and evasion occupied authorities after the war. Moreover, they also help us understand how government agents attempted to reconnect military service with masculinity, a link that women's wartime service had disrupted.

## Soldiers without an Army: Khrushchev's Troop Reductions

By 1954, Ministry of Defence officials' concern about the participation of young men in DOSAAF training and conscription spilled out from internal debates to the pages of the press. From 1945 to the end of 1953, for instance, *Voennye znaniia* focused almost exclusively on Second World War battles, weapons, and veteran biographies, despite the ministry's and Komsomol officials' behind-the-scenes preoccupation with training imperatives and service evasion. An abrupt shift occurred in January 1954, however. That month, the journal used the word "conscription" for the first time and after that, it turned from only discussing the last war to focusing on content devoted to promoting and even glamorizing service in the contemporary army.[91] In a January 1954 story, for instance, a young man's time came at last when he and his friends were finally called up together, fulfilling all his dreams as he "put on the military uniform, received his weapons, and earnestly prepared to take the oath."[92] As the journal increased its content aimed at young men being called up for service, it began publishing a monthly column called "Stories about Military Service," which ran for several years beginning in early 1954 and contained exceedingly benign coverage of contemporary service, such as nature walks, library excursions, and friendship opportunities. In March 1954, *Voennye znaniia* belittled the US Army for *its* alleged problem with draft dodging, declaring that young American men suffered from "militariphobia" [*voennoboiazn'*] and an "aversion to military service." Soviet conscripts, on the other hand, considered service "a sacred thing" and would never try to avoid it.[93] Drawing attention to the issue flagged it as a common concern for editors and readers alike. The issue of evasion even made it into the widely circulated satirical journal *Krokodil* with the "Hypochondriac" cartoon that opened this chapter, encapsulating Ministry of Defence anxieties: if even the masculine archetype of the muscular proletarian wished to evade service – as opposed to "types" the army might expect to do so, such as women, non-Russian minorities, or conscientious objectors – then Soviet masculinity really was in trouble. Service evasion also appeared elsewhere in popular culture, such as in the acclaimed 1957 film, *The Cranes Are Flying*, in which the anti-hero bought himself a deferment while the hero died bravely in service.[94] As an official DOSAAF publication, *Voennye znaniia* shifted in 1954 from an emphasis on the organization's civilian defence mandate to one more overtly courting conscripts, in a manner which was also implicitly gendered, signalling a shift away from the inclusion of women. DOSAAF, after all, was mandated to train both men and women. The army, on the other hand, was male by design after the war. Shifting the focus of the journal wrote women out.

The increasingly public discussions of service and evasion by 1954 coincided with Stalin's death the year before and the re-evaluation of many of his policies as part of Nikita Khrushchev's de-Stalinization program. As we will see in later chapters, de-Stalinization in the mid-1950s did not consistently factor into narratives about military masculinity. For conscription discourses, however, the shift was quite clear. Stalin forbade public discussions of nuclear weapons and what they might mean for Cold War geopolitics, essentially freezing Soviet military doctrine from 1945 to 1954.[95] After his death the Soviet press, especially military journals like *Voennye znaniia*, discussed nuclear weapons and military service much more openly. In consolidating his leadership in mid-1955, Khrushchev, arguing that the future of the military lay with nuclear weapons, not conventional forces, initiated significant troop cuts. In August 1955, he announced that 640,000 servicemen would be demobilized. In May 1956 he called for a reduction of 1.2 million, in January 1958 another 300,000, and in January 1960, 1.2 million more.[96] In his memoirs, Khrushchev pointed to the changing nature of war in the nuclear age rather than on the socialization of servicemen as his rationale:

> Once it was important how many troops, how many rifles, how many bayonets a country had. But we live in a new and different age. The number of troops and rifles and bayonets is no longer decisive. Now the important thing is the quality and quantity of our nuclear missile arsenal. The defense of our country and our ability to deter imperialist aggression depends on our nuclear and thermonuclear fire power.[97]

But military leaders, having endured a fragile relationship with the government since Stalin's time both before and after the war, experienced fractured relations with Khrushchev due to these cuts. The DOSAAF journal *Kryl'ia rodiny* wrote in early 1957 that defensive training was particularly crucial

> in the present time, as our state reduces the armed forces and a section of youth of conscription age will not serve in the army ... These young people cannot be careless in their military preparation. Each young man, Komsomol member, and Soviet patriot can and must gain the necessary elementary military knowledge in DOSAAF so that, when it is necessary, he can carry out his responsibilities in the defence of our native country with honour.[98]

In addition to worrying about battle preparedness, military leaders expressed concern for the social welfare of demobilized men without career options as well as for would-be conscripts denied the opportunity to develop martial fitness – denying them, in essence, the opportunity to be properly socialized in Soviet masculinity.[99]

In late 1956, Komsomol authorities pointed out to the armed forces leadership that in the immediate aftermath of the first round of cuts, before conscription methods could be amended, there was a group of conscripts already called up that would not actually serve. The Komsomol was concerned that the released men would not only miss necessary training in military affairs but would become deficient in "patriotism" and "honour" as well,[100] citing an increase in reprimands for "drunkenness, hooliganism, and inappropriate behaviour towards civilian populations."[101] Komsomol leaders feared that the non-universal conscription resulting from the troop reductions had already affected discipline and morale within the ranks. In the navy as well, sailors were increasingly reprimanded in the late 1950s for behavioural infractions including drinking and fighting.[102]

However, such concerns were not evenly distributed among all conscripts. As we have seen, when it came to the Komsomol and armed forces' preoccupation with evasion in the borderlands, non-Russian nationalities all too often bore the brunt of accusations of improper training or insufficient interest in serving. In 1960, the Komsomol Central Committee singled out "unworthy" conscripts from Azerbaijan, Armenia, and Georgia for drunkenness, robbery, and "hooliganism in relations towards women" while travelling from their points of conscription to points of service. Local committees were blamed for failing to properly train Caucasian conscripts in military behavioural codes and for failing to secure the "moral temperament of every young man" from the area.[103] Even worse, officials feared, some troublemaking conscripts were taking it upon themselves to train others in such allegedly subversive behaviour, including the best ways to evade service.[104] According to central Komsomol officials, the blame should be placed on local youth leaders in the Caucasus who did not value the "friendship of the peoples" ideology of Soviet multinational cooperation and thus did not raise their young men in those principles either. These youth were simply not interested in defending the country, officials concluded. Further, the Caucasian Komsomol groups did not make use of an "excellent popular tradition" of preparing youth for military service by sending letters to their families from other servicemen from the same area, "relating all the beneficial influences of service in the Soviet army to the upbringing and conditioning of young men."[105] Even worse than not enjoying reassurance or encouragement from older peers in service, officials reported with disdain, was the fact that Caucasian conscripts encountered local prosecutors at military commissariats who informed servicemen of potential punishments for evading service, either by intentionally injuring themselves or through other means. Such fear tactics were not condoned, and officials expressed concern that local military officials had resorted to such measures rather than making more of an effort to educate youth about the benefits of service.[106]

Ellen Jones has pointed out that "a conscript army that relies on post-adolescent males will inevitably reflect the behavioral problems associated with that demographic group."[107] Yet at the same time, as we have seen, youth discipline was of particular concern in the postwar era. Anxiety about the loyalty of many non-Russian nationalities was expressed as concern with the behaviour of the conscription-age young men of those groups. This strategy indicated that officials hoped to protect military masculinity as the domain of Russians and delegitimize Caucasian and Central Asian claims to it, through questioning the latter nationalities' dedication to military service. DOSAAF and the Komsomol would be tasked with taking on young men's training and military socialization in the absence of army service, but both institutions seemed to recognize that this endeavour relied on a spirit of voluntarism missing in Soviet military identities since the war.

Conscription after the Second World War illuminated the desire among policymakers in the military to shape youth behaviour not only for the Cold War but also for domestic deployment to promote an ideal type of manhood. That ideal militarized masculine identity by prioritizing discipline, service, physical fitness, and morality, and, most importantly, it constructed and occupied a space for men alone, without women's participation (or interference). Military training after 1948, at a time of peace and with the army depleted of men, signalled government concern with the social and cultural cultivation of a new generation of young men. When those men did not want to participate in building this militarized masculine identity, however, the Ministry of Defence, through DOSAAF, struggled to make sense of their lack of interest, casting blame on the Komsomol, community leaders, and on young men themselves. Framing the issue as an effort to conscript Soviet manhood after the war helps explain why a victorious postwar country at peace should panic over a perceived dearth of soldiers. The social upheavals that followed the war also raised concerns among policymakers that young people without a moral centre were turning to crime in higher numbers. These fears did not necessarily match evidence from crime statistics, but they nonetheless inspired a "moral panic about nonconformist youth" in the late 1940s.[108]

These stories of service expectations and evasion at a particular moment in Soviet history offer a portrait of military agents attempting to recycle a static, uniform image of the Soviet soldier revived from the Bolshevik past – the defender of the revolution and linchpin of Soviet manhood, citizenship, and ideology – for a postwar generation. But they also reflect a cohort of young men who reached conscription age in the 1950s and chose not to respond to these directives to accept and perform military masculinity. These institutional narratives exhibit a deep concern among policymakers also with the public's perception of widespread evasion, regardless of its accuracy. Military and Komsomol attempts to impose order and uniformity on a plurality of masculine identities speak to a number of issues, including the surveillance of male bodies as they approached conscription age, the consistent sense of disappointment and anxiety regarding the failure of conscription-age youth to live up to the state's physical and cultural expectations for future servicemen in the Soviet army, and the conscripts' own persistent subversion of these expectations, particularly in the Soviet Union's national republics and non-Russian areas. But policymakers also revealed disappointment in their own institutions and the ability of narratives from the centre to direct men's participation in military culture.

In the next chapter, we continue to examine military institutions and the frustrations of state actors in trying to define and enforce appropriate masculine behaviour for boys at officer academies, and the challenges faced by their instructors at the schools and in DOSAAF, both of which influenced the broader search for masculine role models in military settings in postwar literature and film. Under a regime no longer willing to promote women's service or employ women veterans in military industries, it would fall to surviving male veterans to perform as role models for boys before they reached the age of conscription. But state efforts to define and control instructors proved as disappointing to DOSAAF and school officials as conscription did to the Ministry of Defence and the Komsomol, showing that broader cultural tools would need to be engaged outside of military training points in order to more fully re-militarize masculinity in Soviet society.

*Chapter Two*

# Looking for Role Models in Education and Literature

From March to October of 1957, the editorial board of the DOSAAF journal, *Voennye znaniia* (Military Knowledge) held a series of conferences to discuss local readership in cities throughout the Soviet Union. The participants revealed their frustration and confusion as they tried to discern the needs of the young male readers they hoped were about to begin their military careers. One editor stated the problem succinctly: "Very few youth of conscription age read *Voennye znaniia*, although the journal is meant to be read by this contingent of readers."[1] Some recommended placing copies in dormitories, schools, and all libraries "frequented by youth."[2] Others pointed out that one reason youth might not be interested in the journal was that the articles were "dry" and aimed at specialists. For young men "just beginning to study military affairs," a more enticing approach was needed to stimulate and maintain their interest.[3] Other participants lamented that contemporary young people did not sufficiently hate "the enemy," whoever that might be. One board member noted that although the journal usually presented articles about heroic military victories, "in modern conditions, we need to write more articles that cultivate hatred for our enemies and bring our youth up in the spirit of hate."[4] That participant's insistence in 1957 on reviving the Stalin-era encouragement of hatred as a "civic emotion" might have betrayed his generational divide from his young readers; leaders after Stalin generally did not spend as much time on this negative sentiment.[5] Others thought that *Voennye znaniia* should try to rival popular general-audience journals like *Ogonek* (Little Fire) to ensure a broad readership.[6] One editor complained that *Voennye znaniia* featured too few articles about the Civil War of 1918–21, a war in which he himself had served. Another countered that lamenting the lack of stories about Civil War heroes or attempts at high literature was futile. "Conscription-age youth rarely read" anymore, he concluded, and so the actual literary content of *Voennye znaniia* did not really matter.[7] Komsomol administrators further complained to each other in the context of military preparation in 1958 – alluding to the "hooliganism" labels increasingly prevalent in Soviet culture in the 1950s – that the new generation coming up for service since the Second World War included too many "young guys who don't work for long periods of time and live off their parents."[8]

These editors' mission to define the parameters of appropriate fiction for impressionable cadet readers (followed by the more practical tasks of soliciting and publishing it) illustrates a bigger concern: by the time the *Voennye znaniia* editors met in 1957, authorities in military and youth institutions had been grappling for more than a decade with the question of how to properly socialize the first postwar generation of boys in military masculinity. These conversations and concerns repeatedly centred on the problem of where to find and how to establish appropriate military role models in a society with such a depleted male population. The result was the creation in Soviet culture and society of homosocial male spaces imagined as martial brotherhoods and reproduced in military education discourses. These spaces drew on literary and film heroes, able-bodied veterans, and examples of military discipline to establish a corps of male role models for boys after 1945, an effort deemed particularly urgent because so many boys would not have had fathers at home.

This chapter examines the cultivation of militarized masculine role models for boys and young men before they reached the age of conscription. As we saw in chapter 1, conscription became a fraught site for authorities who were concerned that men were avoiding both DOSAAF's voluntary training and the army's service imperatives. The discussion here returns to that site but adjusts the lens to better illuminate boyhood as a stage in a serviceman's life cycle and education as a means of building militarized masculine families. The following discussion focuses on training narratives from two related organizations, the Suvorov officer academies and DOSAAF, which worked in tandem to ensure that young men's lives regularly intersected with martial categories in Soviet society. Yet Suvorov and DOSAAF administrators worried about the new generation's fitness to serve. Encouraging proper masculine behaviour through the cultivation of role models, both real and fictional, aided officials' efforts to ensure that boys formed appropriate military camaraderie that could be deployed as a cultural force in society. The key role models that authorities identified were the officers employed as instructors at the Suvorov schools or DOSAAF clubs. Mostly able-bodied veterans retained in the military rather than redeployed to the much-needed industrial labour force, these men established a bridge between cadets and administrators and served as a middling brotherhood that anchored the new, masculinized family of a postwar military culture that was increasingly being constructed without women. One editor at the *Voennye znaniia* conferences articulated a central issue for the journal, DOSAAF, and the military more generally when he stated, "We need to show youth that they are our means of representing the face of the army."[9] Yet glimpses into the Suvorov schools and DOSAAF societies demonstrate much more disarray and anxiety about the masculine fitness of potential role models, including defence instructors, than officials would have liked. By the mid-1950s, policymakers led by the Main Political Directorate of the Army and Navy turned their efforts towards developing literary and film heroes to model proper engagement with the peacetime forces.

## War Orphans and Boyhood at the Suvorov Academies

In August 1943, already looking ahead to the postwar reconstruction of the officer corps as well as the more immediate situation of war orphans, the Communist Party established a network of military secondary schools. Named for the eighteenth-century general Alexander Vasil'evich Suvorov, the schools reflected Stalin's wartime practice of invoking past military heroes to help motivate servicemen and civilians.[10] There were nine schools in total, established in strategic regions of the country: Krasnodar, Novocherkass, Stalingrad, Voronezh, Khar'kov, Kursk, Orlov, Kalinin, and Stavropol'.

The original goals of the schools were to facilitate the "full preparation of boys for military service in the officer corps and to give them a general secondary education." With admission of candidates starting at the age of ten, the course of study lasted seven years.[11] The program stressed physics and mathematics as well as physical training and military doctrine. Russian was the language of instruction at all schools.[12] Graduates of the Suvorov schools could then be admitted to prestigious post-secondary military institutes without having to take entrance exams. Thus, while originally providing a home, education, and discipline for the orphaned sons of Second World War servicemen, the schools quickly became a "farm league" for post-secondary officer academies.[13] Special consideration was afforded to aspiring students whose fathers had fought in the war, as it was believed that this lineage would ensure that the student would possess the ideal characteristics of a future officer.[14] Authorities believed that even in the months following the Allied victory, when the Soviet Union faced enormous challenges of economic and social recovery, parents would do anything necessary to ensure the possibility that their sons could follow a course of officer training in a military academy. Despite the six new academies that opened their doors at the end of 1945, for example, school authorities claimed that there was room to admit only 3 per cent of students hoping to attend.[15] To be considered for admission, students had to submit an autobiography, a health certificate, and confirmation of their parents' acceptable social position. If the applicant's father (not mother) was a Second World War serviceman or veteran, all other application requirements were waived.[16]

The Suvorov academies became one avenue for redefining the postwar military for men and re-establishing service as participation in a masculine family comprising fathers and brothers. Boys orphaned by the war received preferential admission in return for their service to the state. As an institution originally conceived to raise the orphaned sons of servicemen, the Suvorov schools assumed the functions usually associated with families, attempting to prescribe attitudes towards such topics as friendship, comradeship, and brotherhood to the young cadets. General Suvorov himself had characterized his relationship to the troops under his command as that of "a father to his children" in the eighteenth century.[17] The network of officer academies in the USSR, of which the Suvorov schools were a part, became the most important source of new officers after the war and a key system for popularizing military careers among young men.[18] Ellen Jones' work on the multiple sites of intersection between the army and society has shown the significance of education in conditioning boys not only in tactical work but in assuming the social role of a soldier.[19]

This chapter treats these academies as masculinized, homosocial spaces in which brotherhood and paternalism were emphasized and nurtured at the same time that the opposite was happening outside the schools' doors. Indeed, postwar society was characterized by an increased visibility of women, mothers outnumbering fathers, and new meanings of "family." In 1946 there were ten million fewer men than women in the 20–44 age group, with an even greater disparity in the countryside.[20] Deliberately devoid of women, the Suvorov military families united to create a plurality of masculinities that included nurturers as well as disciplinarians. The military rhetoric of family and the efforts to raise children collectively, outside the purview of biological family, drew on the experiences of revolution-era Bolshevik ideology and experimentation. The children's homes of the Revolution and Civil War era, however, had attempted to socialize childrearing much more thoroughly than the Suvorov academies did. As Lisa Kirschenbaum has noted, "Rhetoric attached the sentiment or even sentimentality of 'family' to hopefully modern and scientific, but potentially cold, forbidding, and bureaucratic institutions."[21] Instructors were charged with developing both "friendly and parental love" for the students as the best way to establish a true collective among them.[22] Yet the Suvorov "families" operated without the usual maternal figures that other socialist childrearing institutions offered. The peculiarly masculinized families raising young officers socialized them for a world without women. As such, authority had to be derived through means other than sex differentiation, including generation, status, and the parsing of the ideals of comradeship and brotherhood to form smaller social groups in which the strong dominated the weak.

In the schools' first months in late 1945, Suvorov authorities viewed the academies as crucial not only for replenishing the army's officer corps for the postwar era, but also for attending to the social and moral training of a new generation of young men. Those men were not only to become more "cultured, disciplined, and efficient" and gradually "lose undesirable habits," but would above all strive to "acquire a soldier's look."[23] Administrators seemed confident in 1945 that war widows would overwhelmingly seek to enrol their sons in a Suvorov school in order for them to avoid the postwar hardships that would plague civilians. According to the schools, mothers routinely insisted on putting out their own money for uniforms, training, and food, as they were certain that their sons would be raised well and would leave as "good officers."[24] The absence of fathers in the lives of these cadets was taken as a given. Handing their boys over to this state institution indicated not only a continued loyalty to the military, even in families that had lost a father or husband in the war, but also a tacit admission that the boys would be better off raised in a disciplined, homosocial atmosphere teeming with potential father figures than they would be at home with their mothers.

## Cadets and Community Surveillance of Masculine Behaviour

In the late spring of 1945, with a long, vicious war finally drawing to a close, Suvorov cadets filled out a questionnaire on the meanings of "friendship" and "comradeship." These questionnaires were later quoted with delight by school authorities eager to prove to General-Lieutenant V.I. Morozov and army authorities that the Suvorov students understood their duties to the collective. Suvorov administrators had been motivated to conduct the survey, however, because of a perceived crisis in camaraderie among cadets. The image of student friendship and comradeship that authorities sought to construct from the replies makes visible the tension between the familiar socialist script regarding collectivism and the Suvorov boys' efforts to subvert it using their own emerging codes of appropriate masculine behaviour. The replies repeatedly return to the language of family, expressing opinions about who could and should be part of it and who deserved ostracism from the cadet community. Membership in the Suvorov family was crucial to the cadets, and being cast out from the fraternal unit could be psychologically and culturally damaging. At the same time, however, the boys themselves actively policed the boundaries of acceptable community behaviour and established their own rules for their martial brotherhoods.

In their replies, the students regularly recited the correct Soviet line on the importance of the collective over the individual. "The bonds of strong friendship in one brotherly family can overcome any obstacle in life," one wrote.[25] Student Sh. wrote that "people who are united in a strong friendship in a single brotherly family can overcome any obstacle and impediment," and that "comrades need to be good brothers, helping each other in work and study."[26] Student P. wrote that "friends love and respect each other, they are candid with each other, help each other in work, study, and in all family matters; that people are genuine friends only when their friendship is connected with community, unified life goals … a single world outlook, a single political view and activity."[27] For Student R., "iron friendships" were crucial for military success.[28] Many respondents connected friendship and loyalty directly to military victory. Student Kh. insisted that "without friendship in the army, there is no unity between troops. And if there is no unity, then our army will be weak: that is the role friendship plays."[29] Student K., meanwhile, tied proper behaviour to a boy's filial responsibility, demanding that his friends be proper sons when they were home and be sure to help their mothers.[30]

Approved answers about collectivism only got respondents so far, however; some also expressed remarkable openness about the social challenges to full membership in the Suvorov brotherhood and persistent fractures in the cadet community. Student M. warned of "rude mockery and nicknames taking place among students of his company, ruining children's friendships," adding that "these blemishes" on the community had to be eradicated.[31] Student Kh. rooted disunity in discipline problems among individual cadets. "For the sake of friendship," he wrote, "you need to pay attention to your comrade's poor behaviour, help save him from it, and constantly worry that your comrade should take the correct path." He added, "Comrades must not make fun of the innate shortcomings of other students, but must grapple with all the shortcomings in their behaviour" in order to help overcome them.[32] This type of comment suggests that a cadet's flaws or behavioural infractions were not only the fault of that individual but also that of the community. Invoking the language of family and generational difference, another Student Kh. responded that disciplinary infractions among cadets led to "fallings-out, fights, lies, and deception." He demanded that "adult comrades" – either administrators or instructors – "help everyone equally and not offend their younger comrades."[33]

Although this questionnaire offers only a small sample, the sentiments that the cadets expressed echo E. Thomas Ewing's findings about unruly behaviour and disciplinary issues in Soviet civilian boys' schools. Refocusing military participation on boys and men after the war and excluding girls and women was not the only effort the Soviet government undertook to implement gender segregation. Between 1943 and 1954, primary and secondary schools in major cities were divided according to sex, thus interrupting the coeducation that had been a key Bolshevik social measure since 1918. Education officials imposed the separation, according to Ewing, with the goal of boys having "fewer distractions, gender-specific pedagogy, and a more 'masculine' environment."[34] Sex-segregated schooling was a product of government interest in "the preservation and promotion of masculine privilege."[35] The decree that ended coeducation in 1943 cited the need for more attention to educating boys and girls in separate spaces for their future roles as "soldiers and mothers." The reformed schools would "educate boys to be future fathers and courageous fighters for the socialist homeland and girls to be the conscious mothers and educators of the new generation."[36] This retreat from coeducation and emphasis on schooling boys alone as future soldiers, even in civilian settings, occurred at a moment in the war when the visibility of servicewomen in the press was increasing. By 1943, major newspapers like *Pravda* and *Krasnaia zvezda* were carefully including references to "women soldiers" alongside "men soldiers," exemplifying what Anna Krylova has called "the rupture of the automatic association between combat and masculinity."[37] Ewing argues that separate schooling never achieved the promised results for boys in particular. The widespread breakdown in discipline at boys' schools allowed authorities to blame the absence of girls' supposedly calming influence. As a result, officials pulled higher quality teachers and resources from girls' schools, reassigning them where they were believed to be most needed – to discipline the boys.[38] Although the experiment with separate schools for civilian children was short-lived, it shares with the Suvorov academies the gendered behavioural assumptions policymakers made about boys during and after the war. The Suvorov schools were part of a much larger trend in postwar Soviet society towards re-establishing militarized spaces as masculine and raising boys to revere soldiering.

Despite promoting comradeship and loyalty among cadets as the questionnaire answers suggest, authorities identified serious disciplinary problems, such as when cadets created their own martial brotherhoods outside official sanction, with rules and boundaries that school officials could not access. These incidents involved small groups of cadets engaging in aggressive physical contests with each other, using negative nicknames, splitting into smaller, exclusionary social groups, and practising *krugovaia poruka*, a term whose definition shifted depending on the context, as explored below. Authorities believed all these activities were a major impediment to developing socially correct officers. One lengthy report in late 1945 by Suvorov authorities on *krugovaia poruka* and other infractions, including cheating and the use of negative nicknames, raises more questions than it answers about boys' social conditioning and agency at the schools. Nonetheless, it offers a glimpse of the struggles between administrators who were intent on delineating the boundaries of acceptable behaviour, and a cadet corps who wanted to establish those boundaries on their own.

The concept of *krugovaia poruka* has a long history in Russia. Best known as a legal framework within tsarist peasant communities drawing on sentiments of collective responsibility to ensure taxes were paid, it also appears in Soviet history in factories and other sites of communal work. Although it is generally translated as "collective security," it also took on the meaning of a cover-up when used by Suvorov authorities. In particular, Suvorov assessments refer to officials' anxieties when groups of cadets banded together to mask the misbehaviour of a comrade from school authorities.[39] "Comradeship and friendship should be free from *krugovaia poruka*," the report began. It defined the practice as "collective concealment" in one of two ways: either the activities of one cadet were uniformly condoned by the others, or the collective disagreed with the activities of a misbehaving comrade but still concealed them. Cadets might engage in the second group behaviour, officials surmised, out of pity for the wrong-headed comrade or fear of reprisal if his name were revealed.[40] In most cases, authorities attributed the students' engagement with *krugovaia poruka* to ignorance or a misunderstanding of communal ideals, noting that the students seemed to operate under the principle "a comrade does not betray," while pointing out that such a motto was an "incorrect understanding of the moral basis of comradeship and friendship." Administrators tried to convince students that a true friend and comrade would unmask the culprits of misbehaviour.[41] To do otherwise was to endorse values at odds with the cadets' burgeoning military identities, such as cowardice and dishonour.[42]

With more evidence, historians also need to ask further questions about the role of sexuality, a drastically understudied subject in Soviet history, in the mutual surveillance of homosocial spaces like the Suvorov academies. As historians of sexuality have found, policing behaviour within groups of men is often meant to enforce heteronormative compliance and unmask deviance from communally accepted behaviours.[43] The Suvorov disciplinary records examined here, while far from comprehensive, did not mention sexuality even covertly. The only possible hints come in the few but insistent critiques of "pair-friendships," which authorities considered to be "the worst, most unhealthy form of individualism."[44] While not definitive, this language could certainly be read as concern about relationships between cadets becoming intimate.

School officials denied the possibility that the younger generation could have appropriated collectivist vocabulary and principles to establish an authority separate from that of their elders. They suggested instead that the students engaging in *krugovaia poruka* were naive rather than malicious, simply children who did not know any better. By using the historically meaningful term *krugovaia poruka* for the cadets' behaviour, though, school officials indicated a much broader understanding – and perhaps fear – of boys' agency in developing their own codes of community discipline and surveillance.

These narratives from state actors shaped by institutional archives are incomplete without the voices of the Suvorov students themselves. On the one hand, concern about discipline and rule-abiding behaviour for future army officers should not be surprising; it would have formed the basis of the academies' very existence. On the other hand, gender analysis helps illuminate some practices particular to the Suvorov academies. Reinforcing these codes of conduct at schools dedicated to taking in and training orphaned boys as officers – in the absence of similar opportunities for orphaned girls – demonstrates a deliberate attempt to forge a link between masculinity and military authority. For the boys themselves to disrupt that forging with their own ideas about masculine community, boundaries, and leadership – and for school officials to dispatch alarmed reports on those disruptions – suggests that officials placed high stakes on the success of this training.

**Defence Instructors as Surrogate Fathers**

In its 1952 New Year's issue, *Krokodil* drew on familiar imagery. The journal often depicted the arrival of the new year with an image of a young boy, implying that the socialist future was securely in male hands. To welcome 1952, the usual boy, carrying a placard announcing "Peace to the world!" marched past a brawny soldier. Standing next to his rifle and guarding a post that stood in for the Soviet Union as a whole, the soldier smiled at the boy in approval – an unmistakable nod to their masculine bond as guardians of peace (Figure 2.1).[45] In a similar image from 1953, a boy wearing coveralls with "Peace" stamped across his chest addressed a hulking soldier, who again carried his rifle at his side and gazed down at the boy in approval. The boy thanked him, on behalf of those in the "camp of peace," for his service to the country (Figure 2.2).[46]

These public images underscored the social importance of able-bodied young veterans as role models and defence instructors, particularly from the end of the war through to Stalin's death. The officers responsible for teaching students occupied a middling space between the authority of the men who ran the Suvorov academies and DOSAAF, and the boys who were enrolled in their programs. Both institutions carefully deployed men possessing desired social characteristics as instructors, as authorities searched for a way to sell

— Здесь я ступил на твёрдую почву!

Figure 2.1 "I'm on solid ground here!"

*Krokodil*, 30 December 1951, 3.

Figure 2.2 "The camps of peace all over the world thank you for your many years of service!" *Krokodil*, 20 February 1953, 2.

military training to a generation that had watched with horror as the Second World War raged – a war that, in the vast majority of cases, had killed these boys' fathers and displaced their families. The Suvorov academies and DOSAAF slotted young, yet experienced, instructors into social roles as surrogate fathers or older brothers. Assessing the make-up of the instructor corps in August 1951, DOSAAF authorities determined that 87 per cent were Second World War veterans, with 59 per cent still in the officer reserves. Age was flagged as a key category: 84 per cent were under 40 years old.[47] These figures suggest that in terms of age and experience, instructors might be able to offer facsimiles of filial relationships lost in the war. "The best propaganda for getting military issues to the masses must be to use former *frontoviki*, the demobilized troops," an editorial in *Voennye znaniia* urged in 1948.[48] At a time when the military was about to begin demobilizing millions of troops and officers in the face of serious labour shortages in Soviet industry, the fact that presumably healthy and able-bodied officers remained in service as instructors – symbolically remaining in uniform in some capacity – suggests that they carried more cultural than economic purchase.

Suvorov administrators maintained a list of features desired in the officers serving as instructors at the schools. These men were required to be "genuine patriots," "faithful sons of our Soviet homeland," and "models ... of military discipline." They also needed to be able to assert their authority over the students. A report on instructor characteristics noted:

> Training cadets is impossible without authority. Officer-instructors must secure authority over their students through the strength of their service status [in the army]. Authority is created not with the presence of certain qualities, but with their outward display. Only through living by example will the authoritative instructor have power among students.[49]

Establishing such a relationship with the students was the instructor's responsibility, and the proper behaviour of students was best achieved by example. The report on *krugovaia poruka* reminded Suvorov administrators that "with all his being, the instructor should embody the ideal qualities of a Soviet man" in order to win students' "confidence, respect, and affection."[50] The instructor was expected to be an ideological leader for students and a widely read role model who participates in study circles; he was also to be reasonable towards subordinates, neat, and physically fit.[51] And, as Suvorov leaders wrote in late 1945, he "doesn't have to be a smart aleck (*vseznaika*) about it, but he should know enough" in fields like mathematics, science, and Russian language.[52]

Young men in service needed to meet the following expectations, *Kryl'ia rodiny* advised in 1954: "Soviet youth must be bold, brave, physically hardened, not afraid of difficulties, and able to surmount any obstacles in their path." In order to develop these traits, boys needed proper training and role models. "Boldness and bravery must combine with outstanding knowledge and a perfect grasp of weapons and battle technologies. The Soviet army, the leading army in the world, needs those who are courageous, fearless, physically hardened, and at the same time cultured and educated, knowing the affairs of soldiers and officers well."[53] The common use of the word "courageous" (*muzhestvennyi*) in describing expected military traits in Russian offers gender scholars both an opportunity for rich analysis and a conundrum. Serguei Oushakine has led the field in both Russian and English language scholarship by reclaiming the words *muzhestvennost'* (noun) and *muzhestvennyi* (adjective) as gendered. They can be and usually are translated as "courage/courageous" or "bravery/brave," but they share the root *muzh* with the word for "man." Russian does not have a separate word for "masculinity," but over the past two decades scholars like Oushakine have been using *muzhestvennost'*. By evaluating Soviet sources that use the word, scholarly analysis has also opened new avenues of interpretation, especially regarding its military uses: it might mean courage and nothing more, or the source could be speaking from an implicitly gendered point of view that insinuates "masculinity" as a virtue.[54]

The championing of ideal instructor attributes gave way in 1953 to concern about the lack of suitable personnel, with DOSAAF authorities increasingly dissatisfied with the availability of specialists for instructor duties. In particularly short supply were those trained to operate tanks, self-propelled guns, artillery, and mortars, as well as road workers, bridge workers, and mine-laying instructors.[55] Disappointment with instructors' preparation and behaviour was not always kept from public view, either. The official DOSAAF journals *Kryl'ia rodiny* and *Voennye znaniia* reported on it in the early 1950s. Inexperience and poor leadership were most frequently cited as instructors' greatest weaknesses in DOSAAF training clubs. "There are not enough well-prepared [DOSAAF] instructors," *Kryl'ia rodiny* lamented in 1952.[56] A letter of complaint in May 1954 from ten parachutists pointed in particular to inadequate leadership, with the authors stating that their instructors "do not have enough experience to teach children."[57] Nowhere in discussions of instructors or lack of specialists was it acknowledged that there might simply have been an overall dearth of men in the population or that those men were otherwise engaged. Nor, moreover, was the possibility ever raised of recruiting instructors from the ranks of servicewomen who had been demobilized after the war.

Instructors were held accountable for their students' actions when disciplinary infractions occurred. At the Suvorov schools, authorities' concern with *krugovaia poruka* among cadets at times extended to instructors, who were implicated in covering up student infractions. "There is nothing more disgraceful than when officer-instructors, having received word of a misdemeanor, try to hide [it]," one school official wrote in a disciplinary report.[58] As paternal figures, instructors could find themselves blamed for failing as parents, since they had been entrusted with the task of inculcating proper militarized behaviour in their charges, only to witness cadets' determination to forge their own social networks and hierarchies. The students' own negotiation of power in establishing competing collectives either fell under the radar of authorities or it was assumed that the students simply did not understand the collective responsibilities expected of them. Instructors, whose authority was tenuous, had to rely on befriending children and earning their respect, while also pleasing the school authorities as role models of Soviet servicemen.

Instructors were also implicated in behavioural infractions. Late in 1945, a list of incidents across the Suvorov system incensed administrators. Some officers were caught shirking their duties monitoring students at night, leaving the dormitories unattended. At the Tula, Kuibyshev, and Kursk schools, administrators chastised officers who skipped morning exercises and other activities, leaving some students in charge of the others. Three officers from the Kazan school "in a state of intoxication" drove a car through a fence. During a competition for throwing iron grenades held in Stavropol', a cadet lobbed one at another student's head. Gross negligence among instructors was a major concern for authorities: the Kazan and Tambov academies saw students break their legs on skiing trips, while in Krasnodar, instructors who failed to properly organize shifts watching the students allowed two unattended students to drown. Inappropriate disciplinary techniques also drew attention: in Stalingrad, a student who had been listening in at an instructor's door at night was punished by confinement in a plywood cell purposely built by the instructor himself.[59]

Disciplinary issues among instructors did not appear in the military press as often as more benign calls for further training did, as noted above, but they appeared at times, usually with few details. We know only that a "great violation of discipline" occurred among trainers at DOSAAF's Vologodskii aeroclub in 1955, for example, which led to the dismissal of the senior instructor corps.[60] Officers serving as instructors at the schools posed a real dilemma for administrators who needed them but also lamented their potentially bad influence on cadets. Since instructors were meant to embody "ideal" Soviet officers and serve as makeshift father figures, the schools placed significant emphasis on correcting and reinforcing instructor masculinity.[61] The men reserved for Suvorov and DOSAAF instructor posts were afforded a place in a surrogate family structure as generational intermediaries. Generally older than DOSAAF's ideal demographic but younger than administrators (and with more combat experience than either), instructors wore the badge of wartime service increasingly necessary for validation in postwar society. They offered a way to complete the new masculinized family structure embraced by the military at a time when traditional gender roles and family hierarchies had been disrupted. But when their own behavioural infractions threatened to detract from their mission training the next generation of servicemen, authorities broadened their search for role models.

## Masculine Role Models in Literature and Film

The Soviet Union operated based on what Mark von Hagen has called a "bellicist worldview."[62] In the lexicon of the revolutionary state, military service should not have needed to be resold to a new generation. Nevertheless, after 1945, and in light of the remobilization campaigns of 1948, the military found itself doing just that. Aided by the Komsomol, military authorities had to repackage service as a particularly masculine endeavour in order to avoid calling on women again. They also had to resell military service as a legitimate way of serving the state and the revolution at a time when the chances for battle heroism – a romantic notion for young people – were remote and life in the peacetime forces seemed to be an impossibly dull series of drills and ceremonies.[63]

Historians and literary scholars of the postwar era have described how the regime, as part of this effort, prioritized the creation of literary war heroes aimed at a younger generation eager to immerse itself in stories of glory and heroism – one that was curious about, rather than traumatized by, war. One example was the protagonist in the Komsomol-promoted story *Alexander Matrosov*, by Pavel Zhurba.[64] First published in 1949, it was set during the war and featured a young male hero, an orphan-turned-soldier who learned discipline and the importance of (surrogate) family through service to his country. Matrosov was a leader among the other boys, a good friend, and a man who gave up a chance at romance with a woman in order to pursue his dream and answer the call to serve alongside his comrades in the military. A loyal Komsomol member throughout, he was eventually killed in battle but memorialized as a man who fought bravely. As Catriona Kelly has written of Matrosov, he "became a vital force in mediating the philosophy of the earlier generation to his peers, a link in the great continuity of socialist tradition."[65] For a generation increasingly disgruntled with the present and, in the eyes of central authorities, too disrespectful of the past, Matrosov served as an inspiring military and masculine hero.

Juliane Fürst's analysis of the heavy publicity surrounding Alexander Fadeev's popular 1946 novel, *The Young Guard*, also demonstrates the broader government campaign to encourage reverence for the military in young people. "Not since the days of the Civil War had the opportunity to capitalize on youthful emotions been as strong as in the aftermath of the Great Fatherland War," she writes. "The regime was determined to maintain the momentum of the war years," in particular by whetting youthful appetites for stories of war heroism.[66] In the case of *The Young Guard*, Fadeev fictionalized the true story of a Komsomol resistance group in 1943 whose members were caught and executed by the Germans. It became, according to Fürst, "the Harry Potter of its time." By the late 1940s every young person in the country knew the names and heroic deeds of the Young Guard members.[67] These and many other works of literature of late Stalinism used the war as a setting to depict bravery, perseverance, and victory among servicemen. Along with *Young Guard*, the most famous example was Boris Polevoi's 1947 novel, *A Story about a Real Man*, which was made into a film a year later. The hero, a fighter pilot who lost both legs in the war, became a "real man" when he pulled himself out of his self-pity and, with the help of an inspiring mentor, Soviet prosthetics, and a renewed commitment to becoming the hero his country needed, successfully returned to the skies.[68]

These literary and film classics of the late 1940s took place during the war, a setting with ready-made heroic narratives. They comprised the first of two main eras for postwar military fiction, lasting from the end of the war in 1945 to Stalin's death in 1953. The second era began with Nikita Khrushchev's consolidation of power in 1956 and the inauguration of de-Stalinization and the Thaw in Soviet literature. Although works from this second era were still set during the war, Stalin's death in 1953 had opened a space for writers and filmmakers to reconsider the kinds of war themes and soldier-heroes available in literature and film. This group included some of the Thaw's most famous war novels, such as works by Yuri Bondarev, Grigorii Baklanov, Konstantin Vorob'ev, and Konstantin Simonov. The Thaw also introduced new film narratives for military topics such as in director Alexander Ivanov's *Soldiers* (1957), which all but blamed Stalin for the catastrophic war.[69] Thaw-era military fiction and film focused on individual experiences and trauma in Second World War settings rather than the narratives glorifying Stalin and country that this genre had emphasized before the leader's death.[70] These two main eras of military fiction – before Stalin's death in 1953 and after the emergence of Thaw literature in 1956 – both focused on the war as a setting, however, leaving a dearth of representations of the peacetime forces in the mid-1950s. Suvorov academy and DOSAAF administrators, who were concerned with cadet discipline and instructor misbehaviour, wanted masculine heroes in the contemporary forces, not those from the larger-than-life war years, who might appeal to boys and young men. Between 1953 and 1956, role models in the peacetime military were still needed as cultural icons for the young men whose martial fitness routinely disappointed policymakers.

Military authorities were concerned about what young men were reading – or not reading – and how that would affect their training in military matters. The *Voennye znaniia* conferences in 1957 that opened this chapter were only one part of a bigger conversation then taking place amid the social and cultural reorganizations of de-Stalinization. In May 1955, the First All-Union Conference on Military Fiction was held in Moscow, at which hundreds of representatives of publishers, journal editorial staff, and writers' groups from around the country debated the goals and accomplishments of military fiction.[71] The war had proven an inexhaustible source of inspiration for writers, but the conference also drew attention to the dearth of work on the peacetime forces of the 1950s. One attendee lamented the rigid, garrison-based settings of military fiction, advocating for stories in which soldiers were more well-rounded and resembled civilian literary characters. Another lieutenant in attendance criticized the small number of works produced about the contemporary forces, counting only three in the ten years since the end of the war: Vladimir Komissarov's *Guards Lieutenant*, Vitalii Petl'ovannyi's *The Trumpets Play Retreat*, and Ivan Stadniuk's *Maxim Perepelitsa*.[72] Attendees blamed the lack of writing about the postwar forces on two factors. First, during the war, most military fiction had been written by servicemen. These writers were not interested in writing about the peacetime forces after their demobilization; thus, the war continued to dominate military literature. Second, conference discussants blamed the widespread perception that peace made for boring reading.[73]

Ivan Stadniuk's 1952 novel, *Maxim Perepelitsa*, offered a method for making military fiction more interesting to young readers, even if the plot did not revolve around an exciting, romantic wartime drama. As Alexei Surkov, the First Secretary of the Directorate of the Writers' Union of the USSR, argued at the 1955 conference, new fiction should explore "the psychological changes in a young high school graduate, when he first encounters the rigors of military discipline."[74] *Maxim Perepelitsa* did just that. Released as a film in 1955, *Maxim Perepelitsa* was a huge success. The young pre-service hero was something of a clown in his Ukrainian village, always pulling pranks and making jokes, enjoying his easy life devoid of responsibility, purpose, or discipline. Opening with a village celebration of the men leaving for basic training, the film characterized army service as a privilege reserved for the most deserving men. Tellingly, the story avoided emphasizing any coercive powers of conscription, all but presenting army service as completely voluntary and merit-based. Although the *kolkhoz* (collective farm) leaders considered him ill-suited for service, Maxim insisted that he would change if he were permitted to join the army. "A man like that doesn't belong in the army!" bellowed an elderly villager. "He will spoil the honour of a soldier."[75] But the village leaders begged to differ (thus again promoting the fiction that they were gatekeepers of an exclusive club). "But comrades, why keep him out of the army?" one asked the group. "Let him go, for in the army he will become a man!"[76] After winning the villagers over and entering basic training, Maxim at first continued his jokester ways – masquerading as an officer to entertain his fellow recruits or conniving to get more food or do fewer chores. But his training regimen eventually had an effect, and Maxim became a disciplined, honourable soldier. The army had indeed made a man out of him, transforming him from an aimless teenager enjoying the easy life – a life his elders had fought to make possible – into a soldier grateful for the opportunity to serve.

Although the themes of peacetime service and comedy were not common in postwar military films either before or after the Thaw, a strikingly similar comedic film came out the same year: *The Soldier Ivan Brovkin*. Its hero, Ivan, was a local buffoon more interested in leisure pursuits on his *kolkhoz* than in duty and discipline. His father, a serviceman who had been well liked in their village, had died in the war, leaving Ivan with big shoes to fill. Ivan's path to service was similar to Maxim's, with everyone involved avoiding any coercive talk while emphasizing Ivan's desire to join the armed forces and reform his errant ways. Ivan not only needed to undergo re-education in disciplined masculinity, but he also needed to prove that he was worthy of his father's legacy of service. Through his military training, Ivan grew into a man, one who was mature, reliable, and strong in body and character. This transformation was not an easy one. Indeed, he "need[ed] the help of the entire Soviet army to make a man of him."[77] The film challenged prevailing views among young people after the war, as discussed in the previous section, that peacetime service was dull and unchallenging. Ivan's training regularly featured difficult tasks requiring concentration, discipline, and perseverance. When Ivan returned home one year later on leave, his *kolkhoz* chairman expressed disbelief: "Look what the army does to a man!" he exclaimed. "One year, and Ivan Brovkin is unrecognizable."[78] Gathering around Ivan, the other villagers agreed that he was now a heroic man like his father. Ivan and Maxim represented unusual protagonists in postwar literature and film, expanding the "conventional gallery of heroes," as Josephine Woll has written.[79] By offering young men in 1955 examples of ordinary youth coming into contact with the army for the first time, the stories of Ivan and Maxim stood in marked contrast to the larger-than-life heroes of war dramas.

Neither film's popularity was universal, though. The Ministry of Defence newspaper, *Krasnaia zvezda*, published a series of letters from servicemen criticizing *Maxim Perepelitsa* in particular, arguing that it made a mockery of service. One letter signed by several officers took issue with the portrayal of army discipline: "Of course the army contains individual soldiers who are undisciplined, who have one shortcoming or another ... But all that is unnecessary, negative, and not typical in the Soviet Army." Others disagreed with the central premise of the film, that a "rural bully" could be transformed into a stoic, honourable soldier. "It is hard to believe that an undisciplined soldier could suddenly reform and, shortly after his rehabilitation, receive two stripes and an easy promotion to junior sergeant," wrote another officer. For these men, the film reduced the very serious theme of military service to "vaudeville."[80]

Military literature and film sought to reinforce the exclusion of women and images of femininity from postwar martial identity. *Maxim Perepelitsa* advanced the idea that military service made a man more attractive to women. Maxim's love interest, Marusya, repeatedly emphasized to him that his service was both important to the country and personally appealing to her. For his part, Ivan Brovkin won the *kolkhoz* chairman's daughter, Lubasha, as his prize for completing his transformation. His underdeveloped masculinity had prevented him from successfully courting her earlier in the film. Even as they grew closer, Ivan signalled to Lubasha that she would never be able to understand the fierce bonds between men in service. At the same time, both films treated women as a distraction and a liability for soldiers. In class, Maxim realized that he had missed crucial information on tank deployments because he had been daydreaming about Marusya, to whom he regularly wrote letters. Maxim then learned that his team leader refrained from writing to his girlfriend in order to better focus on training. A young serviceman's military success and promotion in the film depended on not allowing civilian women to distract him. In keeping with this theme, Ivan was repeatedly distracted from key tasks when Lubasha entered the scene. At various times, he damaged a roof, lost track of some pigs, and wrecked a new car, all because he had been trying to get Lubasha's attention. Not permitting himself to lose focus over a woman was only one part of the masculinity these heroes needed to develop; in his physical presentation, Ivan also needed to undergo transformation in order to develop his martial masculinity: as Josephine Woll has noted, Ivan's long blond curls served as a visual cue of his prettiness, weakness, and effeminacy.[81] The scene in which his hair was cut short in preparation for army service proved to be a key moment in his recalibration of masculine identity and repudiation of femininity.

Both films' musical scores also played a role in establishing and reinforcing the boundaries of masculinity and army service. In *Maxim Perepelitsa,* the women of Maxim's village supported him but could not take his journey with him. During the company's march through town to the now-famous song *V put'* (Let's Go), written for the film by acclaimed Soviet composer Vasilii Solov'ev-Sedoi and still a beloved anthem of today's post-Soviet Russian army, women's only role was to watch the procession. Smiling women were seen in summer dresses and countryside kerchiefs while throwing flowers at the troops.[82] The song's lyrics also reinforced women's exclusion from military culture, implying that women could only wait at home for letters from their male companions in uniform. In a key refrain, the soldiers sang, "Soldiers, let's go, let's go, let's go (to war)! / And for you, my darling, there's always the post office."[83] Similarly, the songs in *Ivan Brovkin* drew a line between men's access to military service and women's roles at home. In the scene accompanying one song, as the marching soldiers passed a group of young women (*devushki*) working in the fields, their commanding officer ordered them to stop and help the women with their work, as they would never be able to finish it on their own. In the last verse of the song, it was revealed to the audience as well as the company that the commanding officer had married one of the young women from the garden.[84]

Like these films, the literary aspects of DOSAAF's publications treated women solely as mothers and wives left behind by the Soviet serviceman. In *Kryl'ia rodiny*, these messages often came in the form of songs or poems accompanied by drawings of reserved, grieving women. The poem, "A Maiden's Lyric," published in March 1956, included a sketch of a young woman with a long plait and a polka-dot dress, clutching a tree trunk and gazing off into the distance while her "red-winged ace" flew off in an air force jet.[85] Another 1956 poem, called "To a Son," featured an image of a middle-aged woman staring out the window at an evening skyline, a plane jetting past overhead:

> I look from the window at the starry sky.
> The great distance is both quiet and clear …
> You stand on guard, as a light over our home … All my thoughts – about my son's fate,
> The confidence and happiness of our people
> You carry … in your strong hands.[86]

"I Am a Pilot's Wife" (1957) similarly painted women as mere bystanders to military service and technology, relegated to the home to idly observe as a new age passed them by:

> For twenty years you have flown away with love
> Saying at parting: "I know, you are waiting!"
> Your green lights blink from great heights,
> And you nod your wing to me in parting.[87]

Poems published in DOSAAF magazines like *Kryl'ia rodiny* and *Voennye znaniia* were not high literature. The audience for both publications would have been servicemen and DOSAAF regulars; poems like these would have had to serve this audience with narratives approved by DOSAAF and the Ministry of Defence. At a moment of postwar recovery, images of women waiting for men to return from service would have held significant meaning for many families whose soldiers had not come back. These portraits of women as witnesses, not participants, appeared regularly in DOSAAF's magazines and made clear that women could not access the same martial categories as men. For the air force in particular, as these poems from *Kryl'ia rodiny* demonstrate, the state-sponsored image of the worried yet patient wife and mother fed a gendered narrative about technology, one in which only men could fly. Women, on the other hand, were seen as passive and fearful. This postwar revisionism in a country that had celebrated women's aviation in the 1930s extended beyond the simple poems in *Kryl'ia rodiny*: in chapter 5, we will encounter more examples of how aviation was gendered male at the precise moment that the state was training and deploying the first woman cosmonaut, Valentina Tereshkova.[88]

Military policymakers, including those in the Main Political Directorate charged with commissioning appropriate literature for cadets, DOSAAF participants, and conscripts, had trouble generating appropriate soldier-heroes in the 1950s. While popular, *Maxim Perepelitsa* and *The Soldier Ivan Brovkin* contained virtually the only postwar military heroes in literary culture at the time. During postwar years marked by concern with misbehaviour among cadets and instructors alike, literature and film were not fully able to fill the void in contemporary heroism. In later chapters, we will see the many ways that this emphasis on heroic, military-credentialled men persisted in popular culture into the 1960s in satirical cartoons, in the cult of the atom that elevated nuclear physicists to celebrity status, and especially with Yuri Gagarin and the inaugural cohort of cosmonauts, who proudly wore their air force uniforms and modelled (peaceful) military authority on the world stage.

In their studies of early Soviet history Eric Naiman and Thomas G. Schrand have found that the approach to women's equality in official party ideology resulted in a tendency to "erase the feminine." Writing about the 1920s and 1930s, respectively, they found a gender paradox whereby government directives to emancipate Soviet women implied that feminine spheres of power would only be absorbed into hegemonic masculine society.[89] After the Second World War and the initial swell of expressions of pride that Soviet women had fought alongside men both in civilian mobilization efforts and in military combat, the state returned to an agenda of erasure. This strategy involved remilitarizing Soviet men and remasculinizing military service, both in practice and in cultural narratives.

Both the Suvorov academies and DOSAAF used familial vocabulary and social networks to re-establish military culture after the Second World War. Beginning with the creation of closed communities represented by the Suvorov officer academies in 1945, the military, in which servicewomen had been highly visible during the war, was reinvented as a space of fraternity and patriarchy, a masculinized structure devoid of women and populated by men playing a variety of familial roles. The "brotherly family"[90] consistently glorified in the pages of *Voennye znaniia* referenced the close bond of Second World War servicemen who had fought and died together, but at the same time it indicated a renewed cultural space for a generation moving together through the ranks, albeit one that had lost countless male family members and potential role models.

The Suvorov academies attempted to create an insular atmosphere in which comradeship was recast as fraternal and friendship existed to the exclusion of women; to this end school authorities nurtured the creation of a male homosocial space that attempted to remake relationships of lost fathers and brothers. The approach lacked consistency, however, and, with the campaigns against *krugovaia poruka* in the academies, socialist ideology sometimes undercut cadets' own ideals of brotherhood and loyalty. Still, the training of a new officer corps after 1945 became less about military preparation and more about the social and cultural grooming of a new generation of boys. In a country looking to reassert the political and cultural power of masculinity following a devastating war, such a task took on increasing importance.

In Part II, we look more closely at the militarized spaces that the Cold War made possible outside official military structures in order to investigate the ways in which martial identity continued to be viewed and recreated as a key component of masculinity. Narratives and visual imagery drawn from a satirical magazine, nuclear physics laboratories, and the chronicles of cosmonauts feature actors outside the military negotiating participation in, and exclusion from, militarized brotherhoods throughout the early Cold War. The existence of both voluntary and compulsory service evasion, disciplinary issues, and a dearth of peacetime role models in military literature and film suggests that the postwar recovery, and the promotion and cultivation of a militarized masculinity, would need to take form not just in military circles but in the popular imagination. The military needed to rely on media images and military-adjacent institutions such as science, technology, and space exploration to recreate the masculine archetype of the soldier in Soviet culture. How this cultural reconstruction occurred will be explored in the next three chapters.

# PART TWO

# Military Masculinity outside the Armed Forces during the Early Cold War

*Chapter Three*

# Gender and Militarism in Foreign Affairs Cartoons

The Spanish woman whose curvy form took up the entire back cover of the Soviet satirical journal *Krokodil* was striking for several reasons. Her bright red dress was cut high up on her thigh and plunged low down her back. One foot, visible as she danced, arched elegantly in high heels. In contrast to the seductive image, she wielded a chained set of handcuffs in place of castanets, and she performed her dance atop a giant, bloody axe. She also bore the face of General Francisco Franco (Figure 3.1).[1] By the time the image appeared in July 1963, *Krokodil* had established a postwar pattern, one that changed very little over two decades, of portraying European and American politicians, diplomats, and military leaders and broader themes of militarization in gendered and sexualized ways. At the same time that officials at the Suvorov academies, DOSAAF, the Ministry of Defence, and the Komsomol were privately attempting to reinvigorate military masculinity for a postwar world, a more public cultivation of masculine norms was taking place under the guise of humour in the popular and widely read *Krokodil*. Both this chapter and the two that follow move outside the official purview of the armed forces to trace conversations, directives, and negotiations about masculinity and military identities elsewhere in Soviet society. Together, the chapters in Part II demonstrate that the creation and maintenance of martial brotherhoods and militarized notions of postwar manhood were far more visible in cultural sources outside institutional archives than in the official documents examined in Part I.

This chapter examines *Krokodil*'s persistent use of heteronormative and misogynist imagery of European and American diplomats and military figures to link masculinity with Soviet Cold War military fortitude. Through the medium of cartoons, *Krokodil* made publicly visible the gendered peculiarities of postwar militarism. Approximately one-third of the total cartoons in each issue between 1945 and 1964 featured images

Figure 3.1 A Spanish Dance with Castanets. *Krokodil*, 10 July 1963, 16.

of countries deemed to be Cold War enemies, such as Britain, Spain, West Germany, Yugoslavia, and especially the United States, in gendered presentations that openly depicted power relationships between countries as masculinity contests. The cartoons cast both Soviet and foreign actors in specific visual roles, which were intended at various moments to support, mock, undermine, or refresh official positions. In its efforts to remobilize Soviet masculinity after the war, the state-run media, via *Krokodil*, demeaned capitalist and fascist masculinity and linked issues of sexuality to postwar reconstruction and Cold War power. By portraying foreign military authorities as feminized, queer, or in some way sexually deviant, *Krokodil* introduced an explicitly gendered framework for adjudicating Soviet military strength. One way that military identities could be prescribed outside the regular forces, in other words, was to establish a visual lexicon in the popular press that set the boundaries for what Soviet military masculinity could *not* be.

Literary scholars and cultural critics have approached the genres of humour, satire, and joking in Soviet culture in a variety of ways. For example, they have drawn distinctions between covert or underground satire that critiqued the system and government sponsorship of satirical texts like *Krokodil* that were deemed healthy to socialist life. As Serguei Oushakine has warned, however, research into Soviet "jocularity" must move beyond a dichotomy that assumes that officially sanctioned humour only advanced "propagandistic clichés," or that unofficial forms contained "subversive meanings that might (or might not) have been smuggled under the cover of ideologically sound cultural forms."[2] Historians have assumed that state-sponsored satirical voices like *Krokodil* focused on "safe targets" like good-natured but inefficient workers or on moral improvement, functioning more as an extension of socialist realism than a deep social critique.[3] This chapter takes a different approach, examining instead the broader social space that *Krokodil*'s cartoons on foreign affairs opened. The cartoons were propagandistic, to be sure, but their reliance on explicitly gendered imagery created a space in which official propaganda overlapped with – and itself mobilized – subversive narratives. The result, whether obvious to the cartoonists and editors or not, resembled the institutional actors we have already met in the Ministry of Defence, DOSAAF, and the Komsomol in their attempts to establish and reinforce a specific version of military masculinity after the war.

The cartoons can be interpreted in many ways: as Soviet Cold War propaganda more generally, as an exasperated response to American support for West Germany, or as impatience with the perceived Western indifference to the continuation of fascist rule in Spain or NATO's exploitation of France. In domestic terms, the possible interpretations are similarly wide ranging; imagining foreign affairs as extensions of family life, households, marriages, caregiving, and betrayals resonated with a Soviet public preoccupied with its own domestic recovery after the war. Interpretations other than those I put forth in this chapter are certainly possible, and Soviet historians have used *Krokodil* cartoons as evidence of a variety of social trends, mores, and challenges. But using an approach similar to that used in my analysis of Marshal Nedelin's parabolic response to Andrei Sakharov that opened this book, I show that interpreting these *Krokodil* cartoons only as off-colour jokes or metaphors about larger issues in Cold War politics misses a crucial opportunity to expand our inquiries into the ways that historical masculinities have been constructed and disseminated. The *Krokodil* archives reveal little about the germination of gendered foreign affairs imagery. Some of the cartoonists themselves, in short interviews in the West after the end of the Cold War, have not revealed much about the creative process beyond confirming a lack of freedom in their artistic choices and a pervasive fear of editorial censorship or other punishment.[4] This chapter therefore interprets the cartoons as visual sources, focusing on two commonalities in the vast majority of the images: they feature military characters and situations, and they feature heavily gendered or sexualized situations. The confluence of these categories made visible a particularly Soviet regeneration of military masculinity in the postwar world.

Scholars of masculinity have long argued that masculinity is defined not only by what it is, but also what it is not – femininity, most obviously. At the same time that the postwar military was remasculinizing, excluding women and attempting to guide the social conditioning of a new generation of boys and young men, *Krokodil* was openly mocking foreign generals and NATO's political leaders by portraying them in the most insulting terms – as women. The foreign affairs cartoons with explicitly gendered images fall into four main categories, each of which will be explored in more detail: cross-dressing men, courtship and marriage, violence against women, and the "proper" martial power of the brawny counterpoint, the Soviet proletarian man. By using images of enemy masculinities abroad to signal the limits of acceptable military categories of masculinity at home, the cartoons in these categories opened a rare space where politics, sexuality, and incorrect military identities were revealed for public consumption, scrutiny, and mockery.

## Sex, Humour, and Visual Culture

Political cartoons belong to the broader genre of visual culture that can include architecture, paintings, sculpture, photography, film, animation, illustrations, and posters. Historians studying these forms in the Soviet Union have found that they were far from rote forms of propaganda; rather, they comprised a rich and politically complex visual lexicon that helped to shape Soviet society and culture throughout the century. Visual cues played a role in Soviet culture in the 1920s as a key means through which the Bolsheviks conveyed the rules and standards of a new political and social system to a largely illiterate population.[5] Identifying enemies and othering groups or behaviours falling outside the new norms were standard features of early Bolshevik visual culture, with *kulaks* (so-called rich peasants), priests, or White Army opponents represented as the most common foes. During the Stalinist 1930s, socialist realism became the official aesthetic in the arts and in literature, and it dictated acceptable articulations of Soviet life and the socialist future, emphasizing realism over the avant-garde or caricature. Images of machinery, the peasantry, and the great leader himself had their own specific purposes and forms in the campaign to modernize society and encourage allegiance to Stalin as a unifying, visually tangible guiding force for people who lived in different time zones, spoke different languages, and experienced Stalinism variously in their daily lives.

Although they shared features with other visual forms, political cartoons comprised a distinct genre. The didacticism of Soviet cartoons, like that expected of all cultural forms, was both enhanced and tempered by the medium's ties to humour and satire, giving it a unique tilt within the broader category of the visual arts. Before the 1917 Revolution, cartoons were strictly monitored by the tsarist censor and their creators were not given much latitude for political or social commentary. Free from censorship for a time after the Revolution, by 1922 cartoons had become one of many propaganda tools that the new Soviet regime routinely used.[6] *Krokodil* was founded in 1922 as the official (and only) humour journal in the Soviet Union.[7] Published three times a month, by 1949 *Krokodil*'s circulation was second only to *Ogonek* in the category of general interest periodicals.[8] Circulation in fact increased exponentially from 100,000 in January 1945 to 700,000 in January 1956. Published by *Pravda*, the official newspaper of the Communist Party, *Krokodil* was a state publication that was subject to the same controls as other forms of mass media. Its cartoons echoed the official line on any given topic, but it was also afforded a surprising amount of flexibility in its content. Even at the height of Stalinist censorship in the 1930s, *Krokodil* cartoons were able to attack approved targets, particularly dishonest or inefficient bureaucrats who made daily life more difficult for ordinary people.[9] As a humour journal, *Krokodil* had a specific purpose: to entertain, but also to engage in a unique form of covert narration, saying what could not be said elsewhere in society. Sociologist Michael Mulkay has argued that there is an assumed division between humorous and serious modes of discourse, and that this assumption allows humour to be enlisted in the service of the serious. By shrouding its message in a veil of absurdity, the agent of humorous discourse can purport to be "only joking."[10] The message can be (and usually is) entirely serious; however, by hiding behind a humorous façade, the agent has much more freedom to engage in a taboo discourse. Writing on Russian humour in particular, Emil Draitser agrees that the relationship between the humorous and the serious is codependent, and that "humor licens[es] speech about the unspeakable."[11] The few studies of Soviet cartoons of the Cold War era in existence acknowledge *Krokodil*'s covert narration of a variety of pertinent issues, such as decolonization, race, and global alliances, but they do not address the gendered imagery dominating many of these cartoons.[12]

One way of approaching sexual topics considered taboo is under the guise of humour. Sexual repression in Soviet society has been well documented. Under Stalin and his successors, school curricula did not teach sexual education, birth control information was scarce, and sexuality was never openly discussed.[13] Soviet citizens "were convinced that only perverts and decadents talked freely about sex," wrote Igor Kon, the pioneering historian of sexuality in Russia.[14] This "sexophobia," as Kon labelled it, continued through the era of de-Stalinization. Stalin's 1936 Constitution recodified conservative expectations for women and overturned early Bolshevik efforts to build a more progressive society free of bourgeois gender roles. The Khrushchev era and after remained just as puritan. According to Kon, while in power Nikita Khrushchev was once sent into "paroxysms of rage at the sight of a nude female body" in a painting.[15] Unlike post-Stalinist painting, which sought to distinguish itself in form and content from what had been permitted under Stalin, political cartoons portraying foreign relations in gendered ways changed very little after Khrushchev came to power.[16] Queer sexualities, the subject of many of *Krokodil*'s foreign affairs cartoons, were discussed even less. The immediate postwar period in particular did not feature any regeneration of interwar queer activism in the Soviet Union as it did in many European capitals.[17] While McCarthyism in American politics linked communism with queerness, the Soviet world view associated capitalism in the United States and Western Europe with "deviant" sexuality, even if public opinion in the Soviet Union did not endorse such an association to nearly the same extent as McCarthyism.

Humour was a way to engage in sexual discourse covertly. Mulkay has described how "sexual jokes circulate, not simply as sources of amusement, but as carriers of sexual information, attitudes and emotions which have restricted passage within the serious mode."[18] Projecting sexual humour onto othered groups enabled discussions of otherwise taboo topics without violating Soviet codes of respectability. In his pioneering study of sexual humour, Gershon Legman observed that "people do not joke about what makes them happy or what is sacred to them. They joke only about what frightens or disturbs them."[19]

Sexually frank political cartoons published in a national, state-run magazine were produced and received differently than bawdy jokes told in private, however. Describing privately circulated Soviet jokes, Draitser observes that sexual jokes, "with their aggressive, intentionally iconoclastic, often primitive and crudely biological nature, represented a defiance of the officially proclaimed 'happy Soviet family.'"[20] *Krokodil* hid these taboo themes in plain sight, which suggests that an outlet for discussing them indeed existed and even thrived in puritan Soviet society. By opening them to public scrutiny in such a highly visible way, *Krokodil* also revealed that anxieties about military preparedness and codes of masculine martial conduct warranted the strongest response possible, one that could only be delivered through the use of taboo gendered and sexualized imagery.

## Franco in a Skirt: Cross-dressing and Misogyny

Casting aspersions on European norms of masculinity was not an immediate feature of *Krokodil* after the war but rather something that emerged gradually during the second half of 1945. The cover of the 30 July 1945 issue showed the continued cooperation of Allied soldiers (Figure 3.2).[21] On it was an image of three cars sporting American, Soviet, and British flags. Between the cars stood three soldiers in relaxed pose, sharing a cigarette lighter and leaning against the car with the Soviet flag. Said the Soviet soldier, "Remember, John, back at Yalta I told you, here's to a speedy meeting in Berlin!" Published in the summer of 1945, this cartoon painted the three soldiers as allies, emphasizing their camaraderie and cooperation in defeating the Nazis and reaching Berlin. Of course, the American soldier needed a light from the Soviet one, underscoring the idea that he would not have made it to Berlin without Soviet aid. All three figures were drawn identically and realistically, with high cheekbones, short, neat hair, and immaculate uniforms, absent the caricatured features

Figure 3.2 "Remember, John, back at Yalta I told you, here's to a speedy meeting in Berlin!" *Krokodil*, 30 July 1945, 1.

that would appear by the end of the 1940s. Their Allied masculinity that was cast as cooperative and mutually beneficial would not survive long after the end of the war. By early 1948, Allied imagery had morphed from depicting a brotherly camaraderie of soldier-equals to something to be ridiculed. As part of a two-page spread of various foreign diplomats engaging in behaviour deemed inappropriate, two unnamed Western politicians sat on a park bench, wrapped in each other's arms. A pair of lovebirds on a branch above the men mirrored their pose, and the tree trunk beside them displayed their carved initials underneath a rough drawing of hearts that had been pierced by Cupid's arrow (Figure 3.3).[22]

But these images of men were rare in foreign affairs cartoons. *Krokodil*'s main method of satirizing postwar Europe and the perceived American-led militarization there was to dress foreign leaders as women, implying that women and femininity compromised military decisions and weakened martial authority. The cartoons framed Cold

Figure 3.3 "An International Picnic." *Krokodil*, 30 April 1948, 7.

War political relationships as seductions, marriages or, in the most damning scenarios, prostitution. Imagery of this kind appeared in the last issue of 1949, for example, as part of a two-page spread entitled "New Year's Carnival on Wall Street" (Figure 3.4).[23] The celebration depicted was of a line of chorus girls performing, but the dancers were in fact a group of male political figures from Marshall Plan countries. Belittling the Marshall Plan and its recipients was a running joke in

Figure 3.4 New Year's Carnival on Wall Street
"Today, 16 'girls,' Marshall Plan costumes, big war program, dancing to an American tune!"

*Krokodil*, 30 December 1949, 9.

*Krokodil* after the plan commenced in 1947. Cartoons frequently portrayed Western European countries as pawns of the United States, willing to do anything for American aid. In this scenario, the dancers showed off what they had received from the Plan – which was nothing but rags. Yet they continued to "dance to the American tune." The use of the transliterated English word, "girls," rather than the Russian equivalent, *devushki*, on the poster further removed this postwar scenario from the Soviet world. The cartoon indicated that this type of show, either with real girls or men acting as girls, would not be seen in the Soviet Union.

The cartoons with cross-dressing characters worked through a canon of women's archetypal roles. The Marshall Plan dance troupe exemplified one such type – the impoverished servant woman or girl, who was assumed to be available for humiliation or exploitation. Another cartoon in this category, from 1950, dressed Franco in a long, patched skirt, apron, and peasant woman's kerchief (Figure 3.5).[24] As their new servant, Franco waited on Uncle Sam and John Bull, who represented the United States and Britain. Franco welcomed the two now that he no longer worked with Hitler, saying, "We'll work well together, mister! My previous master had the same taste as you!" Deploying another archetype, some cartoons depicted cross-dressing men as caricatures of mothers. In one image, a man dressed as a nursemaid held a "baby" – in fact a man in military dress with a Hitler moustache – who screamed, "I want an atomic bomb!" (Figure 3.6).[25] Calling from Bonn presumably to the United States, the "mother" said, "Quickly, sir. Without this toy our baby won't calm down." The Federal Republic was not portrayed as a real infant but a grown man acting like an infant, thus demeaning his masculinity perhaps more than portraying him as a woman. Another female stereotype that *Krokodil* depicted was the thoughtless, bejewelled aristocrat, as was the case with US Senate Foreign Relations chairman Alexander Wiley in the wake of the East German uprising in the summer of 1953. Wiley was known at home and abroad as a supporter of German rearmament within a European army and of the West German chancellor, Konrad Adenauer. Fearing that the uprising would scuttle Adenauer's upcoming reelection, Wiley had publicly supported German reunification under a Western system.[26] *Krokodil* commented on the issue by dressing Wiley in an elegant gown, gloves, and high heels, with a fur stole and a decorated hat befitting a fine lady. The purse draped over the senator's arm was a missile, though, and one foot had stepped into a mock tank, causing Wiley to flail and nearly fall. "Careful, dear," the caption warned, "you're setting off on the wrong foot" (Figure 3.7).[27]

Figure 3.5 *An Experienced Servant*
Franco: "We'll work well together, mister! My previous master had the same taste as you!"

*Krokodil*, 20 March 1950, 5.

Another set of tropes revolved around courtship, marriage, and sex, with General Franco the most common target. In 1946 a demure Franco in a negligee and heels smiled from a balcony as Western leaders serenaded him (Figure 3.8).[28] In 1951, as a courted woman he sat on a bench with Uncle Sam, blushing and fanning himself (Figure 3.9).[29] With dollar-sign spurs and a missile holster at his side, Uncle Sam had the appearance of a Cold War cowboy. "For you, señora, I would sacrifice anything!" a

Figure 3.6 *A Call from Bonn*
"I want an atomic bomb!"
"Send it as soon as possible, sir. Without this toy, our baby won't calm down."

*Krokodil*, 10 July 1961, 9.

Figure 3.7 "Careful, dear, you're setting off on the wrong foot."

*Krokodil*, 20 August 1953, 2.

Figure 3.8 *A Spanish Serenade*

*Krokodil*, 30 March 1946, 12.

Figure 3.9 *A Generous Yankee*
"For you, señora, I would sacrifice anything!
I'm even prepared to return his Gibraltar to you!"

*Krokodil*, 30 May 1951, 5.

smitten Uncle Sam said, gesturing behind him at a cowering John Bull. "I am even prepared to return his Gibraltar to you!" Franco was a favoured target for *Krokodil*'s cartoonists, and he was almost never portrayed in anything but women's clothing between 1945 and the early 1960s. Over that period of time, he was consistently depicted as he was in Figure 3.10, in a dress and heels, adorned with swastikas and carrying a bloodied axe, on the arm of a European leader (in this case, Charles de Gaulle).[30]

Courtship motifs in the cartoons sometimes ended in weddings, with the bride always a foreign military figure in drag. In 1950, Adenauer played the bride (Figure 3.11).[31] He carried a bag labelled "Ruhr," an important coal-mining region in western Germany. By pairing him with French foreign minister Robert Schuman in a wedding scene, presided over by a burly personification of Wall Street, *Krokodil* expressed disapproval of the Schuman Plan, which would lead to the formation of the European Coal and Steel Community in 1952. The cartoon adorned Adenauer with swastikas to insinuate that he had Nazi ties. Images of

Figure 3.10 *Krokodil*, 10 April 1963, 16.

Figure 3.11 *A Marriage of (American) Convenience*

*Krokodil*, 10 June 1950, 9.

German militarism from the war, including swastikas, were common in *Krokodil*, suggesting that the new West Germany was a reincarnation of the Third Reich – a very powerful image for Soviet readers. Yet Adenauer could hardly be viewed as a threat to the Soviet Union when depicted this way, despite his swastikas, because he was meant to look absurd. The cartoon commentary can be read on multiple levels: as a denunciation of the French and German economic union, a mockery of sexual difference, and a reminder that "deviant" masculinity was a Cold War threat to Soviet stability and recovery.

A similar cartoon appeared late in 1953, after Adenauer's Christian Democratic Union Party had won the West German election the month before (Figure 3.12).[32] The caption featured "Wall Street," as marriage broker, saying to the groom, a menacing but cartoonish Nazi soldier, "I have chosen for you, Herr Wehrmacht, the most suitable party." Figure 3.13 also featured a German military bride in drag, wearing a wedding dress reminiscent of fatigues and a battle helmet.[33] The American groom held the bride as if he had come to her rescue and was carrying her away from danger. Lipstick marks in the shape of a swastika dotted the American's face. American aid to West Germany still touched a raw nerve in *Krokodil*, and mocking German masculinity through these cartoons shored up Soviet visions of manhood.

The final female archetype *Krokodil* regularly used in its cross-dressing cartoons was the prostitute. Here, again, General Franco was a favourite target. As part of the "New Year's Carnival on Wall Street" spread at the end of 1949 (which also featured the Marshall Plan dancers in Figure 3.4), a cartoon showed a smirking Winston Churchill arriving at the party with a buxom date on each arm, both of whom were dressed in short, sleeveless dresses and heels. The dates were Franco and former Greek prime minister Constantine Tsaldaris (Figure 3.14).[34] Tsaldaris had been lobbying to establish a European army, and the Cominform that year had already seen fit to label him a war criminal along with Franco.[35] A similar scene appeared the following year, when *Krokodil* published a nearly identical cartoon containing a swaggering male Wall Street figure in a tuxedo escorting two men dressed as women. This time Yugoslavian leader Josip Broz (Tito) replaced Tsaldaris, and the caption was much bolder about framing the political situation as both sexual and capitalist exploitation: "Tito and Franco, as usual, will be selling themselves on the streets of New York" (Figure 3.15).[36] While those two images were drawn in a more cartoonish style, *Krokodil* also cast male actors as prostitutes in a grittier way, betraying

Figure 3.12 *A Marriage Broker from Wall Street*
"I have chosen for you, Herr Wehrmacht, the most suitable party…" (Christian Democratic Union Party)

*Krokodil*, 20 October 1953, 16.

Figure 3.13 *The Age of Love*

*Krokodil*, 30 December 1958, 16.

Figure 3.14 *New Year's Carnival on Wall Street*

*Krokodil*, 30 December 1949, 8.

the emotions still raw from the war. In 1946, a full page was devoted to a relatively obscure part of the German postwar trials – the question of complicity of Finnish leaders in German operations in the north, including Operation Arctic Fox to take Murmansk. Convicted of "anti-Soviet plans," former Finnish president Risto Ryti and foreign minister Väinö Tanner were depicted wearing dresses and heels. One even applied blood-red lipstick as they stood on the street, leaning against a lamppost (Figure 3.16).[37] Both wore fox stoles around their necks, a detail that played on the German code name.

Figure 3.15 "Tito and Franco, as usual, will be selling themselves on the streets of New York"

*Krokodil*, 30 December 1950, 9.

Official rhetoric maintained that the Bolshevik revolution had freed Soviet women from the need to resort to prostitution. As Elizabeth Wood has written of revolution-era ideology, "prostitution had to be viewed as a consequence of capitalism, a dependent variable that arose from poverty and exploitation."[38] The cartoons treating Franco, Tsaldaris, and Tito as participants in capitalist exploitation by the United States and Britain cast that exploitation as sexual. In Figure 3.16, however, *Krokodil* seemed to blame and shame the prostitutes for courting their own degradation. The sinister-looking Ryti and Tanner, moreover, had not only made themselves available for German use, but their grins suggested that they took pleasure in it and eagerly accepted gifts.

The fact that these figures, and the other ones featured in the cartoons discussed so far, were deliberately depicted as cross-dressing

Figure 3.16 *Both Fur and Sin*

*Krokodil*, 10 February 1946, 3.

men underscored the messages about exploitation. In the cases of women drawn as women, which we will encounter in the next section, the characters remained within acceptable boundaries of femininity and thus required rescue or protection. A different level of misogyny was at work in images featuring men wearing women's clothing, however: the only reason to portray them in this way was to undermine and discredit those depicted in the most severe way possible. Dressing the figures as women demonstrated one of the ways in which humour and satire could be used, in Jacqueline Tavernier-Courbin's words, as a "substitute for aggression."[39] Such usage coded political or military leadership by women as not only absurd but compromising and even dangerous.

These cartoons showed a marked break from established visual norms for depicting enemies used during the Revolution, the Civil War, and the Second World War. Soviet propaganda of the 1930s had demonized both homosexuality and fascism as related evils, with *Krokodil* cartoons playing on that familiar trope, especially in its references to West Germany.[40] But the explicit visual cues in these images also differed from those used in the past. Victoria Bonnell has shown that artists under Lenin and Stalin prior to 1945 assigned animal images to denote the enemy. Bonnell observes that "images such as serpents, eagles, crows, spiders, dogs, and birds performed an important function in Bolshevik political art: they served to dehumanize the enemy, to transform people into nonhuman and often repulsive creatures."[41] Yet after 1945, very few images in posters, illustrations, or cartoons depicted the enemy in animal form.[42] Although the United States occasionally appeared in *Krokodil* as a malicious eagle or crow and the United Kingdom as a weakened lion,[43] the overwhelming majority of foreign affairs cartoons involved human forms. After 1945, as we have seen in the previous discussion, *Krokodil* preferred to dehumanize enemies using gendered imagery. At the time, these representations were unprecedented in Soviet visual culture. Images of cross-dressing Western leaders, for example, served to dehumanize and undermine Cold War enemies. They also presented a cogent vision of deviant military actions and behaviours to the public and to young men of service age. As Susan Reid has found regarding paintings in the immediate postwar years, "what the party most urgently needed from art and literature was instructive role models and images of comradeship to recuperate disaffected young men."[44]

Significantly, the new uses of gendered and sexualized images of foreign leaders after 1945 persisted with remarkable consistency through the mid-1960s, at which point portrayals of enemies became more varied. For example, the many cartoons devoted to criticizing American involvement in the Vietnam War after around 1960 did not use the type of gendered imagery seen here that dominated commentary on European and American politics and military engagement from 1945 through the mid-1960s. But the consistency with which *Krokodil* relied on the same tropes of cross-dressing, women's domestic service, bridal subordination, and prostitution to depict Cold War military disputes for two decades after the war – at a time of enormous social changes brought by de-Stalinization in particular – indicates a dedication to replicating and reinforcing this particular brand of imagery regarding martial identity in Soviet culture.

## Assaulting Marianne

The images of women in *Krokodil*'s foreign affairs cartoons examined so far map a complex terrain, with the cartoonists using the femininity of cross-dressing as a weapon with which to mock Western military men. Another subgenre of cartoons of this period used images of women in peril to comment on appropriate military behaviour. Many of these images focused on one woman – Marianne, the personification of the French republic since the revolution at the end of the eighteenth century. Marianne was the only woman who appeared regularly in these cartoons, and she was the only woman to represent any of the countries featured. Other traditional female national symbols, such as Germania and Britannia, never appeared; instead, Germany and Britain were represented by male forms, usually West German chancellor Konrad Adenauer and the enduring eighteenth-century caricature of Englishness, John Bull. The cartoonists' use of Marianne in *Krokodil* exemplified the historic Russian admiration for the French Revolution, out of which her image was born. Marianne's association with liberty in France was underscored in numerous cartoons that contrasted her image with that of French leader Charles de Gaulle, who was demonized, along with leaders such as Franco and Adenauer, for what the Soviet Union perceived as overreliance on American military aid.[45] *Krokodil* repeatedly presented visual depictions of Marianne under attack – quite literally – by Western military and political leaders, giving Soviet readers not only a particular angle on French politics but also a broader image of improper masculine behaviour.

To contrast alliances in the socialist world with those in the West, an October 1949 cartoon used a common Marianne-related image: in the top frame, two men, from the USSR and Bulgaria, adorned with medals although not officially in uniform, shared a cigarette and a flask. In the bottom frame, a sinister Uncle Sam held a knife to Marianne, grasping her around the neck with one hand and aiming the knife at her torso with the other (Figure 3.17).[46] Beyond the routine denunciation of the Western alliance and American domination of Europe, which was common in *Krokodil*, this cartoon demonstrated Soviet notions of the proper relationship between men while also demonizing men who committed violence against women. Male friendship was a powerful bond in Russian life in particular. Sociologists have noted the significance of this bond, and according to one observer, "a male friend is a brother, a drinking companion, a soul mate and a bulwark against the outside world."[47] Accusing the enemy of abusing the unique fraternal bond that Russians valued between men was a way to deepen public opinion against that enemy. As we have seen, most post-1945 foreign affairs cartoons worked to impugn European and American masculinity with depictions of cross-dressing or implied queerness. In this particular image of Uncle Sam threatening Marianne, however, *Krokodil* criticized a type of masculinity that crossed the limits of heterosexual respectability and proper behaviour.

In a 1955 cartoon, Marianne again came under attack (Figure 3.18).[48] In the top frame she held a shield with the French emblem and the word "sovereignty" on it and faced off against a severe-looking German military figure. In the bottom frame, her shield served as the table on which the Germans signed a document called the "Parisian Agreement Ratification." Playing on the famous Spartan battle directive, the caption warned that Marianne could either fight with her shield, or surrender on it. Another cartoon featured a rotund American military figure installing missiles in the kitchen of a defenceless-looking Marianne, who this time represented Western Europe as a whole, with her generic peasant clothing and Dutch wooden shoes (Figure 3.19).[49] "You're worrying for no reason, ma'am!" the grinning American said. "I'm doing this for your safety!" His position atop a ladder, attaching a missile to her light fixture, while she remained seated at the table, denoted an unequal power relationship between them. She appeared fearful as his weapons broke her window and knocked her dishes to the floor in a rather chilling allusion to domestic violence.

In French history, Marianne has long served as a symbol of liberty or of the victory of the lower classes during the French Revolution. Her use in these cartoons went beyond the symbolic, though, because she was also used to represent women's battlefield leadership. Eugène Delacroix's iconic 1830 painting, *Liberty Leading the People*, for example, featured a triumphant Marianne standing among her troops after a battle,

Figure 3.17 *Friendship … and friendship*

*Krokodil*, 30 October 1949, 3.

Figure 3.18 *With a shield … or on it*

*Krokodil*, 20 January 1955, 1.

Figure 3.19 "You're worrying for no reason, ma'am! I'm doing this for your safety!"

*Krokodil*, 30 January 1958, 1.

raising a rifle in one hand and a French flag in the other, with smoke rising from the ruined fields.[50] Her bared breasts in this painting and in many other depictions of her represented liberty and her heroic triumph (although at other times, her partial nudity could signal her violation). In keeping with the puritan values of Soviet society, Marianne remained fully clothed in *Krokodil*'s renderings. However, the cartoons also denied the martial authority she was frequently, if not consistently, given in French visual culture. Although Marianne was armed in some of the cartoons, such as Figure 3.18, she was never permitted to brandish a rifle as she did in Delacroix's painting. Her postures in *Krokodil* were defensive, helpless, and non-combative. Well into the 1960s, *Krokodil* continued to run images of Marianne under assault, a consistency and longevity that suggests official fondness for this particular visual tactic. In 1963, the journal was still depicting West German politicians as Nazis; in Figure 3.20, a Nazi literally tied Marianne up and shoved

Figure 3.20 "Now France will breathe easier!"

*Krokodil*, 10 February 1963, 12.

her to the floor.[51] "Now France will breathe easier!" the caption read, as the men above Marianne (including de Gaulle) signed a Franco-German military agreement on her back. Rendering helpless this iconic female figure in Euro-American nationalist discourses served to neutralize women's battlefield contributions. Assaulting Marianne so regularly in *Krokodil*'s foreign affairs cartoons, in other words, not only highlighted the savagery of Western military men, but it also served to nullify women's military roles. This project had engaged Soviet policymakers since 1945.

## The Soviet Counterpoint

As we have seen, *Krokodil* took aim at the Soviet Union's Cold War enemies by maligning their military masculinity in a variety of ways, including demonizing cross-dressing, suggesting queer relationships, and depicting violence against women. To contrast these enemy images, *Krokodil* published foreign affairs cartoons demonstrating a Soviet masculine ideal. A June 1949 issue featured a rare full-page illustration of a soldier (Figure 3.21). He was surrounded by peace imagery and cradled a cherub while a dove sat perched on the end of his rifle. (The rifle was slung behind him and clearly not a main focus of the image.) The soldier towered over his capitalist foes and glanced confidently, and with pity, down at them. The image marked the anniversary of the Nazi invasion in June 1941. The caption read:

> Companies of Wall Street gentlemen
> would burn the world down whenever possible.
> But there's many a slip 'twixt cup and lip,
> because the world is now in safe hands.[52]

To celebrate Soviet Army and Navy Day in 1951, *Krokodil* published another strong soldier image, once again featuring a formidable but peaceful male figure in an officer's red greatcoat holding a dove. For its part, the dove held a "peace" banner in its beak. With one hand calmly held out as if to stop the enraged capitalist warmongers beneath him, the soldier rebuked his foes' efforts to militarize and articulated the Soviet Army's peaceful and defensive ambitions: "Your attempts are in vain, gentlemen! We will not go on the offensive" (Figure 3.22).[53] Size served as an obvious visual tool in these images. Not only were the drawings of the Soviet soldiers more realistic and less cartoonish, but they were three times as large as the capitalist figures on the edges

Figure 3.21 *In Safe Hands*

*Krokodil*, 20 June 1949, 5.

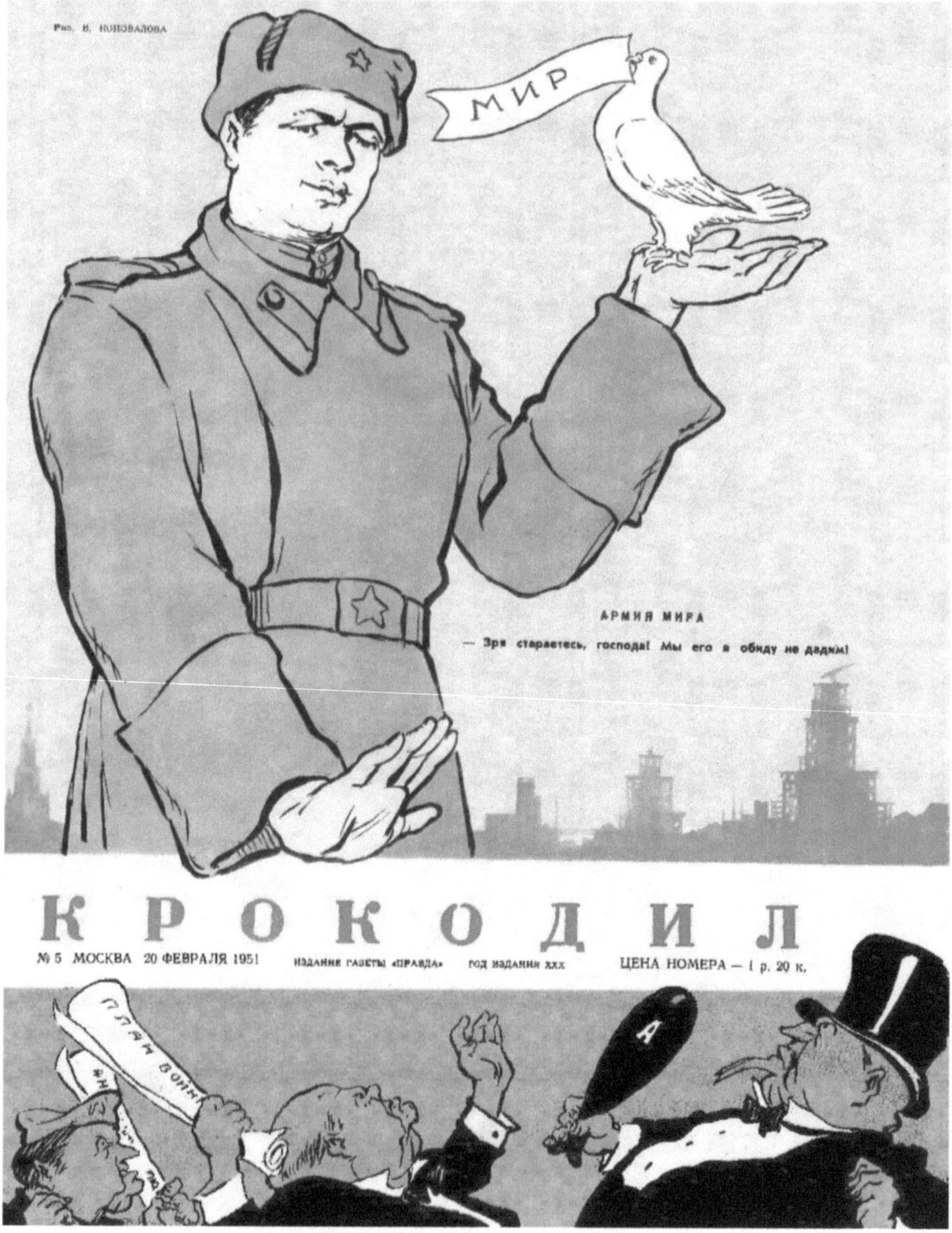
Рис. В. КОНОВАЛОВА
МИР
АРМИЯ МИРА
— Зря стараетесь, господа! Мы его в обиду не дадим!
КРОКОДИЛ
№ 5 МОСКВА 20 ФЕВРАЛЯ 1951
ИЗДАНИЕ ГАЗЕТЫ «ПРАВДА»
ГОД ИЗДАНИЯ XXX
ЦЕНА НОМЕРА — 1 р. 20 к.
ПЛАН ВОЙНЫ
А

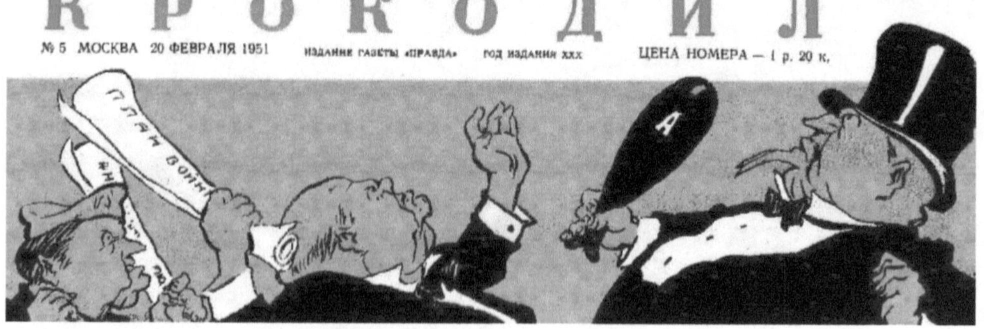

Figure 3.22 *The Army of Peace*

*Krokodil*, 20 February 1951, 1.

of the page. "Like Gulliver towering over the Lilliputians," as Victoria Bonnell found with respect to early Stalinist political posters, "the male Stalinist hero ... was depicted as larger than life."[54]

Yet the role of the soldier as a Soviet Gulliver was more complex in *Krokodil*'s visual culture. The journal frequently represented Soviet soldier masculinity, as we saw in chapters 1 and 2, but the images always conformed to certain rules: they referenced the Second World War, as in Figures 3.21 and 3.22, or the soldier appeared alone or with other Soviet actors, such as the boys in Figures 2.1 and 2.2. When placed in a visual frame with foreign military characters after 1945, the Soviet man became a worker, not a soldier. For example, the cartoon on the cover of an October 1952 issue of *Krokodil* suggested the ease and dominance of male service without actually depicting a Soviet soldier (Figure 3.23).[55] The cartoon showed a brawny young man dressed in worker's coveralls, cap, and boots, striding purposefully towards his goal. Behind him staggered a small military figure representing the "capitalist economy." With war materiel strapped to his back, the capitalist was hunched over, struggling to keep pace with the stronger Soviet man. He muttered, "How can I keep up with him if he walks firmly, while my legs give way!" The capitalist's legs were weighed down with tanks as shoes, while the Soviet man walked easily in his work boots. The contrast between the erect posture of the Soviet man and the limpness of his foe underlined the representation of male vigour or the lack thereof as a key visual marker for masculine identity.[56] Another cartoon from 1949 reinforced the practice of using classic socialist iconography to represent Soviet strength: the image of a young, strong, Soviet male worker contrasted with the image of elderly, weakened, civilian men of the West, the latter apparently despairing over their obvious inferiority. The Soviet worker's muscled forearm clutched a flag reading "For Peace," rising from the very centre of Moscow as if the city itself, or the seat of government, could produce such a perfect male body from its streets, schools, and institutions (Figure 3.24).[57]

These cartoons fit the general Soviet press strategy that denied any Cold War military aims or even engagement and emphasized the USSR's interest in purely peaceful endeavours, despite the West's continued warmongering. The valiant Second World War soldier melted back into the regular labour force in these images, but his visual dominance over foreign military figures nonetheless reinforced his authority. These cartoons correspond with what Eric Hobsbawm found in his pioneering work on socialist iconography: by the early twentieth century, female figures had all but disappeared from socialist visual culture, and

Figure 3.23 "How can I keep up with him if he walks firmly, while my legs give way!"

*Krokodil*, 20 October 1952, 1.

Figure 3.24 "It's the arm of Moscow again!"
"Alas, sir, this is the voice of peace!"

*Krokodil*, 20 August 1949, 1.

the proletariat was represented by a muscular male worker with sleeves rolled up and shirt unbuttoned (if not missing altogether).[58] According to Toby Clark, "the picture of the fit, lean and muscular socialist overpowering the sated, flabby and enervated capitalist has been one of the most enduring themes in Soviet propaganda."[59] Figures 3.23 and 3.24 demonstrate the continued significance of socialist muscle in postwar Soviet iconography.

The image of the ordinary male worker taking on Western military aggression appeared again in a 1954 cartoon. It depicted a Soviet worker in an atomic power station who used atomic energy in a positive way, to unmask a suspicious-looking enemy who was using it in a negative way, to build atomic weaponry (Figure 3.25).[60] The muscular Soviet worker's sleeves were rolled up and his grip firm on the controls. His countertype was wrinkled with age, doing his best to crouch in the dark with his atomic bomb cradled in his arms. As we will see in chapter 4, Stalin's death ushered in an era of greater publicity for Soviet atomic research and development, which was previously kept secret because of its politically sensitive nature. This cartoon foreshadowed the "atoms for peace" moment in popular culture under Khrushchev, when the military co-option of nuclear technology was played down if not wholly denied in favour of progressive, peaceful uses. This movement conferred celebrity status on the physicists tasked with developing the technology that would build the socialist future. The image of the power station worker in this cartoon coded atomic physics as masculine but peaceful. This cartoon also exaggerated the impotence of the enemy. Everything about the Soviet man was erect: his posture, his extended arm, his control lever, even the pen in his shirt pocket. Everything about the enemy, on the other hand, was flaccid: his stance, his bent knees and arms, even his curled fingers. His attempt to acquire potency through possession of the missile was thwarted by the Soviet worker's illumination of the scheme, which safeguarded both his country and his masculinity against an opponent out to subvert both.

Persistently endorsing the image of a healthy, able-bodied, and muscular postwar Soviet man required special dedication from policymakers and cartoonists who witnessed a much different reality in the general population.[61] It also ran contrary to trends in other art forms after the war that confronted the realities of male war wounds. Especially in literature and film, male characters with visible injuries could signal heroism, shame, or the grim price of victory, depending on the medium, form, and time period.[62] Scholarly work in history, literature, and film studies has by now so thoroughly disproven the idea that

Figure 3.25 *A question of using atomic energy … for new illumination*

*Krokodil*, 10 July 1954, 3.

Soviet iconography uniformly privileged the robust male bodies seen above that *Krokodil*'s insistence on reproducing them is meaningful in itself. It suggests that cartoons joined paintings as a particular form of visual culture that promoted able-bodied men not seen as regularly in literature and film. Claire E. McCallum has found that, unlike in literature and film, postwar paintings kept men's war wounds from the public eye, except in explicit battlefield contexts.[63] While images of disabled veterans abounded in late Stalinist and post-Stalinist culture, this did not apply to *Krokodil*'s foreign affairs cartoons. Showing images of healthy, able-bodied male worker-soldiers was necessary to establish a counterpoint to the images depicting foreign military and diplomatic leaders as less capable men.

It is difficult to ascertain just how audiences would have read these cartoons. Unlike military-themed DOSAAF publications like *Voennye znaniia*, *Krokodil* was a general interest magazine not particularly aimed at conscription-age men. How might women readers or queer readers have interpreted these images? Codes of masculinity do not fall only to men to reproduce and reinforce. In reference to German history, Belinda Carstens-Wickham has argued that a preponderance of political cartoons featuring images of gender and sexuality roles outside the accepted mainstream signalled a political culture driven by patriarchal ideology. Moreover, the repeated use of such imagery in the popular press influenced citizens' understanding and perception of the political issues at hand – in this case, Cold War militarism.[64] *Krokodil*'s cartoons were aimed at a diverse audience in a general interest publication, yet the editors presumed that the audience shared their patriarchal view of the world. The visual norms these cartoons created indicate a way of seeing dominated by male producers at the editorial and artistic levels, and indeed of a patriarchal outlook in Soviet society that privileged heteronormative martial male dominance.

*Krokodil*'s foreign affairs cartoons used highly specific images of masculinity to comment on Second World War grievances and define Cold War Euro-American relationships. The masculinized national identities in the cartoons fused the Soviet government's twin concerns of Cold War politics and domestic masculinity. *Krokodil* also portrayed muscular, larger-than-life Soviet men as a fitting counterpoint to Cold War Western militarism. Vladimir Kazanevsky has noted in Russian and Soviet image censorship practices dating back to the nineteenth century a tendency to distinguish between "funny cartoons, which raised careful laughter, and the socially significant ones, which played a leading role in the reconstruction of social life."[65] As the Soviet Union's state-sanctioned humour journal, *Krokodil* allowed both, within limits. It would be a mistake to dismiss these cartoons as crude Cold War propaganda, however. In a society unaccustomed to publicly discussing gender roles, particularly for men, *Krokodil*'s foreign affairs cartoons opened a remarkable space in which to visually situate postwar gender expectations. By portraying European and American diplomats and military figures as cross-dressers, in the guise of servants, brides, or prostitutes, or as domestic abusers, as in the Marianne cartoons, *Krokodil* demonstrated that the state did not remain silent on issues relating to sexuality in the postwar era. Further, the European and American figures were drawn as unworthy inheritors of military masculinity after the war, which had the effect of awarding global masculine authority to the Soviet Union.

Outside of official military institutions, Soviet artists and journal editors produced, and *Krokodil* readers consumed, a specific and deeply gendered visual lexicon of soldiering in the postwar era. The consistency with which misogyny and homophobia were used to draw clear lines between Soviet and enemy masculinities from the end of the war though the 1960s indicates that authorities repeatedly chose, and relied on, such imagery as a tool for fortifying Soviet military brotherhoods. The cartoons mocked the idea of women in military roles and supported images of a female figure like Marianne, who, rendered helpless, needed protection and was unable to fight her own battles. Cartoonists portrayed Western diplomats as sexually available or otherwise subordinate in gendered ways. And they reinforced male muscularity and physical robustness as key attributes of a safe, peaceful society protected by the Soviet men who would become soldiers of the Cold War. Along with displays of military masculinity among nuclear physicists and cosmonauts, two examples of which we will examine in the following chapters, the images in *Krokodil* contributed to the delineation of boundaries and behaviours for militarized identities outside the armed forces. We now turn from state-sanctioned narratives to those composed and reinforced by men in a particular militarized industry in the Cold War – the nuclear physicists who told their own stories of encountering, resisting, and endorsing martial identity.

*Chapter Four*

# Telling Manly Stories about Nuclear Physics

In the anecdote that opened this book, Andrei Sakharov told us a story about nuclear physics – and about virility, privilege, and military masculinity in the early Cold War era. We do not know for certain whether Marshal Nedelin raised his glass at that private banquet to a group of scientists, smirked, and actually said, "Let's drink to getting hard," framing the relationship between physicists and military officials as one where the former could only "pray" to produce phalluses as erect as the latter's.[1] Sakharov had no reason to make it up. But this chapter is concerned not with truth or even authorial intent in physicists' memoirs, but rather with the way they told the story. In a very different tale about science, manliness, and privilege, physicist Evgenii Feinberg, writing in 1998, reacted to a rhetorical question about the moral nature of his work on the hydrogen bomb project in the early 1950s: "[You ask], how could [we] become active participants in the creation of this monstrous weapon that for almost half a century already has brought terror to all humankind? ...To accuse scientists like this is absurd, like accusing Prometheus of bringing fire to earth – something that not only did enormous good for humankind but has also produced evil."[2] These distinct, competing, but also complementary presentations of the self in the personal narratives of Soviet physicists underscore the complexities of masculine identities that both produced, and were produced by, the Cold War. Consciously or not, Sakharov retroactively read into his life story the pacifism that defined his later life as a dissident in order to draw a line between the "hard" militarized pursuit of weapons production and his perceived subordinated status. Feinberg, however, invoked the metaphor of Prometheus in defending himself and his colleagues, drawing an image for the reader of men who were god-like, standing over the work that would dictate the new terms of modern civilization.[3]

This chapter continues from chapter 3 in exploring the processes by which military masculinity was re-established outside the armed forces. It analyses the role of the memoir in narratively arming a brotherhood of physicists working on atomic weapons development in the 1950s and emplotting their access to, and fraught relationship with, categories of military masculinity. The memoirs reveal at least three coexisting masculinized identities for these scientists: in one strand of the story, they felt powerless and in the words of one of them, "impotent,"[4] constantly surveilled by the state and othered by men in the military institutions dictating their work. This first layer of narrative, in which the memoirists described themselves as subordinate, fuelled the other two. In the second layer, they upheld patriarchal privilege in their laboratories and protected their own masculinity by building and reinforcing workplaces hostile to women. Finally, in the third layer, the physicists inhabited roles that were no longer subordinate but god-like, as they armed themselves with the knowledge and technical expertise to design weapons that could destroy the world. With this understanding of their own privilege, the physicists positioned themselves not as participating in military masculinity but surpassing it, claiming a masculine status above even the generals to whom they initially reported feeling submissive. That nuclear physicists should present dynamic and shifting versions of themselves and each other in these texts vis-à-vis martial identity reflects the deep ambivalence scientists on both sides of the Cold War felt about the military applications of their work.

By investigating personal narratives written by several physicists who worked on the first Soviet nuclear project, this chapter continues to explore the contentious relationship between military masculinity and power in postwar Soviet culture. So far, we have seen the various ways that Soviet officials tried to manipulate, define, and produce military masculinities from above, attempting to control both the image of masculinized military fortitude after the war and men's participation in it. How the men in these institutions might have responded to these directives is a matter of conjecture, however. Without access to draft dodgers' motivations or *Voennye znaniia* readers' reactions, for example, one is limited in drawing conclusions about how state imperatives might have been understood on the ground by men in military industries. This chapter focuses on the ways in which a sector of men in a particular Soviet military industry, nuclear physics research, shaped their own stories about postwar and Cold War masculinity. This is not to suggest that martial identity dominated physicists' sense of selfhood. On the contrary. Many of them went out of their way to advocate for the peaceful uses of nuclear technology, such as in medicine or energy production, and they would have wanted to be remembered as pacifists or dissenters in response to the military uses of nuclear research.[5] Reading the physicists' texts within the context of renewed postwar attention to Soviet men and service, however, shows that even as civilians, this particular group of Cold War inventors shared in, and perpetuated, conversations about military masculinity taking place in the other sites examined so far.

Personal narrative evidence is a source of conflict for historians. Many argue that memoirs, autobiographies, and other "ego-documents" can provide access to voices outside the traditional archive, especially those historically marginalized from official records.[6] However, critics question the authenticity of such sources, rightly interrogating memory, voice, and self-presentation. Personal narratives in general provide the historian with much greater insight about the time of writing than the time being remembered. Yet as this chapter shows, personal narratives are key tools also for gender historians in investigating the time period being remembered, because of the insights memoirs offer into masculine subjectivity and the memoirist's self-presentation. Soviet nuclear physicists, after all, have hardly been marginalized in terms of traditional records. How, then, should the historian read the life stories of a group of historical actors who enjoyed publicity and even celebrity in the early Cold War era, but who nonetheless often saw themselves as marginalized and persecuted? Male voices have historically been privileged, particularly in military industries, and analysing the personal narratives of men must take into account the ways in which the physicists here have already positioned themselves as authoritative voices. As literature scholar Peter Middleton has cautioned, "We can also read representations of consciousness, self-consciousness, articulacy, and inarticulacy in men's texts as claims about men's subjectivity." We will see this dynamic again in chapter 5 in regard to the space program with the diaries of General Nikolai Kamanin. In some instances men's narratives contain the potential for self-promotion rather than self-reflection especially, as Middleton frames it, "when men try to look at their power."[7] For these physicists, their authority wavers and often clashes with expressions of marginalization rooted in their memories of subordination under the Soviet political system.

This chapter focuses on a selection of personal narratives written by physicists – including Yuri Orlov, Vitalii Ginzburg, and Roald Sagdeev, as well as Feinberg and Sakharov – who worked at Arzamas-16 in the 1950s, the isolated nuclear research site located 400 kilometres east of Moscow. It was established in 1946 and was often compared to Los Alamos, not only for its research but for the community of physicists living on site. Many who lived and worked there nicknamed it "Los Arzamas."[8] These physicists wrote their memoirs decades after the events discussed occurred and from different platforms; some wrote as Soviet dissidents, others as scientists still working in post-Soviet Russia. In order to arrive temporally at the point in which they decided to write about their past selves, they engaged in the "historicization of the self," emplotting their early Cold War–era nuclear research into arcs that allowed them to become the heroes of their own stories, told on their own terms and with their own lexicons.[9] Since the revolution, the personal narrative had been a key way of sharing Soviet citizens' life experience. By the time Sakharov picked up a pen in 1978, autobiographical writing, and the process of exploring and measuring one's own revolutionary consciousness, was well ingrained in Soviet culture.[10]

Whether characterizing themselves as subordinate, Promethean, or something in between, in producing such ego-documents even many years after leaving Arzamas-16, these writers absorbed culturally gendered affirmation that, as men, as scientists, and as the inventors of crucial Cold War technology, their voices mattered. Ultimately, this chapter demonstrates that re-establishing military masculinity after the war relied not only on the policymakers' prescriptions for young men discussed in chapters 1 and 2, or on the visual presentation of correct masculine codes in chapter 3, but on the complicity of men themselves in military industries, such as the laboratories developing nuclear weapons at Arzamas-16. It also shows that narratives about martial identities forged after the war reinforced the ways these men wrote about their experiences even decades later.

## Masculinity and "Scientific Impotence"

In the Cold War, science became one of the main sites of competition between the Soviet Union and the West.[11] The early Cold War years proved a critical time for Soviet physicists, particularly those who were involved in the nuclear project. While Soviet work on the atomic bomb began during the Second World War, the project assumed an increased urgency after the United States displayed its own nuclear capabilities in its destruction of Hiroshima and Nagasaki in 1945.[12] The Soviet government recruited the country's best scientific minds to populate dozens of newly constructed institutes, sometimes encompassing entire "science cities" in remote regions of the country, such as Arzamas-16, which led the hydrogen bomb effort; Dubna, which brought scientists together from around Eastern Europe at the Joint Institute for Nuclear Research; Cheliabinsk-70; Krasnoiarsk-26; Tomsk-7; Akademgorodok; and many others.[13] These research centres were dedicated solely to the development of nuclear weapons and other technological advancements that the leadership viewed as crucial to the country's military preparation in the Cold War era.

Historians generally agree that, as a group, the nuclear physicists were treated well, earning high salaries and enjoying comfortable living quarters, for example, at a time when much of the Soviet population remained subject to wartime rationing. During the war through to his death in 1953, Stalin was invested in physicists and their capability of building nuclear weapons, while his successor, Nikita Khrushchev, was too preoccupied policing geneticists to persecute physicists – and indeed, as we will see later in the chapter, helped elevate them in popular culture.[14] New research on *sharashki*, forced labour camps where scientists and intellectuals worked on dictated research topics as prisoners, has highlighted an aspect of the Gulag, political repression, and scientific work little acknowledged in Soviet history, one salient to any discussion of identity and selfhood for Soviet scientists.[15] *Sharashki* did not generally include nuclear physicists, although many physicists still lived and worked under a cloud of suspicion. Late Stalinist policymakers accustomed to making accusations of sabotage in key Soviet industries still suspected that physicists might attempt to undermine the nuclear program.[16] Thus, physicists experienced an uneasy relationship with their own privilege.

The ways in which the physicist-narrators wrote about this tension suggest that their self-assessments of their masculine identities were unfixed and shifting. In her pathbreaking studies of masculinities and social groups, R.W. Connell has written that subordinated masculinity relies on men in dominant, or hegemonic, positions coding other groups of men as lesser in some way.[17] In their narratives, however, the physicists used a vocabulary of subordination about themselves, especially in discussing their physicality, their sense of persistent surveillance, and their lack of choice regarding career assignments. On physicality and their sense of their own bodies, Sakharov and Ginzburg felt the need to explain why they did not serve in the Second World War. Sakharov wrote: "As for myself, I had doubts about my physical fitness for the front because of a chronic heart condition. I can say in all honesty that I've never wished or tried to duck responsibilities – with respect to army service or anything else. As things turned out, I never joined the army, as most of my generation did, and I stayed alive while many others were killed."[18] Later, Sakharov referred again to physical and militarized categories in describing his first meeting with his graduate supervisor, Igor' Tamm, in January 1945:

> Tamm asked after my father, and then almost immediately launched into questions on science. He conducted this examination calmly and tactfully, but he quickly penetrated to the bottom of my rather modest, though solid and, I think, not superficial knowledge of science. (My own self-appraisal could be summed up without false modesty by the military classification: *Fit, but untrained*.)[19]

Ginzburg, who described himself as "not particularly athletic," was diagnosed with a thyroid condition that kept him out of military service. "I cannot say that I was bursting to go to the front," he wrote, "but I was not in the least trying to avoid it."[20]

In the same vein as his depiction of Marshal Nedelin's virility joke at the November 1955 banquet, Sakharov suggested elsewhere that, as civilians without access to martial authority, he and his colleagues at Arzamas-16 were disciplined and surveilled:

> During the May holidays we went hiking in the woods that surrounded us on all sides. Absorbed in conversation, we didn't realize that we had entered the boundary zone … We were taken to a truck and ordered to sit on the floor with our legs stretched out in front of us. Four soldiers sat on a bench across from us brandishing their submachine guns. We were told that if anyone tried to escape or pulled up his legs, they would shoot without warning … Half an hour later, having satisfied themselves that we were not prisoners on the run, they graciously let us go.[21]

Tamm's colleagues also recalled his irritation at having to submit his permit to a soldier at the guard post in order to leave the premises. He had his privileges revoked at least once for failing to do so.[22]

The comfort of the laboratory's homosocial spaces (to be further explored in the next section) could not always provide the physicists with a sense of authority over their lives and careers. For example, many admitted to feeling disempowered not only by their inability to choose their own path in science, but by their knowledge that their research would be used for military applications. Of thermonuclear testing, Sakharov wrote, "In 1948, no one asked whether or not I *wanted* to take part in such work. I had no real choice in the matter."[23] In describing his resistance to employment assignments following his diploma work at Arzamas-16 and graduation in 1956, Sagdeev wrote that "I, too, was a victim of conscription. I was brought to this place against my personal will."[24] Even his assignment to work with Igor' Kurchatov, one of the country's most eminent physicists, provided no consolation for his inability to choose his own path: "While my newly acquired colleagues and neighbors in the dormitory were openly rejoicing at their huge luck to be a part of Kurchatov's empire, I was unable to overcome the deep internal resentment I felt against the authorities who had deprived me of the free choice of a future profession. In the gloomiest moments, I compared myself to a kind of intellectual serf."[25] Similarly, Orlov wrote, "They say that after the war Stalin himself signed the order for the formation of the physics department. It was actually a contract between scientists and Satan."[26] Describing their lack of research choice as "conscription" is noteworthy. As we saw in chapter 1, both the word and the concept held great sway in postwar military institutions; drawing on this martial lexicon in their memoirs suggests that these scientists, even decades after the events described occurred, continued to negotiate, and perhaps even feel burdened by, their relationships to military authority.

Physicists' reports of excessive government control went beyond laboratory placements to surveillance of their research in progress. *Krokodil* lampooned government interference in scientific research in 1953 with a cartoon in which a scientist, gesturing at a sinister figure in a long dark coat lurking outside the laboratory, asked his colleague, "Why did you get the head of the local committee to co-author your scientific work? In order for him to help?" Looking cynical, the other scientist replied, "No, in order for him *not* to hinder" (Figure 4.1).[27] Writing from post-Soviet Russia and not overtly from a dissident point of view, Ginzburg recalled being denied the opportunity to attend an international conference in 1959, pointing out that he "did not see many good physicists, and did not learn many interesting things. I was very bitter about it at that time, and I am bitter now when I remember this insult."[28] Acclaimed physicist Vladimir Veksler recalled harbouring a "lack of faith in authority" throughout the 1950s, bridging both the

Figure 4.1 *Costly Help*
"Why did you get the head of the local committee to co-author your scientific work? In order for him to help?"
"No, in order for him *not* to hinder."

*Krokodil*, 28 February 1953, 3.

Stalin and Khrushchev eras. He declared that the political encroachment on physicists' research caused "scientific impotence."[29]

Physicists like Sakharov, Orlov, and Sagdeev wrote as dissidents and as activists against further nuclear testing. This point of view informed their rhetoric about having moral concerns over the consequences of their work, and it potentially explains their expressions of helplessness in choosing their career paths. "We, the inventors, scientists, engineers, and craftsmen, had created a terrible weapon, the most terrible weapon in human history; but its use would lie entirely outside our control," Sakharov wrote. "The people at the top of the party and military hierarchy would make the decisions."[30] This distancing of oneself from any agency in inventing these weapons is typical of a kind of memory work engaged in by citizens of oppressive systems, especially those seeking to avoid accusations of collaboration.[31] Physicists' activism against nuclear testing was not only a Soviet dissident phenomenon, however. While Soviet physicists reported clashes with Stalin, Beria, Khrushchev, and military leaders like Nedelin, their American counterparts might have faced their own issues of subordinated masculinity: When J. Robert Oppenheimer became more publicly opposed to nuclear testing after the bombing of Hiroshima, President Truman apparently called him "that cry-baby scientist" in a note to Secretary of State Dean Acheson.[32]

The physicists coded themselves as subordinated men, recalling a past in which they lacked choice and suffered under the domination of military masculinity. The lack of freedom in closed science cities was quite real; I am not suggesting that these examples were simply the rhetorical flourishes of men engaged in exaggerated and self-serving post-Soviet memory work. But as we will see below, the physicists were inconsistent in their portrayals of pacifism and in removing choice from their narratives about their work. At other times, they colluded (consciously or not) to create their own comfortable spaces in which they could work collaboratively as a brotherhood bound by their common understandings of masculinity, heterosexuality, and intellectual privilege.

## The Gendered Cold War Workplace

Without discounting their narratives of subordination, to focus only on that first layer of their texts obscures the physicists' engagement with the "collective practice" of masculinity in a space such as the laboratory.[33] Their stories of powerlessness appear at various points throughout their memoirs but never dominate. Instead, such stories drove the writers to ensure that lack of freedom, choice, and power would not define their texts: in effect two more layers were added to their narratives, ones that demonstrate more active participation in crafting the boundaries of acceptable masculine behaviour. Physicists' self-presentations shifted significantly when they discussed three related areas: their marriages and private lives, their descriptions of women with whom they worked, and their participation in constructing and maintaining the laboratory as a homosocial space, in which bonds between men were emphasized and in which women were marginalized. How the physicists talked about women, in other words, reveals their complicity with a Soviet patriarchal dividend that persisted despite women's nominal equality.[34]

Women were consistently othered in all the personal narratives considered here, beginning with the physicists' discussions of marriage. Sakharov, in keeping with his self-fashioning as a physicist-philosopher, humanist, and pacifist, portrayed his family life as tranquil and loving, painting himself as a responsible family man. He was married to Klavdiia Alekseevna from 1943 until her death in 1969, and they had three children, two of whom were still young during his years at Arzamas-16.[35] He referred to her by the informal name, "Klava" in his memoirs and generally wrote about her in diminutive ways.[36] He declared that she "didn't have the emotional strength" and "lack[ed] the stamina" to work outside the home, for example. "Klava's lack of occupation aggravated her psychological problems. I am to blame (if any blame attaches) for not insisting that she study or find a job and for not fully appreciating how important this was."[37] Moreover, he often passed judgment on his colleagues' marriages and relationships, speaking in particularly disparaging terms about infidelities in his circle. "[Yakov] Zel'dovich had a number of other affairs," he wrote. "Too many – most of them strictly sexual liaisons." He concluded, "I don't like some of the stories I've heard."[38]

Infidelity influenced Orlov's discussion of his family life as well. He married in 1951 and became a father the next year, a time he remembered as happy and fulfilling. "At night, while rocking the baby carriage with my left hand, I calculated conversions of orthopositronium into parapositronium with my right," he wrote.[39] However, exiled to Yerevan, where he lived apart from his wife and children from 1956 to 1961, Orlov admitted he could not maintain the role of loyal husband and father that he had embraced in Moscow. "She worked as an electronics engineer in [physicist Abram] Alikhanov's institute," he wrote of his second wife, Ira, but her scientific qualifications were quickly superseded by descriptions of her only in leisure pursuits or as his mistress – and an unfaithful one at that, he claimed.[40] "Lively, talented, she played the piano, played table tennis, and rode a motorcycle ... My Yerevan friends tried to make me listen to reason, and essentially they were right."[41]

Other scientists engaged in what Sagdeev called "endogamy within their profession," especially within the small group of colleagues and mentors directly surrounding them.[42] Both Sagdeev and colleague V.I. Gol'danskii married the daughters of their respective supervisors, David Frank-Kamenetskii and Nikolai Semenov.[43] Sagdeev and Gol'danskii's masculine identities fused the scientist, the husband, and the son-in-law. Sagdeev wrote of this coalition between family and science in his recollection of his doctoral defence in front of a committee that included the acclaimed physicist and future Nobel laureate Piotr Kapitsa, who articulated a metaphor of love and fidelity to parallel the challenges of academic work: "Kapitsa probably sensed my uneasiness and said, 'Don't worry. All of us had to do it. After all, you should remember – love is passing, but the diamond ring remains forever.'"[44] In describing a colleague's marriage and its tragic end, Sakharov wrote in a surprisingly offhanded way:

> In 1950, when I was living at the Installation [Arzamas-16], I dropped by to see [Nikolai] Dmitriev on my birthday. I wasn't allowed to go to Moscow and didn't know what else to do to mark the occasion. He had just married a girl named Tamara, and the two of them began giving me a lesson in how to drink pure alcohol: I'd never touched anything stronger than vodka before, and then only a drop on rare occasions ... Zel'dovich disliked Tamara intensely and seemed jealous of her relationship with Dmitriev. He complained that she was taking up Dmitriev's time with domestic matters – teething rings, diapers, and the like – and keeping him in bed too long; she would ruin his scientific career. In 1955, Tamara jumped from a fifth-floor window a few days after having a thyroidectomy, leaving Dmitriev alone with two children. A few years later, he married a woman from our math department.[45]

Sakharov did not further reflect on Tamara Dmitrieva's suicide, nor was it mentioned in the other memoirs examined here. A 2015 eulogy of Dmitriev similarly avoided the subject, despite discussing other aspects of his personal life.[46] Although only one example, Dmitrieva's erasure from physicist narratives is indicative of a broader trend in writing about women. By writing women and domestic life into their narratives in these ways (and by largely writing about women only *as* domestic life), the physicists created and revealed for the reader a gendered environment in which women could not be described as anything other than a problem to be solved or, in an extreme case like Sakharov's words about Dmitrieva, a distraction that could be erased.

The texts also suggest that for women scientists and support staff working within that space the top of the hierarchy remained elusive. Even by 1970, women held only 94 of 693 positions as full and corresponding members of the Academy of Sciences.[47] As feminist scholars Jill Bystydzienski and Sharon Bird have demonstrated, academic science in the modern era has created a gender division, meaning "the practices and procedures through which students and faculty are recruited, processed, and deemed successful (or not) tend to advantage men (and constructions of masculinity) over women (and constructions of femininity)."[48] For men, it indicates a deep immersion in and allegiance to their imagining of a homosocial world of science. "Revekka Izraileva was the sole woman in our department," Sakharov noted in introducing the reader to his new team upon arrival at Arzamas-16. "In addition to her regular work, she would copy out the boys' scribbled calculations in a clean hand."[49] He did not remark on the patriarchal structure of the institute that would have built such work into women scientists' jobs – and one need not expect him to have done so – but narratives such as these signal complicity in a masculinized culture.

Rather than discussing women colleagues' scientific work, the physicists characterized women as naive, unintelligent, and unambitious in their careers. Sagdeev recalled that during his time at Arzamas-16, he witnessed a trial of a "young girl" recently appointed a medical doctor there. "She wrote a letter to her parents in which she tried to impress them with how significant and important her presence there was," he wrote. "She spoke of the [I]nstallation as the capital of bomb design. Poor girl. Even if she had been intentionally willing to disclose secrets, she knew none of them. Still, the verdict was three years' imprisonment."[50] (Women at Arzamas-16 were repeatedly referred to as "girls" (*devushki*) in several of the personal narratives examined here. Like the corresponding word in English, the word in Russian devalues women's achievements and control over their adult personhood.) Orlov indicated that early in his career, he did not consider the women in his department as colleagues so much as potential dates: "I do not remember going out for long walks at all; just to the movies, maybe, once or twice. I had not yet worked my way up to girls, but there were only three or four in all of our enormous faculty anyway," he wrote.[51] Gol'danskii recalled an incident retold to him by Ginzburg, dismissing it without further comment as just a bit of "nonsense":

> As far as the topic of women was concerned, many years afterwards Vitaly L. Ginzburg teased me about how he had first heard my name. He had been walking with YaB [Zel'dovich] in the corridor of the only wing of the ICP [Institute of Chemical Physics] in use at that time, and some young female colleague had asked YaB in which room Gol'danskii was working. "That one," said YaB pointing out the door, "but bear in mind that a young woman entering that door can be considered to have gotten married.[52]

Before the development of computers for advanced calculations (the first of which were not ready until 1954), Arzamas-16 employed women operators who "follow[ed] instructions that meant nothing to them," according to former physicist Gennady Gorelik, "add[ing] and multiply[ing] incomprehensible numbers without knowing that the result of their work could answer the question of how powerful a thermonuclear explosion would be."[53] During one period at Arzamas-16 in 1949, Sakharov's wife could not join him for six months.

> I lived in the hotel until November. Yuri Romanov and I were inseparable during that time. We worked together in the daytime, relaxed together in the evening, and slept in the same room at night. I was very fond of him … Two young women lived in the room beneath ours – Revekka Izraileva, who worked in Zel'dovich's department, and Lena Malinovskaya, who moved to the Installation at the same time we did and worked in the mathematical department. (Her chief, Mattes Agrest, was wont to observe: "Lena's a nice girl, but she needs a bit of a push from time to time.") In the evenings Yuri and I usually visited the girls. He would dance somewhat awkwardly with each of them in turn, while I would sit and relax; I didn't know how to dance. Sometimes Lena would sing for us.[54]

The stories the physicists told about gendered spaces showed a distinct exclusionary culture in which women could not exist on an equal plane as scientists. In detailing his work with Lev Landau, who would go on to win a Nobel Prize in 1962 (known as "Dau" in several memoirs), Alexei Abrikosov revealed the lengths to which he and Landau went to keep women away from doctoral research:

> Although Dau liked women, he did not think them capable of engaging in theoretical physics … I resolved to show Dau that a woman can become a theoretical physicist. I took as a diploma student one who had passed the theoretical minimum (at the third attempt). I had to do the work for her and of course did not wish to recommend her as a PhD student, but she stubbornly insisted … I went along to Dau and asked him to accept her for my sake. "Is she your mistress?" he asked. "No," I replied. "Well, perhaps you hope she will be?" "Really, Dau, I have no such thoughts." "Then is she a theoretical genius?" he inquired with a highly sceptical expression. "Hardly," I answered, remembering how the diploma went. "Then I will come to your rescue," said Dau; "I will not accept her as a Ph.D. student, and you can tell her that." I did so with great relief. In consequence, she

> changed to another subject and was extremely successful. I see her rarely, but we are on excellent terms. I will add only that I made other attempts to refute Dau's proposition. I once had a very able French girl. But in the end Dau proved to be right.[55]

Establishing precedents of not admitting women was one way to assert a masculinized brotherhood in the laboratory; another was to reinforce the boundaries of that brotherhood whenever possible. For example, Sagdeev wrote about the gendered classroom language his mentor, Andrei Budker, would use:

> I still remember one particular problem, which [Budker] asked with a kind of male bravado. "Imagine for a moment," Budker said, "you are going to meet one of your two mistresses. You approach the metro station planning to take the first train arriving at the station no matter which of the two directions it is traveling. The lucky mistress would be the one to which you are delivered by this particular train. After many trials, statistics indicate that somehow one of the two young ladies would be visited three times more often than the other. How is it possible? Can you give an explanation quickly?"[56]

Later, Sagdeev recalled seeking Budker's help after a fellow student, Vladimir Zakharov, was expelled from the Moscow Energy Institute for assaulting a man Zakharov believed had seduced his girlfriend: "Budker invited Zakharov to tell him the story. After hearing the sordid tale, Budker gave his own assessment: 'Volodia, I believe that you behaved like a real man. For a man who was – and maybe still is – in love, what you did was quite understandable. But if you were also an intelligent man, you would have found a different solution. An intelligent person would never resolve a dispute with brute force.'"[57] Gorelik, who later became a historian of science, used gendered metaphors to write about understanding physicists' motivation in their research: "The passion for scientific invention is like passion for a woman, for poetry, for playing cards, for music."[58] He also recalled Tamm saying, "You can fall in love with a beautiful theory as if with a beautiful woman." Gorelik himself then added, "and when the affair turned out to be nothing more than temporary intoxication, exhausted and miserable, [Tamm] would beg his young colleagues to 'throw me a problem of some kind,' calling it a hangover treatment. He gave the last fifteen years of his life to unrequited love for an enchantingly beautiful and bold idea."[59]

While the physicists devoted little space to their impressions of their women colleagues, they wrote at length about the men with whom they worked, many of whom they held in high personal and professional regard.[60] Orlov described Landau, one of his early teachers, as "tall, lean, with a naturally elegant manner and luminous intellect apparent in his face. He set a great example for me." Orlov added that Landau's keen mind was not the only feature that he admired in his teacher. "Several students claimed that I imitated his hairstyle," Orlov confessed, "but this was not true."[61] Despite the presence of women, the physicists portrayed their world largely as a homosocial one, particularly at isolated locations such as Arzamas-16. In the words of another, they were "brilliant" men who lived and worked "side by side" for years, sharing cottages, meals, and leisure time as well as laboratories.[62] The various departments and divisions frequently held contests or embarked on other playful pursuits aimed at releasing tension amid such stressful work. Gol'danskii reported his victory in a literary contest in the late 1940s in which poems or stories were posted to one's office door for communal debate. His winning poem, rife with crass imagery that spoke to a deep familiarity among the men working at his institute, was titled, "Hymn of the Theory Division":

> Our division is the hub of the institute,
> Longed for by other people,
> Our great Corresponding Member
> Defecates hundreds of ideas a minute.
> We bring the light of science to the plebeians,
> Who are always working so hard on their experiments,
> We are not afraid of [supervisor] Semenov,
> There are none more daring than our boys.
> Landau himself makes the sign of the cross over us,
> We are mighty, healthy, strong,
> Only our asses suffer
> When we prepare classified reports like pancakes.
> Glory to the physicists, glory to the poets
> Surrounding Yakov's throne.
> We feel good in the peacefulness of the office,
> Our balls are not scared by neutrons.[63]

"Corresponding member" (*chlen-korrespondent*) was a specific designation in the Academy of Sciences of the USSR, although as in English, *chlen* can be used as a double entendre, as Gol'danskii seems to do here. This particular memoir collection appears to have been written in English, so one can assume the translation of the original poem is Gol'danskii's.

Practical jokes were also common and further demonstrate the fraternal comfort in which the physicists worked. Some episodes indicate that they felt much more at ease in their surveilled laboratories than their stories of subordination suggest: Gol'danskii told of playing a particular "joke" on Zel'dovich in which he repackaged prints from a foreign scientific journal (the origins of which were unclear) and left them on Zel'dovich's desk with a friendly note implying Western cooperation. "It must be realized how dangerous it was at that time (especially for a person doing top-secret work) to have any contacts with émigrés," Gol'danskii wrote, "in order to understand how upset YaB [Zel'dovich] was and how sorry we were afterward for this joke."[64] No repercussions seem to have come from this episode. Vladimir Zakharov also wrote of a brotherly camaraderie and comfort in crude jokes among the physicists. "I apologise to the reader," he began, "but here is a typical episode" describing Zel'dovich's lewd influence on his colleagues and students: "A discussion is underway at the blackboard. Somebody makes an assertion and enthusiastically tries to prove his point. At last, the man exclaims, 'As YaB [Zel'dovich] says – you can cut off my member if I'm wrong!'"[65]

Sakharov spoke with great admiration of his mentor, Nobel Prize–winner Tamm. The two worked together at Arzamas-16 from 1950 to 1953. "This was the period of our closest collaboration," Sakharov wrote, "and I grew to know him in ways that would have been impossible in Moscow. We worked together uninterruptedly throughout the day, had breakfast and lunch together in the canteen, and ate supper and relaxed together in the evenings and on Sundays."[66] Although both men's wives lived with them on site at that time (which was not always the case), Sakharov's memories spoke of a relationship that rivalled, if not surpassed, marital affection: "Tamm talked about his life and many other things during evenings we spent in his hotel room or wandering along the deserted forest paths of the Installation (one of them was the local 'Lover's Lane')."[67] Contributing to his characterization of the close fraternity that developed among physicists, Sakharov added that, "my longest relationship – spanning four decades – was with Yakov Zel'dovich."[68] This was a longer period of time than Sakharov spent with either of his wives.

That the physics laboratory as a Cold War workplace was rife with sexism, crass language, and performances of male bravado in the 1950s should not surprise us; despite the official ideology of women's equality in Soviet society, sexism and harassment persisted in many workplaces throughout the Soviet century.[69] This first generation of nuclear physicists is remarkable, however, in that these records of how a workplace can develop such a masculinized culture do not come from complaint transcripts or other potential archival sources, but from the men themselves. As they reminisced fondly about their contributions to science, the physicist-narrators made choices about how to construct their narratives, which colleagues and anecdotes to emphasize, and how to frame their participation in the laboratories that developed nuclear weapons. As we have seen, physicists' memories of subordination and lack of choice might have been motivated by a desire to escape accusations of collaboration. Similarly, these men might have highlighted lewd jokes or strolls in the woods with their friends and mentors in order to destabilize another, more prominent narrative, one publicly understood and responsible for their fame: that their work at this time was devoted to creating such devastating weapons.

The lexicon physicists used to discuss their family lives, women colleagues, and male mentors was remarkably uniform across the texts, despite the fact that they were produced at different times in the late Soviet and post-Soviet eras. Further work on gender orders in those eras that might have influenced these narratives is needed. For example, writing from the West in the 1980s or from post-Soviet Russia in the 1990s – both environments with different gender orders than that which the writers would have been used to in the 1950s – might have sparked their nostalgia for an era when they believed women need not be taken seriously. Historically, however, these memoirists' descriptions of their workplaces in the early 1950s matter for narrating their foundational moments of martial masculine privilege. Furthering that trope, the Prometheus metaphor of possessing a great and terrible power because of their scientific work also structured physicists' narratives about the 1950s.

## "Some Kind of God": Re-arming a Soviet Prometheus

As we have seen, multiple narratives of masculine subjectivity coexisted in these personal narratives. Physicist masculinity was subordinate at times to that of the military or the state but was also complicit in building and benefiting from the patriarchal structure of the workplace. Feinberg's invoking of Prometheus and the physicists' god-like power introduces the third layer of the narrative, in which all earlier tales of suffering as serfs, conscripts, and political pawns evaporated. One way that physicists claimed a privileged position in Cold War society was through the "atoms for peace" moment. Fostered by the Khrushchev government, it publicly celebrated physicists as the men responsible for leading the country away from its Stalinist past and towards the modernized socialist future, in which nuclear power drove Soviet achievements.[70] By the early 1960s, the cult of the atom had resulted in songs, poems, novels, cartoons, and films with nuclear science as a theme. It also included the construction of the Pavilion for Atomic Energy, exhibited at the Exhibition of the Achievements of the People's Economy (VDNKh) in Moscow from 1956 to 1989.[71] It was not only the physicists who wanted to publicly emphasize the idea of atoms for peace: the authorities themselves endorsed the peaceful uses of atomic power, as we saw in Figure 3.25 in chapter 3, in an image visually emphasizing the atomic energy station and privileging the masculinity of a man working at a peaceful atomic project.[72] The movement also highlighted generational diversity among physicists: Vladimir Zakharov, who finished secondary school in 1956, reported that he greatly admired the physicists he saw exalted in public culture. We "were mad on physics," he wrote in reminiscing about that era. "In my circle of friends, the famous Soviet physicists were idols."[73] Physicists gained cultural currency from the cult of the atom, enjoying government sponsorship in popular culture and the curiosity of the public by virtue of their secretive profession.

Physicists found themselves centre stage in one of the era's most famous cultural exchanges, *liriki-fiziki*, or the physicists and lyricists debate. It was sparked in 1959 by a letter to *Komsomol'skaia pravda* by a young woman seeking counsel after her fiancé told her that artistic and cultural pursuits were obsolete in the invention-driven atomic age. The debate grew to envelop Soviet society in a broader conversation about the place of the humanities in an era when Khrushchev had put so much emphasis on science and technology.[74] Poet Boris Slutskii penned the debate's defining ode, "Physicists and Lyricists," in 1960, lamenting what he saw as physicists surpassing writers and artists as celebrated contributors to the cultural fabric of society. "Looks as if physicists are in, looks as if lyricists are out," Slutskii wrote. "Nothing Machiavellian – Nature's law, no doubt."[75] One physicist at Akademgorodok in the

1960s called physicists a "very keen tuning fork for the spiritual life of the country," participating in "creative work" alongside well-known poets like Bulat Okudzhava and Vladimir Vysotskii. "They make up a considerable portion of the future 'men of the sixties (*shestidesiatniki*),'" he concluded, referring to Soviet efforts in the 1960s to replicate the creative renaissance of the 1860s, when the term had last been used.[76] (What would become perhaps the most famous portrayal of a physicist in Soviet culture, the character of Viktor Shtrum in Vasilii Grossman's epic 1960 novel about the war years, *Life and Fate*, was not published in the Soviet Union until 1988.)[77] *Krokodil* also showcased the popular cult of the atom, playing down any talk of militarizing or weaponizing science and instead portraying the atom as a harmless young boy. Greeting another boy representing the New Year at the end of 1955, *Krokodil*'s child-like atom asserted a peaceful, non-threatening persona, saying to the New Year's boy, "I think that you and I are going to work well together!" (Figure 4.2)[78]

The cult of the atom and the associated cultural buoyancy of physicists culminated with the production of one of the Soviet Union's most popular Cold War films, *Nine Days of One Year* (Deviat' dnei odnogo goda), directed by Mikhail Romm and released in theatres in early 1962. The film was initiated by a Communist Party leadership intent on continuing to publicize physicists' (peaceful) work.[79] Offering the Soviet public a glimpse into the world of nuclear science for the first time, the film confronted both the dangers of the field and the dedication of its researchers. The protagonist, Gusev, was a nuclear physicist whose exposure to radiation was slowly killing him and destroying his relationships with both his physicist wife and his male colleagues. But his experiments contributed to Soviet military strength and, he believed, would improve humankind, and so he sacrificed his own health for the good of the collective. Despite his intellectual virility, Gusev sacrificed his physical body for his research, suffering battle scars that rivalled those of military servicemen.

The press had mixed reactions to the film when it was released. *Izvestiia* praised the unique role of the hero in the film, finding him "witty and sarcastic," and noting that "this has not always been the case for our positive film heroes. These traits have generally been reserved for negative characters. A good man cannot be sarcastic about anything."[80] *Literaturnaia gazeta* found the film's "extensive deliberations on life, science, the present and the past, [and] intellectual disputes to be refreshing."[81] *Pravda*, however, lamented the somewhat negative view of scientific research found in the film, as well as the lack of a strong

АТОМ:— Я думаю, мы с вами сработаемся!

Figure 4.2 *A Friendly Meeting*
Atom: "I think that you and I are going to work well together!"

*Krokodil*, 30 December 1955, 4.

male authority figure to anchor the hero. The absence of "an outstanding scientific leader" hurt the film, according to *Pravda*, who wanted to see a man "who inspires and teaches youth, like for example, Igor' Vasil'evich Kurchatov. The figure of the fussy director … does not correspond very closely to the reality of life."[82] Despite its negative tone, the review eventually published in *Pravda* could have been much more damning; the reviewer originally assigned to the film was removed after he submitted a piece highly critical of the film's dark plot and the hero's mortality.[83] Scientists themselves were not sure what to make of the film. Several top physicists attended the opening night screening, including Kapitsa, Tamm, and Zel'dovich. Some of them wanted the film shelved. Zel'dovich complained that it simplified science too much: "Every bit of science in the plot was centred on one question: would it irradiate the hero or not."[84] Filmed at the Joint Institute for Nuclear Research in Dubna, just outside Moscow, the film opened the door to a closed world, allowing the viewing public a glimpse of the laboratories, equipment, and especially the men who had been so exalted in popular culture. Actor Alexei Batalov, who played the doomed Gusev, noted the popularity of physics, particularly among young people, and welcomed the transparency he thought the film would bring. "For us, it was like making a picture about Martians," he said. "No one knew how they lived, how they worked, what they talked about."[85] That mystique surrounding their work also seemed to have buoyed the memoirists as they told their stories, lending them pride in their status as unknowable and untouchable.

Because it offered physicists fame and encouraged the public to celebrate their (peaceful) achievements, the cult of the atom, in gendered terms, represented the government implicitly granting authority to non-martial masculinity, and physicists accepting it. However, in their narratives, the physicists who worked at Arzamas-16 in the early 1950s, before the cult of the atom overcame Stalin-era secrecy about nuclear research, suggested that they not only gained access to categories of military masculinity but in fact surpassed them. "I understood, of course, the terrifying, inhuman nature of the weapons we were building," Sakharov wrote of his years at Arzamas-16. "But the recent war had also been an exercise in barbarity; and although I hadn't fought in that conflict, I regarded myself as a soldier in this new scientific war. (Kurchatov himself said we were 'soldiers,' and this was no idle remark)."[86] Here, Sakharov shifted his use of a military service metaphor away from the lack of choice associated with conscription, which we saw earlier in this chapter as defining physicists' first, subordinate, layer of these narratives. Sakharov's claim that he regarded himself as a soldier of the Cold War reframed his service as much more positive, honourable, and fully within his control. Still, the soldier metaphor was imperfect, since soldiering implies an identity defined primarily by taking orders. In this third strand of the narratives, however, the physicists deferred to no one else in the Communist Party command structure.

Writing at the end of the Cold War, when nuclear war had not come to pass, the physicists might have felt emboldened to invoke their superior powers of intellect and invention in casting themselves as heroes of their own stories. As scientists, they saw themselves as above war, not in service to militarism but working to dismantle it altogether. In seeking to overcome the American monopoly on nuclear weapons, physicists, wrote Feinberg, would have the power to declare that no one could wage war.[87] In this third layer of his narrative, Feinberg aimed not merely to accept or perform military masculinity, but to supersede it. He wrote, "Landau more than once said to me, 'Well done, physicists, for making war impossible.'"[88] Empowered by their mastery of such destructive technology, the physicists even implied that their intellect made their minds, and bodies, the most powerful weapons of all. Sakharov recalled taking the train to testing sites, because "there were several of us who were considered too valuable to risk in a plane crash."[89] After the first thermonuclear bomb test in Kazakhstan in August 1953, which had been based on Sakharov's design, he immediately toured the site as if invincible, "nonchalantly walk[ing] across the field" despite the presence of radiation.[90]

In previewing the script for *Nine Days of One Year* in 1960, one reader at Mosfilm also pointed to the idea of deification: "Why does a scientist have to be an Einstein, either a fool or some kind of god?"[91] *Nine Days*, tremendously popular among filmgoers in 1962, capped a decade of ambivalence in masculine identities among physicists and in representations of physics. The Communist Party and Soviet culture in the late 1950s and early 1960s supported an increasingly public discourse that championed not only progress in nuclear research but the heroism of the men responsible for it. At the same time, however, the film's framing of a radiation disaster and the vulnerability of these hero-physicists to the dangers of their work also spoke to unease with the atomic project.

## Telling Manly Stories

These physicists' memoirs are part of a much longer tradition of life-writing in Soviet culture. As Jochen Hellbeck has written of Stalin-era diaries, "To belong to the collective and be aligned with history was a condition predicated on work and struggle, complete with lapses, failings, and renewed commitments."[92] Especially under Stalin, an autobiography was required both for access to Communist Party membership and as evidence for those deemed to be lacking in party loyalty.[93] In the Khrushchev era, narratives and testimonies of Gulag survivors constituted a distinct genre.[94] In the late Soviet period, dissidents' personal narratives joined these earlier texts. They were almost always published abroad and sought, at least in part, to explain and justify activism while garnering support and sympathy in the West.[95] Under *glasnost'*, the "impulse to speak out" led to a new wave of life-writing and preservation, and the writing of personal narratives has exploded since the dissolution of the Soviet Union.[96]

The narratives examined here fall under several of these categories. Sakharov's *Memoirs* is clearly a dissident text. He began writing in 1978 and continued through 1982 while in exile in Gorky. "Autobiographical narratives constitute an important part of mankind's memory. That is one reason why I took up the writing of this book," he told the reader in his preface, written in 1989. "And because much of what has been written about my life, my circumstances, and those close to me is grossly inaccurate, I want to try to set the record straight." In addition, he cited the "extraordinary turns my life has taken" as part of his impetus to write his own story: "This book is not a confession, nor do I lay claim to having produced a work of art. These are candid recollections of the world of science, the world of the Installation [Arzamas-16], the world of dissidents, and, simply, of my life." He had already shared an awareness that his life was not ordinary, however, implicitly casting himself as the lead actor in a story of great importance.[97] Part of the *glasnost'* generation, Sagdeev started writing in 1988 while still working in Moscow.[98] Ginzburg, on the other hand, claimed he very reluctantly wrote his autobiography only because he won the Nobel Prize in Physics in 2003, and a written autobiography was required along with his Nobel Lecture:[99]

> I do not have any wish to come back to my autobiography ... [but] I respect the wishes of the [Nobel] Foundation, so I am writing. Of course, I could confine myself to brief biographical information; writing a detailed autobiography is rather dangerous – it can bring reproach for "exhibitionism" and immodesty. Nevertheless, I have decided to write in a rather detailed and frank way, as it corresponds to my habits and tastes. One more reason to justify this decision is that I am already 87 and will hardly ever have another occasion to write about myself and my views.[100]

Ginzburg's concern about the "danger" of life-writing betrayed his continued consciousness of his past life as a Soviet subject, and of the power of the personal narrative to signal both conformity and dissent.[101]

Historians' use of personal narratives is often part of a recovery project, aiming to overcome the marginalization of various social groups from the historical record. Rooted in Marxism, feminism, subaltern theory, and queer theory, such work has provided a necessary corrective by searching for historical subjects whose stories might have been recorded and preserved outside the traditional archive.[102] For regimes that attempted to control history by destroying documents or selecting which would be written in the first place and then preserved, personal narrative sources provide unique access to historical experiences. In historical research on imperial Russia and the Soviet Union, studies focusing on women's stories have recovered these marginalized voices.[103] Indeed, many women physicists from around the world have sought to step out of the margins to tell their own stories.[104]

Physicist life-writing, a phenomenon common among Cold War–era scientists, disrupts many of the conclusions scholars have drawn about personal narrative evidence. The sentiment of marginalization present in Soviet physicists' memoirs clashed with other evidence of privilege and celebrity, creating a complex terrain for these men's sense of self. They cast themselves and their engagement with nuclear research as particular plot points; even during moments of self-criticism, they created the conditions for their own emplotment as heroes of their own stories, told with their own vocabularies of acquiescence and submission, complicity and resignation, and sometimes virility and privilege. For Soviet physicists, as former citizens of a regime that both curtailed their individual rights and created the conditions for their scientific achievements, masculine identities continually had to be reforged – whether in the universities, research laboratories, or, decades later, in front of a typewriter.

These personal narratives by physicists who worked on Soviet nuclear development illustrate the shifting identities by which this particular brotherhood, engaged in military-adjacent work, might have defined itself. As masculinized subjects, the physicists discuss their surveillance and perceived othering by different groups of men; their exclusion of women and the upholding of patriarchal privilege in the workplace; and their ability to narratively construct identities of god-like hegemony. Read together, the memoirs reinforce a self-congratulatory hagiography of nuclear physicists in Cold War history. The male narrator shows a commitment to casting himself as the lead in his own story as a soldier of the Cold War – sometimes as a reluctant conscript or rank-and-file researcher, sometimes as a deity empowered above the generals at test sites. One curiously absent theme in many of the physicists' self-assessments, however, was Jewishness. Despite the fact that many Soviet scientists had Jewish backgrounds and conducted their work in the late 1940s and 1950s, during a time of heightened Stalinist anti-Semitism, none of the texts examined here reflect on Jewish identity. More research on the particularities of Soviet Jewish masculinity needs to be done. Along with *Nine Days* and the cult of the atom phenomenon in Soviet culture, the physicists' texts reveal the fraught relationship between Soviet men and military masculinity. But before they could write their stories and present themselves as important men of the Cold War, they would witness, and perhaps be influenced by, the martial spectacle of our final group of actors, the male test pilots selected to become the celebrated public faces of the Soviet space program.

*Chapter Five*

# Military Masculinity and the Cosmonaut Brotherhood

It was a celebrity watcher's dream come true: in July 1961 the most famous man in the world, cosmonaut Yuri Gagarin, lunched with one of the most famous women in the world, Queen Elizabeth II, at Buckingham Palace. Only two months earlier, Gagarin had become the first man to successfully orbit the earth, executing not only a covert military challenge to the United States but also a global victory lap for the charming and handsome young Soviet hero. Both at home and abroad he was packaged as a virile man, desirable to women but sexually contained as a committed husband and father, his masculinity predicated on his sex appeal, his technological feat, and his air force uniform. That day at lunch, overwhelmed by the proximity of such a famous icon as the queen, Gagarin dared to lean forward to touch her leg under their lunch table. Having heard of kings and queens only from fairy tales, he wanted to make sure that she was a real, "live" queen, he later told a colleague.[1] That particular transgression not only violated royal protocol but might have played, however subtly, into his image as an attractive young man who was entitled access to women's bodies. The queen, of course, was off-limits. Gagarin's primary chaperone on tour, the space program veteran General Nikolai Kamanin, later described Elizabeth II – who would have turned thirty-five that spring to Gagarin's twenty-seven – as a "pleasant middle-aged woman, dressed very simply, without any decorations or traces of make-up."[2] Women like that, Kamanin implied, should be pleased that a man as handsome and successful as Gagarin would want to touch them. After all, according to Soviet observers, Gagarin received no rebuke for his boldness but only a smile from the queen over her coffee cup.[3]

Gagarin anchors the themes of this chapter, which investigates the cosmonaut program of the early 1960s as the ultimate site where the codes of military masculinity being rebuilt since the war reached their zenith. The early cosmonauts became the most significant martial brotherhood of all in the Cold War, and more importantly, they commanded cultural prestige in Soviet society outside the regular armed forces. As a famously charming man with access to women, technology, and a fascinated domestic and global public watching his every move, Gagarin's status as an icon of Cold War masculinity might seem assured. However, the particular ways in which his masculine persona was cultivated and performed, often in contradictory moments, deserves further investigation. Overturning years of secrecy about the cosmonaut training program, the Soviet government publicized Gagarin's historic flight as soon as he landed. Such publicity was partly meant to announce to the United States that Soviet rocket technology had successfully sent a man to space and could, presumably, launch missiles just as far. Yet the publicity surrounding Gagarin's feat conveyed more than coded military and scientific messages. Not selected for any particular skill on the flight deck, Gagarin was rather a man who, as historian Andrew Jenks has observed, was "straight out of Soviet central casting" – handsome and articulate with a famously bright smile.[4] While the spacecrafts they fronted might have operated on autopilot, Gagarin and his cosmonaut cohort were needed to sell that technology – and a specific formulation of Cold War masculinity – to a domestic and global public. Previous studies of the Soviet cosmonauts have focused on the scientific and political negotiations that led to Gagarin's flight, and more recently, social historians in both Russia and the West have begun to crack the almost hagiographic narrative about Gagarin.[5] However, the gendered aspects of the cosmonauts' public personas have not been fully investigated.

One significant aspect of Gagarin's masculine performance is often downplayed in biographies as well as in accounts of space program participants: his position as a charismatic young military officer. He was a senior lieutenant in the Soviet Air Force at the time of his flight in April 1961, and the air force uniform would become one of the most important factors contributing to his fame and that of his cosmonaut brethren between 1961 and 1963. Continuing from the visual treatment of military masculinity that we saw in chapter 3, Gagarin's uniform was also a key component in maintaining public visibility of military masculinity outside the regular forces. This group of early cosmonauts, known collectively in the press and in participant memoirs as the *shestiorka*, or Group of Six, was led by Gagarin, who became both the first man in space and the first to complete a full orbit of the earth. The group also included Gherman Titov on *Vostok-2*, who piloted the first 24-hour orbital flight on 6–7 August 1961; Andriian Nikolaev and Pavel Popovich, who became the first to pilot spacecraft in orbit at the same time on *Vostok-3* and *Vostok-4*, respectively, from 11 to 15 August 1961; and Valerii Bykovskii, who piloted *Vostok-5* for five days from 14 to 19 June 1963, setting a record for a solo space flight. These five cosmonauts advanced a cult of masculinity militarized by their roots in the air force and explicitly performed as a key part of the story of Soviet postwar recovery. At the same time, this story of cosmonauts in the early 1960s also continued the postwar pattern of writing women out of military institutions. The sixth cosmonaut in the *shestiorka* was the first woman in space, Valentina Tereshkova.[6] She piloted *Vostok-6* from 16 to 19 June 1963, which overlapped with much of Bykovskii's flight, but she was a civilian whose main public role was that of future wife and mother rather than pilot. The five male cosmonauts were enlisted as leaders in Soviet efforts to prescribe Cold War masculinity and embody military attributes missing in Soviet culture after the Second World War, with Tereshkova relegated to a supporting role. The creation of cosmonaut myths and the production of their post-flight images were not dictated by any single agency, nor did they preclude the cosmonauts' own involvement.[7] The process relied on a collaborative shaping of cultural understandings of manliness, building on the soldier archetype but also renewing that image for Cold War publicity at home and abroad.

A space suit on its own can render sex and gender invisible. Before the 1960s, both Soviet and Western science fiction featured robotic spacemen with neutral boxed heads and torsos. Advancing space technology that placed humans in the suits opened a path for revealing the contents of the space suit to the public on earth. As cultural critic Stefan Brandt has written of American space culture, "the body of the astronaut [was] increasingly used as a projection screen for anxieties concerning the stability of gender categories."[8] The narrative of Soviet masculinity projected onto Gagarin, the first man in the world to emerge from that suit, as well as those who came after him, reveals anxieties about the gendered cultural terrain of the Soviet Union after the Second World War, particularly regarding sex, family, authority, and service.

This chapter discusses the first group of cosmonauts, and Gagarin as their *de facto* leader, as part of a larger arc in postwar Soviet history that saw men like him – air force captains piloting space shuttles – reclaiming military masculinity in a salvo that echoed around the world. Historians of the space program have argued that Gagarin's launch and subsequent celebrity deliberately coincided with the new Communist

Party program that the Twenty-Second Congress adopted in 1961, which emphasized the crafting of a New Soviet Man, who would shepherd the country towards full communism by 1980. Gagarin represented that man, described in the following way: "the Soviet cosmonaut is not merely a victor of outer space, not merely a hero of science and technology, but first and foremost he is a real, living, flesh-and-blood new man, who demonstrates in action all the invaluable qualities of the Soviet character, which Lenin's Party has been cultivating for decades."[9] This chapter repositions Gagarin and his *shestiorka* cohort not only as inspiring a newfound drive to locate Soviet manhood in the communist future to come, but as the end result of a campaign that had begun in 1945 to rebuild military masculinity.

The cosmonauts of the early 1960s helped re-establish the martial credentials of Soviet masculinity after the disappointments of the ill-trained DOSAAF volunteers, defence instructors, and draft evaders. Gagarin's domestic and global image drew on understandings of masculinity that anchored Cold War ideology for both Soviet audiences and a variety of global publics. Those understandings included the security of the family, the primacy of military expertise, and the diplomatic acumen to peacefully navigate the new world order. That Gagarin was routinely portrayed as an expert in all these areas is not surprising. As literary critic Lev Danilkin has observed, Gagarin easily "embodied all conceivable manly virtues."[10] But, rather than the personal qualities of individuals, it is the categories themselves that were of primary importance. In attaching certain attributes to Gagarin and his male cohort and positioning them as hegemonic, authorities countered the increasing evidence of plurality in Soviet gender identities since the end of the war, especially for men of Gagarin's generation. At the same time, a major part of this story is how Tereshkova was denied access to military identity or credentials. Cosmonaut publicity campaigns attempted to elevate the masculinity of the serviceman again to premier status in Soviet culture by writing women out.

## Gendering *Sputnik*

Even before Gagarin's flight, public discourse about the machinery of space flight relied on particular formulations of masculinity. In October 1957, the Soviet Union became the first country to successfully launch a satellite, the now-famous *Sputnik*, into space. Links between technological innovation and the success of socialism in the Soviet Union predated the Cold War; the cultural significance of machinery to Soviet industry in the 1920s and 1930s paved the way for a similar emphasis on technology in Soviet culture in the 1950s and 1960s – this time with rocketry. Whereas in the 1920s and 1930s humans were encouraged to become more like machines, in the late 1950s space program representations suggested that machines were becoming more like humans.[11] Technology meant little without a human face. The anthropomorphism of satellites and rockets, moreover, depended on specific visions of masculinity and femininity.

Popular media covering *Sputnik* routinely downplayed the potential military impact of the launch by representing the satellite with imagery of an ambitious, enthusiastic, but otherwise harmless young boy. *Krokodil* consistently published such masculinized *Sputnik* imagery in the wake of the satellite's launch. In these cartoons, *Sputnik* either appeared as a young male figure itself, or in its absence, boys explained its significance to the bewildered women around them. One common female figure in *Sputnik* cartoons was Mother Earth, a proud if passive witness as "her" little boy, *Sputnik*, flew past.[12] In many other cartoons, elderly women failed to appreciate *Sputnik*'s achievement. One cartoon showed a young boy waiting for his grandmother to read him a bedtime story. "Grandmother," he told her, exasperated, "you're telling me stories about flying carpets, when a man-made satellite is already in flight!" The grandmother, who did not reply, wore a kerchief tied under her chin, the visual signal of a traditional peasant woman (Figure 5.1).[13]

A cartoon in the family journal *Sem'ia i shkola* (Family and School) depicted a young boy in a spacesuit, leaning out the window of a spacecraft. He reached out to a witch riding a broomstick as he passed her. "Come sit, Grandmother, and we'll give an old friend a lift," he said.[14] The demonized figure of the *babushka*, a traditional and sometimes sinister old woman, is well known in post-revolutionary Soviet culture, particularly in visual representations.[15] The marginalization of feminized elements – peasants, the elderly, and religion – drew on these traditional visual cues to cultivate meaning for the Cold War, but they also projected a new vision of boys as the future of Soviet technological innovation. Whereas depictions of the older, traditionally dressed peasant woman during the 1920s and early 1930s were more likely to contrast her with the young, modern Bolshevik woman, who wore work boots and coveralls and tied her kerchief behind her head rather than under her chin, *Sputnik*-era images featuring peasant women indicated that only their technologically minded grandsons could show them the right path.

Coding *Sputnik* in visual media as not only human but childlike and boyish accomplished two things in addition to marginalizing women

Figure 5.1 "Grandmother, you're telling me stories about flying carpets, when a man-made satellite is already in flight!"

*Krokodil*, 20 October 1957, 2.

from technology and space exploration. First, it downplayed the technology itself. Anthropomorphizing its image suggested to the viewer that the machine was not virile on its own and would not connect with the audiences to which it was being sold. We saw this tactic in chapter 4 with the domestication of the atom around the same time as *Sputnik*'s launch, with publicity campaigns about atoms for peace cloaking the military uses of atomic technology. Humanizing the satellite made its launch not only a victory for Soviet science and machinery but for Soviet citizens and workers as well. One image in *Krokodil*, for instance, portrayed *Sputnik* as one of several new satellites waiting to go into orbit. Neatly queued and wearing work clothing and caps, they compared notes about their assignments: one was heading to Mercury, another to Jupiter. Their tasks seemed to be open to ordinary (male) workers with the enthusiasm to take on a new task (Figure 5.2).[16] Second, casting *Sputnik* as a boy underlined not only masculinity but youth. As preliminary technology, an achievement in itself but also only a starting point, the satellite had room to mature as a scientific project that would pave the way for more sophisticated rocket technology, a theme expressed in the masculine imagery of a boy who would develop into an adult man.

Figure 5.2 *Krokodil*, 20 November 1957, 1.

## Even Martian Girls Want to Date Gagarin

Less than four years after the launch of *Sputnik*, the Soviet government announced its next technological feat: the successful launch, orbit, and landing of Yuri Gagarin's capsule.[17] In April 1961, he became the first person to successfully orbit the earth. Seated in the cramped capsule of *Vostok-1*, Gagarin was launched from a cosmodrome in Kazakhstan and executed one full orbit before landing again. At the time, the Americans were only weeks away from sending Alan Shepard into space. Astronaut John Glenn later put Gagarin's feat into perspective: "Not only had the Soviets put a man into space first, they had put him in orbit – something we didn't plan to do for several flights to come."[18] Soviet space program officials immediately faced a publicity problem: they wanted to publicize Gagarin's flight and celebrate it as an achievement for socialism, but virtually every aspect of the flight remained a closely guarded secret, from the number of potential cosmonauts training with Gagarin, to the type of craft he piloted, to the very location of the launch site. Asif Siddiqi has shown that this fundamental "rhetorical tension" in publicity plagued the cosmonauts' celebrity tours.[19] The only element of the USSR's achievement that could be publicly promoted, celebrated, and made visible was Gagarin himself – his attributes, personality, and physical body. As his generic flight suit peeled away and the man underneath embarked on a carefully plotted public victory lap, his image as a specific masculine icon came into sharper focus. As with previous Soviet celebrities such as the quota-exceeding coal miner Alexei Stakhanov or the group of pilots who mapped the Arctic in the 1930s, Gagarin's fame relied on his role as an exceptional individual within the collective, a model of a socialist man for the gaze of audiences at home and abroad.[20]

Unlike his predecessors, though, the labour of Gagarin's accomplishment was often downplayed in favour of his personal attributes and, as such, the trajectory of Gagarin's fame differed from earlier worker-celebrities in this postwar country still looking to recharge its notions of masculine heroism. Most notably, the cosmonauts neither needed nor were permitted to touch the controls of the spaceship.[21] Their celebrity was not based on exceptional skill. Indeed, when space program engineers and scientists gathered in 1959 to debate the professional qualifications they should seek in cosmonaut trainees, "fighter pilot" was not a first or obvious choice, and participants in the meetings arrived at it only after much debate. Even then, Soviet cosmonauts of the *shestiorka* cohort had far less experience in the air than their American counterparts, with Gagarin logging about 230 hours before his flight in contrast to the 1,500 hours required of the Mercury astronauts.[22] Before Gagarin's flight, Soviet notions of celebrity had relied on labour achievements or war honours; the cosmonauts represented the first Soviet brotherhood dispatched as celebrities based only on the illusion of both those traits, but without substance. The concomitant tension between ideas of "manned" and "unmanned" space flight[23] permeated discourse about the space program and privileged gendered notions of rationality, able-bodiedness, and control. Both because of space program secrecy and because of the lack of technological skill expected of Gagarin during the flight, his celebrity image in the aftermath emphasized his persona as a new masculine icon. According to cosmonaut Gherman Titov, who trained with Gagarin and was also considered for the position of first man in space before fronting the second flight instead, officials wanted the first cosmonaut to be a man "whose will and energy, industriousness and sincere generosity, self-discipline and high feeling of duty were the best example for those who dreamed selflessly to serve the homeland, science, and the people."[24] In practice, these generic attributes translated for Gagarin in his roles as a husband and father, an air force captain, and a savvy diplomat.

Gagarin's role as a family man was crucial to his celebrity. It not only helped establish space travel as a masculine pursuit but also lent a well-known public face to the government's postwar project of shoring up the war-ravaged Soviet family. While the period of Stalin's rule from the late 1920s to his death in 1953 is generally seen as much more socially conservative than the eras before and after it, family law overall after the Second World War encouraged monogamous marriage and parenthood. (An important exception to the reinforcement of conservative family law after the war, however, was the decriminalization of abortion in 1955, which Stalin had outlawed in 1936.)[25] In part, Gagarin's family-oriented persona drew on the 1944 family law decree: as an incentive to marry and have children, the decree expanded a 1941 "bachelor tax." Men between the ages of 20 and 50, and women between the ages of 20 and 45, were subject to the tax if they had fewer than three children. At the birth of a third child the tax was no longer levied, and the state began paying mothers a child allowance, which began at 300 rubles at the birth of the third child and extended to 5,000 rubles at the birth of any child after the tenth.[26] Postwar family law – which provided state and social support for the large number of unmarried mothers in Soviet society after the war – had a significant effect on men's legal responsibilities and behaviour. While the state took up the role of provider to mothers, the abolition of paternity laws meant that all unmarried men were officially childless.[27] In order to escape the bachelor tax, a man had to marry and father at least three children with the same woman, his wife. The law therefore steered men towards monogamous marriage and fatherhood, despite the fact that they were no longer responsible for paternity payments outside of marriage. Helene Carlbäck has pointed out that the 1944 law made "fertile men" a category of interest and intervention for the government, which sought to replenish the dwindling birth rate as the war came to an end.[28] Particularly at risk, authorities feared, were young men in their late teens and twenties who were susceptible to bachelorhood, aimlessness, and – most worrisome, as previous chapters have shown – evasion of military service.[29] Gagarin's role as a stable family patriarch, the country's most famous devoted husband and father, helped cement the value of those roles in Soviet culture and popular discourse.

But Gagarin's family man image also drew on more recent post-Stalin conversations in government and society about private life and proper behaviour for communist citizens. Taking shape over the latter half of 1961, this particular narrative about Gagarin reinforced the Communist Party's long discussed but newly formalized edict on communist morality that would be announced at the Twenty-Second Party Congress in October. The country's most famous man had to exemplify the new "moral code" intended to pave the way to the communist future. The code's twelve tenets included "moral purity, simplicity, and modesty in social and personal life; mutual respect in the family; [and] concern for the upbringing of children."[30] As Deborah Field has written, "Communist morality imposed both public and private obligations, demanding orderly personal conduct in addition to patriotism, diligence, and activism."[31] Gagarin and his cosmonaut cohort played an important role as models of the party's new program, especially in regard to men. Through the publicity afforded to the cosmonauts, and by extension their private selves, they signalled certain codes of behaviour to be followed by the communist man.

At the same time, however, and within certain limits, Gagarin was also represented as a desirable (hetero)sexual commodity. Playing on his good looks as well as delivering the coded message that operating a spaceship must be a particularly manly endeavour, space program authorities fashioned Gagarin as a man whom women should desire. In a series of public incidents, Gagarin played right into those expectations, announcing at a Swedish press conference in which he had been asked about his wife's choice of dresses that "I prefer her without clothing."[32] As Andrew Jenks has chronicled, even local hosts on the cosmonauts' post-flight tours participated in fostering a sexualized image, with one Komsomol leader coyly telling a group of women meeting Gagarin and Titov, "You see what kind of boys" they are.[33] Gagarin's appeal was apparently not confined to earth girls, either: a month after his flight, *Krokodil* featured a cartoon of a Martian suitor sneaking up behind his date, causing her to blush as he placed his hands over her eyes. "Gagarin?" she asked hopefully (Figure 5.3).[34] Despite the trail of female desire that was meant to follow him, however, the codes of communist morality held; it was clear in the press that Gagarin was not available. Married since 1957 to Valentina Ivanovna Goriacheva (now Gagarina), a nursing student, Gagarin did not need to undergo a public transformation by marriage, as we will see was the case with cosmonaut Valentina Tereshkova. Gagarin's wife was always portrayed as fully supportive, accompanying him on tours and appearing by his side at public events.

Gagarin's safely flirtatious but ultimately conservative image was mirrored by the first American astronauts. Although some later earned a reputation as hard-partying tough guys, owing mostly to their portrayal in Tom Wolfe's 1979 book, *The Right Stuff*, astronauts such as John Glenn played important public roles in the early 1960s as family-oriented, well-behaved men, humbled in the service of God and country. (Religion would provide the major point of difference between the astronauts and Gagarin's cosmonaut cohort, who used their experiences in space to declare the universe to be man's domain, not God's, and to advance the official atheism of Soviet ideology.)[35] As with the cosmonauts, though, the astronauts' pristine images often masked men who "drove too fast, drank too much, and left their pants in unexpected places."[36] Glenn famously took it upon himself to police the behaviour of his colleagues, particularly with alcohol and extramarital relationships, and he participated in at least one major cover-up of an astronaut whom a reporter and photographer had found in a "compromising" situation while the group was staying at a luxury hotel in San Diego during meetings with engineers in 1960. Glenn argued that maintaining the astronauts' public images as respectable and honourable role models was crucial to the continuation of manned space flights, at a time when many at NASA still argued that unmanned flights were preferable.[37] It is not a coincidence that we saw a similar presentation of

ГДЕ-ТО НА МАРСЕ
— Гагарин!

Figure 5.3 *Somewhere on Mars*
"Gagarin?"

*Krokodil*, 20 May 1961, 12.

the self in Andrei Sakharov's memoirs in chapter 4, as he confided with disapproval to his readers that some of his colleagues at Arzamas-16 had engaged in extramarital affairs. For these famous men of the Cold War writing about their experiences (in part to control their legacies), honour and fidelity ranked high.

Soviet space program officials, led by the *shestiorka*'s primary chaperone, General Nikolai Kamanin, went to great lengths to cover up what they saw as dishonourable and immoral activities among the cosmonauts. The most famous incident was not widely known at the time and was revealed only with the publication of Kamanin's diaries in the 1990s. Vacationing in Crimea in October 1961 with his wife, nanny, and small daughters, along with several other cosmonauts and officials, Gagarin was found outside the hotel, unconscious and bleeding from the head in the middle of the night. Emergency surgery saved his life, but he suffered a severe head injury and required three weeks in hospital, which proved difficult to explain to the press. Piecing the story together later, Kamanin concluded that after confirming that his wife was playing cards with others on the trip, an intoxicated Gagarin went upstairs to the room of a 27-year-old nurse and propositioned her. When his wife knocked on the door looking for him, the nurse later said, he jumped off the balcony to escape, plunging to the courtyard below.[38] Although kept from the public, the story circulated quickly among Soviet journalists travelling with the cosmonauts. Iaroslav Golovanov, who covered the space program for *Komsomol'skaia pravda*, heard the story secondhand and changed the profession of the woman Gagarin sought out from nurse to waitress in the retelling. "When Kamanin told me about it later," wrote Golovanov, "he said that the sight of Yura [Gagarin] was terrible: his whole face was covered with dirt and blood. Nikolai Petrovich [Kamanin] admitted that he wanted to shoot himself" for letting this happen, quite literally, to the face of Soviet space travel.[39]

When Gagarin continued his tour in India six weeks later, journalists asked him about the scar over his left eyebrow. The question gave Gagarin pause, Kamanin recounted, before his trademark smile returned. On vacation in Crimea in October, he began, he injured himself playing with his younger daughter, Galka. The explanation was rich with descriptions of his wife and daughters, reminding the journalists that Galka was already seven months old and that his children were the light of his life.[40] He also told Pavel Barashev, a journalist who then printed the explanation in the magazine *Trud*, that he had stumbled while carrying the baby on his shoulders. "Saving my daughter, I raised her high and hit my face against the stone. It will heal before Galka's wedding," he joked, "or even earlier – before the next space flight."[41] The journalist Golovanov noted that in the press corps, at least, the story was obviously a cover-up, and "nobody believed Pashka [Barashev]."[42] Gagarin's sexuality might have been safely advertised to sell him as a man that other men should want to emulate and women should want to marry, but any tales of drunkenness, recklessness, or infidelity were kept carefully from the public.

This anecdote is meaningful beyond its surface appearance as merely a tantalizing bit of celebrity gossip. It implies that a damaged cosmonaut body could not be presented to the public. We have already seen that showing the human face of space travel was crucial to Soviet aims, not only to soften, for public consumption, its military implications, but to use its successes to highlight key social and cultural values for Soviet citizens on earth. *Sputnik* meant nothing as a bit of metal, but everything as the embodiment of an adventurous, future-thinking boy who might deliver the entire Soviet Union its Cold War victory. The androgynous space suit purported to mask not only gender identities but physical imperfections as well. But as soon as the suit was stripped off, the body underneath needed to be unblemished, cleanly showcasing correct masculine features. In confirming the persistent gossip about Gagarin's injury – as well as its cause and cover-up – Kamanin also confirmed that fatherhood was a category that he and other space program authorities had privileged in representing Gagarin's masculinity. The war had already created a space in visual and popular culture for men's private lives and especially for positive depictions of men as fathers.[43] After all, other potential stories to explain the scarring on Gagarin's forehead could have served a narrative purpose in line with Soviet social didacticism: toughness and resilience after a training accident, or honour and heroism in defending his wife from an attack by "hooligans."[44] Instead, the explanation focused on notions of his private-sphere morality and featured Gagarin as a husband and father, making himself available as a role model and caregiver to his daughters and deeply concerned with carrying out his primary goal as a father: to give Galka away at her wedding. (Tragically, he would die before she was eight years old.)

Gagarin was not the only cosmonaut to transgress authorities' behavioural expectations, at least in private. Gherman Titov's drinking led to several interventions from Kamanin; he crashed his car three times in six months, likely from driving while intoxicated.[45] At Kamanin's recommendation, the space program leadership also expelled cosmonaut trainee Mars Rafikov in March 1962 for infidelity and domestic abuse.[46] Three other trainees were dismissed in 1963 after drinking and instigating a fight with a serviceman on patrol.[47] Despite the men's personas as dedicated husbands, the marriages of Gagarin and Titov likely suffered more stress than was apparent to the public view. Kamanin reports episodes of marital discord and disrespectful language that Gagarin and Titov directed at their wives, Valentina and Tamara, who often travelled with the group.[48] Gagarin's family life was burdened by fame by late 1961, according to Kamanin, who lamented in his diary that Gagarin "does not respect his wife, sometimes humiliates her, and she does not have enough tact, education, and other virtues to influence him."[49] Kamanin dismissed Titov's bodyguard in late 1961 for procuring prostitutes (*svodnichestvo*), although his diaries do not dwell on that issue.[50]

In retelling such salacious anecdotes, Kamanin's diaries reveal a preoccupation with delineating acceptable behavioural boundaries for the cosmonaut brotherhood. Moreover, they suggest a link between Kamanin's self-presentation and generational anxieties about military masculinity. He uses examples of the cosmonauts' bad behaviour to establish the generational chasm between himself, a decorated general, and this young cohort of relatively inexperienced pilots who had missed the war. As we saw in chapters 1 and 2, and with Andrei Sakharov's anecdote about being shamed by Marshal Nedelin discussed in chapter 4, this particular generational divide permeated military discourse after the Second World War. According to the journalist Golovanov, "Kamanin kept a tight rein on [the cosmonauts], demanding utter discipline and unquestioning obedience ... To Kamanin it was flattering that these world famous people had to obey him, just like new recruits obey their corporal."[51] The first five cosmonauts (before Tereshkova) were the most famous military officers in the country in the early 1960s, and their success and fame placed military masculinity back in the spotlight after the practical challenges and loss of public prestige that plagued the military in late 1940s and 1950s. Concerns about their misbehaviour, however, show continuity from the late 1940s, when Suvorov cadets, DOSAAF instructors, and draft dodgers also became the focus of an older generation tasked with shaping supposedly wayward young men into proper military actors.

Regardless of any private troubles in their marriage, Gagarin's wife, Valentina, featured prominently in press coverage and buoyed his family-oriented persona. Public discourse about Valentina Gagarina also helped cement space travel as a masculine endeavour that women could not fully understand or access. After Gagarin's flight, for instance, Soviet leader Nikita Khrushchev acknowledged that neither Gagarin nor other space program officials were permitted to tell Valentina Gagarina the details of the flight, and she did not learn about it until shortly before his departure – owing, she later said, to her advanced pregnancy and the fear of upsetting her.[52] Khrushchev praised her "courage" and "great soul" in supporting her husband unconditionally, despite not knowing the details of his work.[53] In her public role as the cosmonaut's wife, Valentina Gagarina implicitly validated women's domesticity as well as their unsuitability for space flight. "Congratulations to Yuri Alekseevich [Gagarin]'s wife, mother, and sister," one reader wrote to the women's journal *Rabotnitsa*. "I wish all mothers could experience such great happiness and live through their own Yuri." Another letter writer thanked Valentina Gagarina, "who was so courageous to see her husband off on this distant path."[54] Other cosmonaut wives were not as supportive, a transgression for which they were publicly judged. Titov, the second man in space, told Khrushchev in a widely reported congratulatory phone call after his flight that his wife, Tamara, had not been pleased to learn of his selection for the flight. "How did your wife feel about [it]?" Khrushchev nudged. "She did not quite approve," Titov admitted, implying that after being told her response was unacceptable for a cosmonaut's wife, "then, she did [approve]."[55]

Documentary films about the Gagarin family were also an important conduit for the domestic cosiness that had become a key feature of Gagarin's public masculinity. In one film, whose apparent purpose was only to chronicle the hero's leisure time, a shirtless Gagarin sunbathed, threw stones into the surf, swam, and went rowing, while Valentina sat on the beach, happily watching him and rocking a baby carriage.[56] By including Gagarin's wife in public discourse about him, authorities cemented Gagarin's image as a family man. Such images also contributed to coding space flight and cosmonaut identity as masculine and normalizing Cold War Soviet masculinity within the family. A profile of Gagarin in the newspaper *Komsomol'skaia pravda* summed up the main categories on which his masculinity was adjudicated:

> He is 27 years old. He lives among us. He sits beside us at films, on Sundays pushing a pram in the park (his family appears to have one more "passenger.") He visits friends, plays basketball and billiards … and now he travels to space. Gagarin … how many times now has that simple Russian name been said around the world? And for [Valentina] he is simply Yura. And to Lenochka he is simply papa. And to the world he is a son that we can be eternally proud of.[57]

## The Cosmonaut's Wife

Valentina Gagarina's role as a cosmonaut's wife – as a civilian woman in a dress and pushing a baby carriage – shored up her husband's masculine image by bearing witness to his accomplishment. She would not be the only Valentina, or the only cosmonaut's wife, to play that role. The other was Valentina Tereshkova, who piloted the sixth shuttle of the *shestiorka* in June 1963 to become the first woman to travel to space. Kamanin's diaries tell a revealing story about how he, and presumably other men in the program, viewed "the two Valyas": Over a weekend in April 1964, a group of 20 Soviet cosmonauts, trainees, and their spouses headed into the countryside near Yaroslavl', 250 kilometres northeast of Moscow, for a hunting trip. Yuri Gagarin and fellow cosmonaut Andriian Nikolaev (who had piloted the third flight of the *shestiorka*, in August 1962) led the way, along with their wives, both named Valya, and several other pilots and military officials in the cosmonaut training program. The hunt was a great success, and members of the group bagged several grouse, hares, and even an elk. Kamanin wrote that the two wives cooked the wild game into a delicious meal for the group.[58] He elided the fact that although both were cosmonauts' wives, one was also a cosmonaut herself. Tereshkova, in fact, had married Nikolaev six months earlier, not long after her flight.

The details of Tereshkova's flight, and the internal debates about sending a woman into space at all, have been well documented by historians of the Soviet space program.[59] Kamanin was a leading advocate, but more so because of Tereshkova's potential propaganda value than any deep-set belief in women's equality. "In my opinion, it is essential to prepare women for space flights," he wrote, mainly because he was certain that women's space travel would happen one day anyway, and "one should not allow an American woman to become the first woman in space."[60] On 16 June 1963, Tereshkova took off in the spacecraft *Vostok-6*, orbited the earth three times, and successfully landed on target in the Kazakh desert. She was, on the surface, the perfect propaganda vessel for the Communist Party's proud slogan of "emancipation" for Soviet women: she had a worker's background, was a member of the Komsomol, had participated in DOSAAF's civilian defence training as a parachutist, and, perhaps most important, her father had fought and died in the Second World War. She was the "textbook all-round Soviet woman."[61] She was also 26 years old, unmarried, a civilian, and ethnically Russian, all factors that combined to underline the cultural categories that the party found at once reassuring (her youth and ethnicity), and open to public correction (her marital status).

Tereshkova's success as a cosmonaut owed a debt to the rich history of women's aviation in the Soviet Union before and during the war.[62] A group of accomplished women pilots, led by Marina Raskova, became national celebrities in the 1930s for their flying feats. Despite their achievements, the leader of the Komsomol in the late 1930s declared that training female parachutists was a waste of time.[63] Support for women's aviation might have collapsed but for the exceptional service of women pilots during the war. It also had the effect of elevating women's military service overall in the national imagination. Tereshkova's ability to train in parachuting through DOSAAF, and her initial selection for the cosmonaut corps, reflected the dawning of a more progressive era than the one that had limited women's aviation opportunities in the 1930s. At the same time, one should not overstate the influence of the war on generating uniformly positive notions of women's air service. Representations of Tereshkova in the Soviet and foreign media, as well as opinions of her expressed by her cosmonaut colleagues and space program authorities such as Kamanin, were gendered to privilege a cult of masculinity that not only drove the cosmonaut program but contributed to the overall marginalization of women in postwar military activity.

This portrayal was in flux throughout the 1960s and beyond, however. As with any treatment of women in the Soviet Union, discriminatory actions and assumptions tangled with the socialist ideology that promised women's equality. Roshanna Sylvester has highlighted this complexity for Tereshkova by arguing that despite treatment and representations of her that were clearly sexist, her celebrated achievement as a woman cosmonaut inspired girls in the Soviet Union to pursue studies in science and technology.[64] This enthusiasm of individual girls and young women was not witnessed in state-sponsored imagery. Rather than using Tereshkova's image to chart a path forward into the age of technology for women, authorities instead reproduced prewar patterns that limited the aspirational opportunities for women. Karen Petrone has demonstrated that women pilots of the 1930s, feted along with their male counterparts for their achievements in exploration and navigation, were limited by a strictly gendered landscape that defined for them what could constitute "heroism." The gender order Petrone found for prewar women pilots was echoed in Tereskhova's time, almost as if the war had never happened. Images of women pilots in the 1930s, Petrone argues, were "part of a gender system that professed equality and valorized some women's deeds but gave priority to heroic masculinity."[65] As we have seen throughout this book, re-establishing that prewar gender system mattered to policymakers uneasy with both women's service during the war and men's perceived aversion to service afterwards.

Despite the feminist achievement of Tereshkova's flight, she was more useful to authorities not as a woman cosmonaut, but as the most famous wife and mother in the country. This more limited identity echoed the permissible path to celebrity for early women aviators like Raskova.[66] It also contrasted with the masculine embodiments of military might, science, technological progress, and diplomatic skill ascribed to Tereshkova's male colleagues. It cemented her exclusion from military identity and participation in the air force brotherhood openly performed by the five men who had flown before her. Despite conducting her work at the same level as her male colleagues in piloting an orbital space flight, Tereshkova's relegation to the role of civilian furthered the postwar project of writing women out of military institutions after the Second World War.

Tereshkova's flight brought gender anxieties into relief on both sides of the Cold War. Feminist activists in the United States heralded her while also bemoaning her flight as evidence that the Soviet Union was years ahead of the United States on equal rights for women.[67] Historian Margaret Weitekamp has shown how the American space program was built on an ideal of rugged, frontier masculinity that had no room, and indeed no vocabulary, for the concept of women astronauts – a group labelled in English as "astronautrixes" and routinely dismissed.[68] In the Soviet Union, pronouncements of official equality for women, while leading to important gains for women particularly in legal terms and in labour, also masked the continued systemic sexism in Soviet society and institutions. Kamanin and others did manage to overcome opposition within the government and military in order to successfully train and send a woman into space long before the United States had even given the matter serious consideration, but the women were never fully welcomed and in fact faced continued hostility from male cosmonauts and engineers.

At first, Tereshkova was portrayed as more than capable of space flight and the required training. In a short film made soon after her flight to chronicle the use of television cameras in documenting cosmonaut training, Tereshkova was shown in a quickly spinning training capsule. The footage seemed designed to prove her physical resilience. "How does she feel afterward?" the narrator asked as the viewer watched her climb, calm and smiling, from the capsule. "Excellent!" After being ushered out by several men in white coats who took various measurements of her, Tereshkova was replaced in the spinning capsule by a male colleague. "He's a professional cosmonaut," the narrator assured viewers, "so this is not difficult." Besides the physical training, the film demonstrated, Tereshkova needed to undergo intellectual and cultural training as well – not only in leisure pursuits she previously enjoyed, but in new activities expected of a cosmonaut and a Soviet public figure. To that end, she was filmed walking alone in the woods, riding a bicycle along the seashore, and reading or studying. One must be intelligent in order to become a cosmonaut, the narrator explained, excelling in physics, biology, astronomy, chemistry, electronics, aerodynamics: in short, "modern science." She was even shown deliberating over math problems.[69] Prior to and immediately following her flight, the conditions of Tereshkova's celebrity included physical fitness and scientific expertise, categories that were not discernibly different from those expected of her male colleagues.

At the same time, Tereshkova's place in the masculinized culture of space travel and exploration remained precarious and subject to remoulding. Questions about her fitness and physical difficulties during the flight began to surface in the press and among her colleagues, fuelling rumours that she had experienced a great deal of trouble with anxiety and exhaustion during the flight.[70] This narrative ignored the fact that it was Titov who had suffered severe nausea during his flight nearly two years earlier, an issue that had led not to his public shaming but to further research by scientists behind the scenes into the causes of his illness and ways to prevent it on future flights.[71] The press also insinuated that Tereshkova's achievement mattered only to women but would remain insignificant to men. In a cartoon in the general interest journal *Ogonek* just after her flight, a boy and girl sat at a desk while *Vostok-5*, Bykovskii's craft, and *Vostok-6*, carrying Tereshkova, sailed by outside the window. Titled, "During exams," the cartoon showed the boy making a play on words regarding the number five, which was both the highest grade possible in Soviet schools, and a reference to the "Group of Five" to which Bykovskii belonged as the fifth cosmonaut. "Ah, it will be a 'five' [*piatiorka*] for me!" he exclaimed of both his exam and the spacecraft, while the girl, watching Tereshkova's craft, added, "and it will be a 'six' [*shestiorka*] for me."[72]

Space program leaders seemed uncertain of just what form Tereshkova's public persona should take, an inconsistency that could be traced back to the internal quarrels within the program over whether or not it was necessary or advisable to send a woman into space at all.[73] At the time of her flight, for instance, Tereshkova was characterized as a sibling within the cosmonaut family. "[Joining] the glorious family of Soviet celestial brothers," General Kamanin wrote, "is their sister of the stars!"[74] She initially joined the *shestiorka* as just another member of the team. Khrushchev's congratulatory phone calls to her and Bykovskii, who had piloted his own vessel at the same time as her flight, were remarkably similar.[75] *Krokodil* had a field day with the theme of women's "emancipation" immediately following Tereshkova's flight, happily poking fun not at the lack of an American timetable for women astronauts but rather domestically, at Soviet men and boys. On the cover of the first issue following the flight, *Krokodil* ran a cartoon showing a girl thumbing her nose at her two playmates, both boys. She asked them, "Now where is your advantage in outer space?" (Figure 5.4)[76] Another showed a woman reading newspaper reports about Tereshkova while her apron-clad husband approached with a vacuum cleaner in one hand and a cooking pot in the other. "I went to the shop, prepared lunch, and washed the floor." Referring to International Women's Day, widely celebrated in the USSR, he added, "Enough, Natasha – today is not the eighth of March!" (Figure 5.5)[77]

At the same time that *Krokodil* celebrated Tereshkova's achievement for Soviet women, the journal underlined her public status as an available, single woman as well as a symbol of emancipation. Another cartoon featured an image of Bykovskii chivalrously offering Tereshkova a bouquet of stars as he flew by her in *Vostok-5* (Figure 5.6).[78] On the same page, two cherubs watched God, who was dressed in a checked suit, preening himself in front of a mirror. "What is the old man dressing up for?" one asked, to which the other replied, "The lady of the cosmos!" (Figure 5.7)[79] This cartoon also mocked the American astronauts' often-repeated claim that space flight brought one closer to God.

In her path to celebrity, Tereshkova traced a delicate line in achieving the proper degree of femininity, one which did not make her appear either overly available to the male gaze, or too masculine. In France in the summer of 1963, a Soviet journalist accompanying her reported that "Valya"[80] was a hit with the media and the crowds, having "overshadowed all the beauties of Paris." She was such a popular starlet that "now nobody even remembers Brigitte Bardot." If Bardot had been there, the journalist continued, reporters would have asked her, "Brigitte, what

Figure 5.4 "Now where is your advantage in outer space?"
*Krokodil*, 30 June 1963, 1.

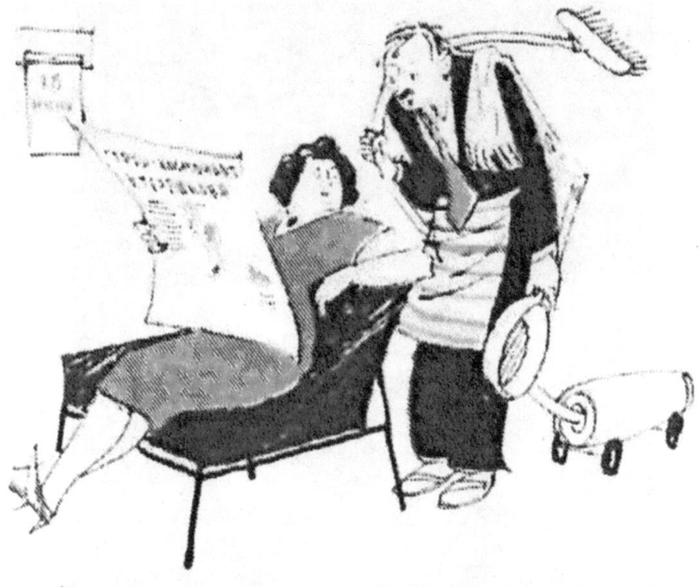

— В магазин сходил, обед приготовил, пол вымыл, хватит, Наташа,— сегодня ведь не 8-е марта!

Figure 5.5 "I went to the shop, prepared lunch, and washed the floor. Enough, Natasha – today is not the eighth of March!"

*Krokodil*, 30 June 1963, 3.

do you think about Valentina Tereshkova's flight?"[81] Brigitte Bardot was not the right sort of image the Soviet government wanted to portray with Tereshkova, however. While "femininity" (*zhenstvennost'*) remained important to Soviet authorities, her image could not betray any "scandal, obscenity, or sexiness."[82] Soviet women like her were supposed to be working towards socialism; they were not single girls travelling the world in the style of buxom starlets pursuing the attention of male capitalists.

To patrol this line in femininity, the men of the cosmonaut program became particularly concerned with women trainees' clothing. Tereshkova was publicly called "Gagarin in a skirt," for instance, a phrase that managed to concede that her successful flight rivalled Gagarin's while

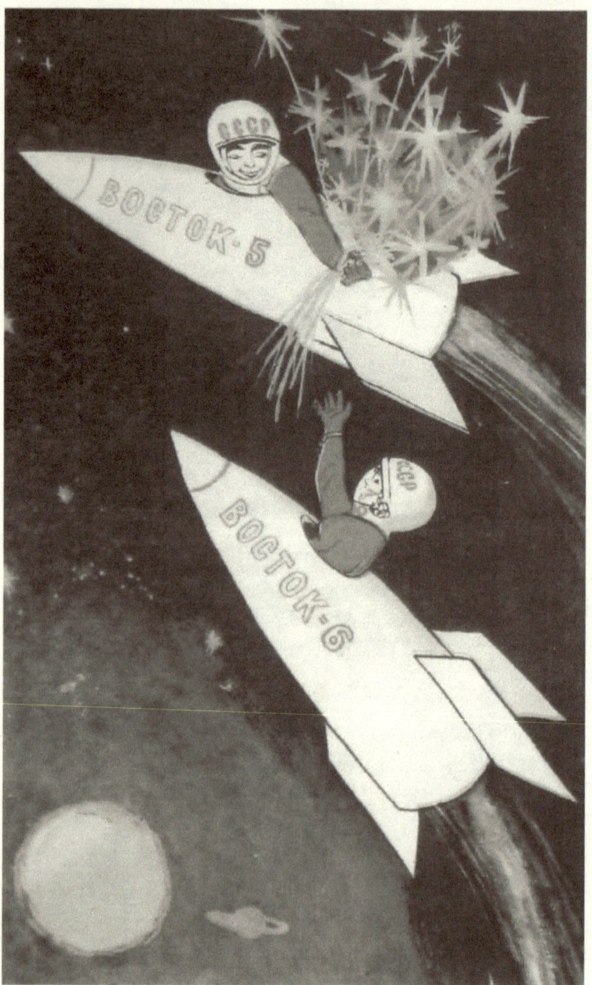


Figure 5.6 *Krokodil*, 30 June 1963, 2.

also denigrating her and positioning woman cosmonauts, through their clothing, as unable to access the military structures of the air force and space flight.[83] The skirt also proved a key symbol for Gagarin himself. Training together at Star City, Gagarin refused to allow Tereshkova and her cohort to wear military uniforms as he and the men did,[84] but he also found their gender-neutral training clothes inappropriate, even away from public view. Valentina Ponomareva, who trained as

— Что это старик прифрантился?
— Тетя в космосе!

Figure 5.7 "What is the old man dressing up for?"
"The lady of the cosmos!"

*Krokodil*, 30 June 1963, 2.

a cosmonaut alongside the *shestiorka* but never flew to space, recalled Gagarin's annoyance that the women trainees walked around in tracksuits during training. "Girls, why do you all go around without dresses on?" he asked. "We did usually go around 'without dresses on,'" Ponomareva wrote in her memoirs, because the standard issue tracksuits were comfortable and convenient, even if their blue and white stripes kept them from being fashionable. "We tried to go to the cafeteria in our tracksuits, but Gagarin ordered this to stop. The guys always came in their military uniforms, even if, like us, they were coming from training. And we had to walk to the cafeteria in dresses."[85] Gagarin also made a point of looking in on the women, not out of romantic interest but because, according to Ponomareva, "I think he felt sorry for us … [He thought] we didn't have the slightest idea about military discipline … or how to prepare for the flight."[86] Kamanin generally defended the women cosmonaut trainees, but even he was prone to commenting on their physical appearance. He assigned himself the occasional role of policing women's physiques, telling one trainee that she was eating "a lot of cakes and chocolate" for a cosmonaut.[87] Women cosmonauts' femininity was surveilled to ensure neither too much nor too little would be put on display, another part of the continued marginalization of women in militarized institutions.

Tereshkova's femininity was ultimately contained when her handlers assigned her a new role as wife and mother. (It is not clear who made this decision or when, although Kamanin surely played a part.) The issue of her unmarried status became subject to official correction soon after her flight, when her public persona shifted to focus on her family roles. To be 26 years old and never married was conspicuous in Soviet society, especially in such a public figure as Tereshkova.[88] Not only that, but it would not do to focus on her success in science and technology as a barrier to her desirability as a wife. Ponomareva cites a poem that a classmate at the training school wrote for her as typical of male views:

> She is a pilot, a parachutist,
> a gymnast and, apparently, a weightlifter.
> But less likely than all of that
> is that she would be suitable as a married woman.[89]

Tereshkova could not be permitted the fate of becoming the world's most famous spinster, devoted to science or her physical training but shunning men. Within six months of her flight, when no relationship between them had been apparent before, Tereshkova married fellow cosmonaut Andriian Nikolaev, who himself was part of the *shestiorka*. The wedding was a public spectacle, with Khrushchev taking the place of the bride's father, who had died heroically in the Second World War. Breaking with Kamanin's earlier motif of celestial brothers and a star sister, Tereshkova was transformed from the younger sister of the group to a wife and, soon after, a mother. Doing so not only safely harnessed her sexuality within the respectable confines of marriage, but it finalized the auxiliary status of her celebrity. As Kamanin's story about the Yaroslavl' hunting party reveals, she was repositioned not as a cosmonaut, but as a cosmonaut's wife. She even took on a hyphenated surname, Valentina Nikolaeva-Tereshkova, so as not to erase the public recognition of her name but to underline her now-married status.[90] She gave birth the following summer, completing the shift in her public role from the celebration of extraordinary feats in space to the celebration of ordinary, expected duties as wife and mother.

The tale of domesticity woven around Tereshkova was complicated by the simultaneously complementary and competing narrative composed for her husband, Nikolaev. Two factors coalesced in his public persona, defining his celebrity and expanding the cosmonauts' martial brotherhood. The first factor was the errant masculinity coded into his bachelor status and male friendships. The only unmarried one of the first five men who had flown before Tereshkova, Nikolaev's marital status was open to public correction just as Tereshkova's had been. Another of the original five, cosmonaut Pavel Popovich, characterized Nikolaev's longstanding friendship with Valerii Bykovskii as central to the cosmonauts' training group prior to Tereshkova's arrival. Popovich called them an "inseparable pair." The two of them had pledged to fly together on their missions before officials stepped in to propose Tereshkova as Bykovskii's flight partner. Titov cited the time he spent with Nikolaev, the bachelor of the group, as part of his wife's objections to his flying.[91] The second factor that defined Nikolaev's fame was his Chuvash nationality, which reversed standard scripts of tradition and modernity by framing "backward" issues such as village life, religion, and non-Russian nationality as masculine rather than feminine. After his engagement to Tereshkova, Nikolaev and his Siberian origins were framed in a traditional narrative that clashed with the emphasis on science and modernity among the cosmonauts. After having several quarrels over her married name, Tereshkova and Nikolaev, at Kamanin's encouragement, eventually agreed that she would keep her name. "But the night before the wedding," Kamanin wrote in his journal, "Nikolaev, under the influence of his relatives, guests from Chuvashia, insisted that Valya use two surnames."[92] Through Nikolaev's public conversion from bachelor to husband (and father), his masculinity shifted to align with Gagarin's, as a modern military man suitably desirable to women but whose virility was safely contained within marriage.

As Tereshkova's individual achievement in space was downplayed in favour of her gendered personal narrative, authorities also continued to emphasize her civilian status in contrast to the military credentials of her male colleagues. Whereas the *shestiorka* men were air force officers with piloting experience, Tereshkova had been plucked from the ranks of the parachuting club at her local DOSAAF group. She was eventually given the rank of junior lieutenant, indicating that officials noticed the gap in military credentials between her and the male cosmonauts. Even so, after he took power in 1964, Leonid Brezhnev refused to allow her to appear in public in a military uniform.[93] She wore simple dresses in group photographs, whereas the men always appeared in uniform. Her tours did not include stops at foreign military bases, the way the men's itineraries did. Denying Tereshkova legitimacy as a military figure – or, conversely, not recruiting the first woman cosmonaut from the ranks of women veterans of the air force from the war – reaffirmed the military as a masculinized space. At the same time, Tereshkova's civilian status softened her achievement and the rocket technology that had enabled it. For global audiences, the Soviet Union portrayed itself as advanced enough in gender relations to allow a woman to fly in space, underscoring the possibilities available to women under socialism, but as Tereshkova's public persona evolved, the government was also careful not to give the impression that its cutting-edge rocket technology was in the hands of women.

In the year after her flight, the image of her face surrounded by a space helmet was replaced with increasingly gendered portrayals of women and space that downplayed any equality she may initially have been allowed with her male colleagues. Soon after her wedding in November 1963, for instance, *Sem'ia i shkola* offered advice to readers on how to prepare children's costumes for the upcoming New Year's holiday, including instructions for dressing young boys as cosmonauts and girls as "star fairies" (Figure 5.8).[94] A month later, *Krokodil* seemed to note the irony of such imagery even while contributing to it. Announcing the new costume for Snegurochka, the fairy tale Russian snow maiden, for the winter of 1963, a cartoon showed her as a young woman in a chic, knee-length skirt covered in stars, wearing cowboy boots and carrying a handbag in the shape of a rocket. On her head sat an open-visor version of a space helmet, but her perfect hair and make-up were still intact under it. She strolled down a runway while admirers looked on. Snegurochka's stereotypically feminine outfit was able to overcome the inherent androgyny of the spacesuit and remind viewers that while a woman might have been able to travel to space, she was a woman first and a cosmonaut second (Figure 5.9).[95]

The Soviet government claimed credit for Tereshkova's achievement as the first woman in space, capitalizing on that publicity for both domestic audiences, shown an accomplished working wife and mother, and international audiences, shown socialist feminism at work. But the conditions of her celebrity had limits. Tereshkova was one of the first individual female celebrities the Soviet Union had decided to showcase, at least since the war, and her cultural purchase extended not only through her own country but globally as well, to an outside

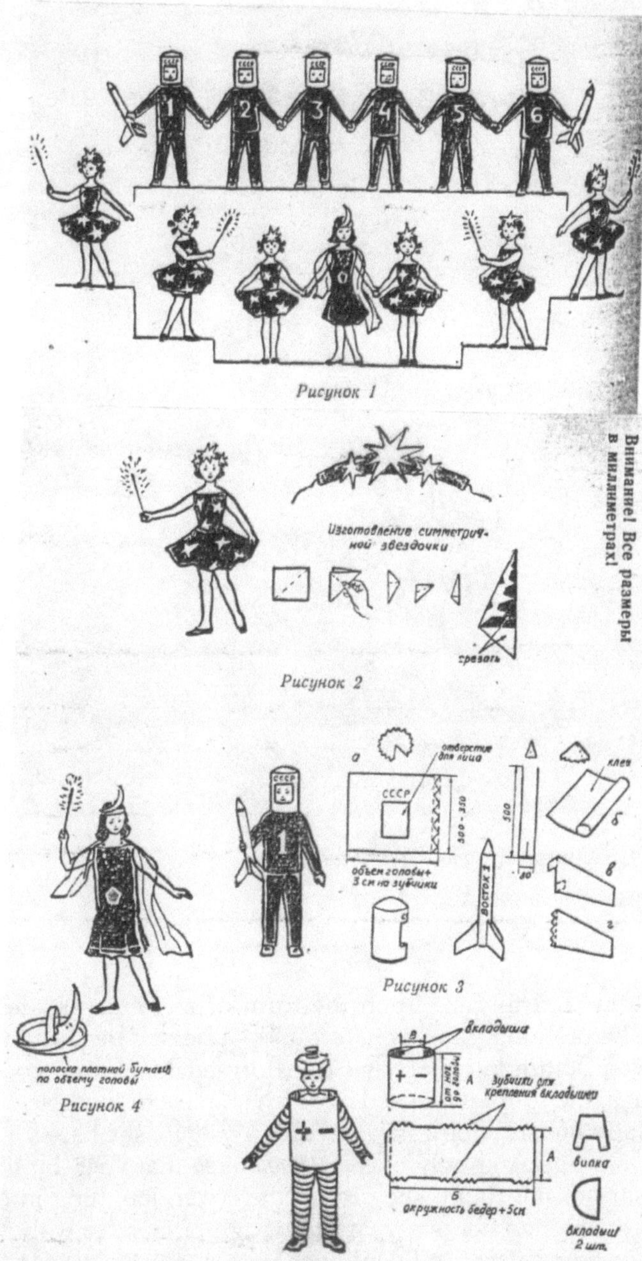


Figure 5.8 *Sem'ia i shkola*, November 1963, 24.

Figure 5.9 *Snegurochka's model outfit for 1963*

*Krokodil*, 30 December 1963, 2.

audience invited to gaze upon the form of an "emancipated" Soviet woman. Before long, however, Tereshkova herself began to fade from view. Even before her marriage transformed her into a cosmonaut's wife, magazine profiles focused not on her space training and flight but on her daily life and domestic activities. By 1965, she barely warranted a mention, appearing only once in *Rabotnitsa* that year: on the second anniversary of her flight, she graced the cover, laughing in her living room as she helped her one-year-old daughter learn to walk.[96] Her use as a public figure was firmly entrenched in domestic imagery.

The masculinization of *Sputnik* imagery and Tereshkova's inability to fully access the privileges of space flight afforded her male colleagues suggest a continued ambivalence in Soviet culture towards women and technology. In the 1920s and 1930s, efforts to mechanize farms and factories met with a series of obstacles, not only cultural but structural: early Soviet tractors were built for men to drive, for example; peasant women struggled to make sense of a new political culture that encouraged them to operate machines but built tractors with seats so high many women could not reach the pedals.[97] As we saw in chapter 4, the masculinized culture of research laboratories also alienated many women from technology and formed rigid cultural barriers to their participation. Cold War–era martial brotherhoods, such as those of the space program, reinforced Soviet cultural norms that insisted on deepening men's ties to military technology like *Sputnik* and the *Vostok* shuttles while curtailing Tereshkova's inclusion in the machine-driven discourse of the Cold War.

## Cosmonaut Masculinity on Tour

In February 1962, ten months after his flight, Gagarin arrived in Liberia to meet with government officials, tour rubber plantations, and offer sound bites to Soviet, African, and global media about his successful mission. Modelling and reinforcing masculine authority at home was only part of the cultural work Soviet authorities needed Gagarin to do. The other part involved sending him abroad as a global ambassador for Soviet masculinity. Gagarin and his *shestiorka* colleagues embarked on a series of world tours, visiting factories in Czechoslovakia, meeting with leaders such as Jawaharlal Nehru in India, and attending receptions with the queen in London.[98] Gagarin's visit to Liberia was only one stop on these tours. Gathered together with Liberian government leaders for photographs, Gagarin donned what the Soviet press called the "Liberian national dress" over his ever-present air force uniform, smiling with the group and playing the role in which Soviet authorities had cast him: the celebrity face of science, military honour, and socialism for the consumption of audiences in Cold War battlegrounds around the world, as well as for the Soviet public at home (Figure 5.10).[99]

The exchange of people and cultures through touring was a relatively common feature of the Cold War, at least after Stalin's death, and Gagarin was not the only individual or group deployed for this type of soft power diplomacy. Historian David Caute has demonstrated that

Figure 5.10 Cosmonaut Iu. A. Gagarin in the "national dress" of Liberia greeting representatives of Liberia, February 1962.

RGANTD, Fond 173, op. 1, d. 27

(personal fond, Aleksandr Aleksandrovich Zvorykin, photographer).

during the 1950s and 1960s, ballerinas, violinists, chess players, and athletes from all sides of the Cold War traversed the globe to advertise their world view and way of life.[100] Deploying Gagarin and his cosmonaut cohort, however, also involved selling to a global audience the masculinized persona authorities had constructed at home. That this task was given to someone already famous at home for his sex appeal and family-man persona ensured that masculinity would play a central role in Gagarin's touring. Now added to Gagarin's domestic duties as a loyal husband and father were the roles of politician and diplomat, an expansion of the expectations for the military masculinity that the cosmonauts represented.

Gagarin's gendered identity mattered to his image as an envoy abroad. The space age was also an era in which a wave of new, young leaders took power in several geopolitically strategic states: John F. Kennedy in the United States, Fidel Castro in Cuba, Gamal Nasser in Egypt, and (if only symbolically) Queen Elizabeth II in the United Kingdom. In addition to his use as a propaganda vehicle for marriage and fatherhood among Soviet men, Gagarin and, in his wake, the *shestiorka* men became key symbols of youth and virility in government. Maximizing their visual effectiveness in photographs and public appearances, officials either paired the aging Khrushchev with a cosmonaut or allowed the cosmonaut to replace him entirely. Khrushchev met with both John F. Kennedy and Fidel Castro in the summer of 1961. Meeting Kennedy in Vienna in early June, Khrushchev was photographed with the young president. The images mirror photographs that same spring and summer of Khrushchev with Gagarin, whose youth and megawatt smile matched Kennedy's.[101] Khrushchev also wanted not only foreign but domestic audiences to visualize Gagarin as a force of renewed vigour in political leadership. Khrushchev's son, reminiscing about Gagarin's welcome in Moscow after his flight, confirms how Khrushchev literally took a backseat to Gagarin:

> [Khrushchev] very much wanted to ride with them in the same car and share their joy; on the other hand, it was their triumph, and, as they say, three's a crowd. It was Gagarin who settled it. He was already in the car, standing there like a marshal about to review his regiments. Yuri smiled at Father and stretched out his hand as though to help him get in. Father took a back seat. Thus they rode the whole route: Leninsky Avenue, the jubilant square that would be named after him, and on to the Kremlin. Yuri and Valentina standing and [Khrushchev] sitting at the back.[102]

Gagarin's physical presence was increasingly required for generating impressions at home and abroad that the Soviet leadership was younger and fresher than was actually the case. Soon after Gagarin's head injury in Crimea, for example, he had been scheduled to sit at Khrushchev's side at the opening of the Twenty-Second Party Congress in October 1961. Khrushchev was reportedly furious that Gagarin would not be able to appear. After much negotiation, Gagarin attended only the fifth day of the Congress and with his head wound still noticeable, leading officials to issue a frantic order to journalists not to photograph his face.[103] The visibility of his body in public space was the entire reason for his attendance, however; if he was not photographed, his usefulness as a masculine icon dwindled. Gagarin and his masculine persona were dispatched around the world to rebrand the Soviet Union not as an outdated bastion of aged, pensioner-revolutionaries but as a modern, technologically sophisticated state where young, handsome men like Gagarin were building communism and flourishing in the comfortable life it provided.

Deploying Gagarin as a masculine icon, and using his famous smile and charisma to disarm global audiences, also masked the militarized implications of his flight. The *Sputnik* launch as well as the *shestiorka*'s manned flights were designed and implemented by an agency known as Experimental Design Bureau-1 (*Opytno-konstruktorskoe buiro-1*, or OKB-1), which was operated by the Ministry of the Defence Industry and whose explicit assignment was to develop and improve intercontinental ballistic missiles (ICBMs) for the Soviet Strategic Rocket Forces.[104] It was well understood in both Soviet and American military circles that, as historian Sue Bridger has pointed out, "Only an extremely powerful missile, one equally capable of delivering a nuclear bomb directly onto American soil, could have propelled *Sputnik* into orbit."[105] The same was true of Gagarin's launch. Given the strong message of peace that the Soviet Union was emphasizing both at home and abroad by the time of Gagarin's tours, the cosmonauts as soldiers could have become a problematic image. Gagarin's celebrity was carefully crafted to downplay, when he was abroad, the military implications of the technology that had sent him to space, while simultaneously signalling his authority as a serviceman to audiences at home. To fulfil these dual representations, authorities relied on Gagarin's nonthreatening personality as an Everyman who enjoyed vacationing with his family or grabbing a beer with the guys.[106] But in more subtle ways, his military credentials and his performance of soldier masculinity lurked just behind his self-deprecating jokes and casual hand-waves. One key aspect of this second image came in the form of the air force uniform that Gagarin, Titov, and the other men in the *shestiorka* always wore in public. Although no one openly discussed the militarization implicit in rocket technology, it hovered plainly in the background, wrapped around cosmonaut bodies.

On tour, the performance of intellectual and political expertise became a key part of Gagarin's celebrity image. He was sanctioned to act as a surrogate diplomat, routinely scheduled to meet with world leaders at most stops – not only because both sides would have seen the publicity benefits of being photographed together, but ostensibly also to discuss major political issues. On a tour through North Africa and West Africa in early 1962, Gagarin's first stop was in Egypt, where he met with Nasser and spoke about the controversial Aswan High Dam project. During a press conference in which Gagarin talked about the Cairo youth festival and the city's new stadium, he also lent support to the dam.[107] Perhaps noting his willingness to comment on political matters, an Egyptian journalist later asked him if he would ever become a deputy to the Supreme Soviet. Gagarin replied, "In our country, deputies to the Soviet parliament are the servants of the people ... All Soviet people participate – for peace, labour, freedom, equality, brotherhood, and happiness."[108] It was a moment intended to secure his credibility as a people's diplomat, but it also underscored the fact that he was not a deputy and did not have the credentials or authority to speak with Nasser and the Egyptian public about the Aswan Dam project or any other diplomatic issue.

Later on that trip, Gagarin was photographed with Liberian government officials before moving on to Ghana, where he met with one of the most powerful postcolonial leaders of the time, Ghanaian president and pan-African activist Kwame Nkrumah. Ghanaian newspapers suggested that Gagarin's influence had motivated Nkrumah to redouble his government's efforts to promote scientific research.[109] According to the Soviet press, meanwhile, Gagarin and Nkrumah became such good friends on the visit that they cemented their intellectual compatibility by exchanging copies of their respective books – implying that Gagarin's ghostwritten celebrity memoir, *Dawn of the Space Age*, was an equal text to Nkrumah's anti-imperialism manifesto, *I Speak of Freedom*.[110] Both Ghanaian and Soviet journalists played into the myth that Gagarin possessed political, military, and diplomatic credentials that rivalled Nkrumah's, and that the two men's qualifications were rooted in their shared understanding of Cold War masculinity. "I see a powerful man tearing asunder the chains of colonialism with powerful hands," Gagarin told the *Ghanaian Times*, speaking not directly of Nkrumah but of African national liberation movements, as often depicted in Soviet anti-racism imagery. "I see before me the image of a man squaring his broad shoulders. His chains have fallen to his feet and his muscular hands, the hands of a worker, are free. I should like to clasp those hands. This is the desire with which I am going to Africa."[111]

Space program authorities repeatedly presented Gagarin as an equal to the world leaders he met. In November 1961, Gagarin met with Jawaharlal Nehru and Indira Gandhi in India, despite later revealing to Indian radio that his political expertise was limited to his certainty that India was a "brother country" to the Soviet Union.[112] In Afghanistan in December 1961, not only did Gagarin address the Kabul Military

Academy, fortifying young pilots with his own story of success, but he also met with King Muhammad Zahir Shah.[113] In March 1964, a trip to Sweden was postponed after the KGB found a bomb at Gagarin's destination. Swedish newspapers were quick to pick up on the implication: "A bomb for Gagarin is a bomb for Khrushchev!" headlines blared, further securing his status as a diplomatic proxy for the Soviet government.[114] However, from Kamanin's point of view, the role of diplomat was too much for Gagarin, and he found itineraries in which he had to meet with foreign leaders exhausting.[115] That would be understandable if true, although as we have seen, Kamanin's diary entries routinely expressed disappointment in Gagarin's celebrity acts and persona, perhaps to buoy Kamanin's own sense of himself as a commander of inexperienced cadets.

Tereshkova was also deployed on global publicity tours. Her experience with celebrity differed markedly from that of her male colleagues in many ways, as in authorities' failure to grant her the diplomatic access to foreign leaders that Gagarin enjoyed. Unlike other touring female celebrities of the time, such as Queen Elizabeth or Jacqueline Kennedy, Tereshkova's publicity tours were more low-key, and she was not expected to comment on political situations. As evidence of the queen's rearrangement of a masculinized political culture to fit her, one might point to her participation in a tiger hunt as part of her tour of India in March 1961.[116] "The mark of a man is his hunting prowess," *Time* magazine declared of the venture, comparing the queen's hunting success to that of King George V, who in 1911 had killed more than 60 animals on his own tour of India.[117] Tereshkova's presence on the cosmonaut hunt in Yaroslavl', by contrast, was, if not an afterthought, then an inclusion on a much different level. Characterized by Kamanin simply as a trip for "Gagarin and Nikolaev and their wives," Tereshkova's role was only to cook, not to hunt, denying her the opportunity to participate fully in the masculinized culture that helped mould a particular identity for her colleagues. She was further distanced from any potential role in the hunt by the fact that she was heavily pregnant that weekend, cementing her transformation from a woman involved in science and technology who could compete with men on the same terrain into a wife and soon-to-be mother. For Tereshkova's celebrity image, the two identities could not overlap.[118]

Gagarin's and Tereshkova's respective trips to the United Kingdom illustrate the gendered differences in their deployment as Cold War celebrities. Visiting the UK in July 1961, Gagarin met with both political and symbolic leaders, speaking with Prime Minister Harold Macmillan and dining with Queen Elizabeth – leading to the incident that opened this chapter, in which he dared to touch her knee under the table. As he was with many other global leaders, Gagarin was portrayed on this trip as the queen's equal, perhaps even her superior, and as an experienced and charming diplomat. Tereshkova embarked on her own high-profile visit to London in February 1964, ending only days before her doctor ordered her not to travel anymore owing to her pregnancy. She accepted an award from the British Interplanetary Society, attended a reception at the Great Britain–USSR Association, and also briefly met with the queen at Buckingham Palace.[119] Kamanin reported that she had a "meeting with parliament," although the *Times* clarified the nature of that visit: "She was presented with books containing coloured pictures of Parliament and an account of how it works. The diplomatic party, which included the Soviet ambassador and twelve of his staff, then walked through to the central lobby, where they met Mr. Wilson, Leader of the Opposition." Marking the fortieth anniversary of the opening of diplomatic relations between Britain and the Soviet Union at an event that evening in Tereshkova's honour, the Soviet ambassador and Tereshkova's chaperone, Alexander Soldatov, read a message from Khrushchev aloud.[120] Finally, upon her departure, Tereshkova informed the British press that her favourite stop on the trip had been at Stratford-upon-Avon because she, like many Russians, was an avid reader of Shakespeare.[121] In sharp contrast to Gagarin, afforded a role as a diplomat armed with mandates to engage in political discussions with foreign leaders, Tereshkova, despite her celebrity as a cosmonaut, was kept her away from the political realm. Whereas Gagarin often spoke in Khrushchev's place abroad, Tereshkova remained silent while the ambassador spoke on Khrushchev's behalf in London. Despite travelling the world with a similar message of peace and prosperity as spokespeople for international cooperation based on the shared global interest in space exploration, Gagarin and Tereshkova represented vastly different roles for Soviet men and women on the world stage and, by extension, at home.

Gagarin's government meetings abroad buoyed his diplomatic masculinity, but only if he received suitable adoration at each stop. In Ghana in early 1962, Gagarin met a crowd of thousands of Young Pioneers eager for his autograph, their "Pioneer discipline" the only thing keeping them stoic and reserved, according to the Soviet press. Dancing and cheering for him in Accra's main square, the children held up banners in Russian that read, "Hurrah! The man from space is among us!"[122] In Liberia, Gagarin was given the Order of the African Star and taken to see local businesses, construction sites, educational institutions, and plantations. At one point, the Soviet delegation passed a crowd singing "Moscow Nights," a famous Soviet anthem.[123] A guide reportedly told *Pravda* correspondent Nikolai Denisov, who was travelling with Gagarin, "Pass on to Mr. Khrushchev our great thanks that he sent Yuri Gagarin first into space, and then to us, in Liberia!"[124]

Many accounts characterize the stops on these tours as places of otherness that could be brought into the Soviet sphere of influence through the force of Gagarin's personality and achievements alone. Soviet observers focused on customs such as dance and clothing, positioning Africans as ignorant but attentive as they listened to Gagarin's explanations of the science of space flight. This insinuated lack of scientific knowledge in the African and Asian countries the cosmonauts visited was a repeated theme. Titov, who often travelled with Gagarin, recounts this story: "One day an Arab journalist asked [Gagarin]: 'Did you have any sort of good-luck charm with you in the cabin of the spaceship *Vostok*?' 'Yes,' answered Gagarin, 'in the pocket of my protective suit was a certificate that I was a citizen of the Soviet Union. That is the most trustworthy good-luck charm!'"[125] The invented contrast between Soviet science and other countries' superstitions or mythologies came up again in Greece and Cyprus, where the press referred to Gagarin as the "Icarus of the cosmos," a moniker with roots in Greek mythology and in Russian folklore as well. In Russian legend, Ivan the Terrible told a serf with dreams of flying that "a man is not a bird. He does not have wings. Those who attach wooden wings to themselves do so in opposition to the will of nature."[126] Conquering the will of nature was part of the promise of Soviet science, and Gagarin reflected on that while speaking to journalists in Cyprus. When asked about the Greek mythological hero, he said, "Icarus had wings made from wax, a material that is not very stable, but Soviet space ships are made from durable modern metals. These metals are produced by the hands of our workers and engineers, our Soviet people – they are the ones who should rightly be called 'Icarus of the cosmos!'"[127] Considering what happened to Icarus in Greek mythology, it is perhaps no wonder that Gagarin was eager to distance himself from the name, but in the process he created a vision of the superstitious other that Soviet science and reason could conquer in the same way they had conquered space.

The idealized masculinity of the conquering hero informed conversations about the tours. *Komsomol'skaia pravda* observed after Gagarin's flight that the work of Jules Verne and other adventure fiction encouraged "boys to dream of setting out for the jungles of Africa, the prairies of South America, to desert islands and unknown lands ... And on 4 October 1957, boys on all five continents raised their heads" to watch the stars and dream of becoming cosmonauts.[128] Outer space, like Africa or South America, was labelled an unknown land, and it was the duty of Soviet cosmonauts to chart it. Whether in space vessels or on victory tours on earth, cosmonaut celebrity and masculinity were tied not only to notions of peaceful diplomacy but also to a vocabulary of conquest.

In March 1968, Gagarin was killed at the age of thirty-four in a plane crash that had been part of a training exercise. The crash had the curious cultural effect of closing one era – the flights and celebrity tours of the first *shestiorka* – while opening another. That new era would see Gagarin's image almost frozen in time and his celebrity cultivated in popular culture as an unassailable hero as well as a reckless maverick, a James Dean figure permanently etched in Soviet collective memory.[129] As Andrew Jenks has written, maintaining Gagarin's role as a pilot-hero at home and internationally was the main reason authorities had grounded him for several years before the crash, but doing so had hurt his image, as well as his self-identification, as an air force pilot first and foremost. "It was a long-standing tradition in the macho world of pilots that one did not respect a grounded commander," Jenks writes, "and Gagarin did not like to have his authority challenged."[130]

An increasingly masculinized Soviet culture after the Second World War set explicit boundaries regarding permissible forms of public authority for the first group of cosmonauts. The space flights and subsequent publicity tours of Yuri Gagarin and the other men of the *shestiorka* attempted to carve out lasting, positive identities for Soviet men of the early Cold War generation while also modelling socialist heroism to the world. Family devotion, military honour, and political diplomacy defined their masculinity. At home, Gagarin's sexually charged but carefully contained image as a desirable but monogamous young man complemented postwar family law policies intent on re-establishing the primacy of marriage and fatherhood for Soviet men. Abroad, being handsome and charismatic was not quite enough; Gagarin also played the role of diplomat in an effort to add intellectual substance to his persona, as well as to attach a fresh face to the Cold War policies of the Soviet administration.

Tereshkova, meanwhile, was paraded in front of both domestic and international audiences not as a symbol of science and technology but as a face of the achievements of Soviet women. At the same time, she was a female body displayed in a deeply conservative way. As an ideal type for marriage and motherhood, her gendered status was sewn into her celebrity in order to allow the public to witness her transformation from adventurous, single girl to disciplined wife and mother who never flew in space again. Tereshkova was viewed and presented as a woman first and a cosmonaut only a distant second, her body deployed abroad for geopolitical purchase in an increasingly complex Cold War battleground, and also at home, as a moral compass for a wayward post-Stalin generation in need of a safely feminized hero. The symbol of her mandated dresses represented the public marginalization not only of Tereshkova within the masculinized culture of space flight but of all Soviet women within military enterprises.

Gagarin's global tours placed him in physical, intellectual, and cultural contrast to the people and places he visited, affirming a Cold War brand of Soviet masculinity that included charisma, diplomatic skill, and authority derived from fronting a technological achievement recognized by a variety of global publics. As a makeshift political leader, his youth and attractiveness trumped the age and experience of leaders before (and concurrent with) him; as a diplomat, his space flight lent legitimacy to his discussions of international affairs on earth; and as a cultural celebrity, he filled a niche in masculine heroism missing in Soviet society since the Second World War. Although the early cosmonauts have been viewed as the vanguard of Khrushchev's new drive towards a communist future in the early 1960s, they also represented the final stage of a project, initiated with demobilization in the late 1940s, to reimagine and re-militarize masculine authority in Soviet culture.

# Conclusion

The processes of re-establishing military masculinity in Soviet society produced multiple narratives about military institutions, service, and men's relationships to martial authority in the aftermath of the Second World War. One set of stories emerged from within traditional military structures such as the Suvorov academies, the Ministry of Defence, and, by virtue of its assumed authority over youth of conscription age, even the Komsomol. The Suvorov schools, established during the war to ensure the survival of the officer corps afterwards, were set up as facsimiles of families disrupted during the war, except with men filling the roles and replacing the women who would have raised the cadets on the outside. Meanwhile, DOSAAF authorities knew that the postwar world would require a reconfiguration of training imperatives and the very spirit of martial voluntarism. What they did not anticipate was the degree to which both voluntary defence activities as well as conscription through the Ministry of Defence would have to be resold to a population of young men increasingly uninterested in constructing its premier masculine identity around soldiering. These institutional narratives suggest that postwar martial spaces fit uncomfortably, if at all, with postwar masculinities in Soviet culture.

Further complicating the picture, a second set of stories were produced outside military structures throughout the late 1940s, 1950s, and into the 1960s that revealed a broader cultural pattern in the reinforcement of masculine military authority. Under the façade of humour, *Krokodil* signalled deep discomfort with the postwar gender order at home and in the new global Cold War. As quickly administered visual cues, its foreign affairs cartoons, persistent in tone and volume for nearly twenty years, attacked femininity and attempted to reinforce Soviet manhood by ruthlessly belittling the masculinity of European and American generals, politicians, and diplomats whose decisions ran counter to Soviet ideology or policy. In telling their own set of stories outside official military structures, nuclear physicists like Andrei Sakharov developed their own angle on concepts and ideals of masculinity. While we might have expected those stories to consist of simple tales of intellectual censorship and feelings of martial inadequacy or "softness," in Sakharov's words, in the shadow of "hard" military leaders like Marshal Nedelin, the physicists' texts revealed a far more complicated picture of masculinity, scientific innovation, weaponry, and service.

By the early 1960s, two decades' worth of attempts to rebuild the masculine iconography of military service reached their peak when Yuri Gagarin, a handsome and charming air force captain and the first man in space, began his publicity tours at home and abroad. The success of his story, however, entailed the crafting of a different story for Valentina Tereshkova. Both versions were predicated on the cosmonauts' conservative image as desexualized spouses and parents, but creating a cultural space for Gagarin and his male cohort to gain access to martial masculinity relied on Tereshkova's exclusion. As officers, Gagarin, Gherman Titov, and Andriian Nikolaev, Tereshkova's cosmonaut husband, neither possessed greater technical knowledge nor performed more specialized feats during their flights than she did as a civilian. In a Cold War reprisal of the very gendered divisions this book has explored coming out of the Second World War, Tereshkova – like a demobilized woman in the Red Army in late 1945 – had her access to military authority deliberately curtailed and eventually revoked in order to provide a feminine-civilian countertype to the masculine-soldier ideal.

The lexicon of family featured prominently in the sites of remasculinization explored in this book. Chapter 2 explored the culture of soldiering both within and outside official military institutions and how the language and metaphors of family were used to frame understandings of honour, duty, and reconstruction. At the Suvorov academies, male war orphans became the foundation for rebuilding the Soviet military family, with Ministry of Defence officials cultivating the academies as hierarchical, homosocial spaces for cadets, elder-brother instructors, and paternal administrators. The cadets' and instructors' occasional deviation from the dutiful roles they were meant to play, negotiating authority for themselves instead of yielding it to more senior men or even to the esteemed war veterans among their instructors, demonstrates that the top-down pathways for rebuilding military masculinity were not always smooth or successful. In another context, men in uniform who deviated from narrowly configured family narratives were vilified in *Krokodil*, as we saw in chapter 3, which used images of foreign military and political figures to police the boundaries of acceptable masculinity. The physicists' memoirs examined in chapter 4 further demonstrated that the concept of family influenced their laboratory interactions, with the most senior men held in high regard as *patres familias*, and that marital fidelity was policed among scientists working at isolated research centres away from their wives. Chapter 5 showed that the first cosmonaut cohort also was subject to familial presentations, with the most famous military officers in the country and the world shaped into responsible husbands and fathers on the public stage, regardless of their private activities. Tereshkova's access to military or scientific authority was also contained by her public marriage and shift to motherhood, which was medically argued to be incompatible with space flight.

Taken together, the persistence of these masculine family motifs across several different sites indicates a stubborn refusal of military institutions to acknowledge and accommodate the women-led families that dominated postwar society. Excluding women from the postwar military also involved creating fantasy-families within military cultures. In the postwar Soviet military imagination, men (and boys, as explored in chapter 2) maintained control over all family roles, as parents, siblings, children, and beyond – all in sharp contrast to what was going on in the real world. As we saw in chapter 1, however, not all young men wanted to participate in that imaginary world, indicating that we can consider would-be soldiers alongside other specific social groups that Soviet historians have recently explored as a way of demonstrating the increased plurality of identities shaping postwar society.

There are more events, stories, and voices that contributed to establishing, maintaining, and challenging the postwar gender order in the Soviet Union. With so little historical work done so far on this theme, there is much room for scholars to continue asking questions about the specific processes that built Soviet masculinities broadly and in the military in particular. For example, although memoirs of Second World War veterans abound, we have few texts recounting service (and virtually none, to my knowledge, admitting evasion) in the postwar years, at least until the war in Afghanistan in the 1980s brought the issue to light again. If the Russian government opens postwar military archives to Western researchers in the future, we might be able to obtain further answers (and generate new questions) about how military masculinity was reconstructed and reinforced after the Second World War. Relying on the peculiar and narrow language of the Soviet bureaucracy in archival records can limit the gender historian's access to cultural patterns, however; scholars have already had far more success investigating masculinity by looking at novels, plays, and films than archival documents.[1] As we saw in chapter 3, the boundaries for acceptable presentations of military masculinity were produced and policed in Soviet civil society, and quite openly at that, but historians have largely overlooked these public pronouncements of gender expectations in the Soviet press. There is more work that historians can do with both archival and cultural sources to reveal gendered notions of martial power and privilege.

While rooted in the first two decades after the end of the war, the themes of masculinity this book has explored had no firm end date, nor did they demonstrate close adherence to the standard patterns of periodization in Soviet history. Historians have recently begun to reconsider those traditional periodization breaks, which have generally corresponded to leadership changes, but they persist. In chapter 1, I suggested that Stalin's death in 1953 influenced the shift the following year to publicly discussing, if still covertly, the issue of young men's service evasion. Chapter 2 also found greater opportunities for unconventional military heroes in literature and film after Stalin's death, such as the unlikely protagonists Maxim Perepelitsa and Ivan Brovkin. Yet chapter 4 saw unexpected leniency in Stalin's treatment of nuclear scientists in comparison to Khrushchev's. On the whole, re-establishing military masculinity became part of the process of reconfiguring the postwar gender order, not a directive tied to any one time or leader. De-Stalinization, while still a crucial topic in this time period, surprisingly did not shape martial masculine discourses as we might have expected. The *Krokodil* cartoons, for example, showed stunning consistency from 1946 to the mid-1960s in their gendered portrayals of Western military figures. Whether it was under Stalin's leadership that orphaned boys were admitted to the Suvorov schools, Khrushchev who insisted scientists be treated like conscripts about to flee, or Brezhnev who forbade Tereshkova from appearing in public in a military uniform even after she was granted an honorary rank, the culminating effect of these microsites of masculinization informed postwar recovery in the Soviet Union as a whole from 1945 to about 1965.

By the late 1960s, however, several factors converged to alter the climate for the institutions and actors this book has investigated. First, the 1967 Law on Universal Military Obligation significantly changed service requirements for conscripted men by lowering it from three to two years, which had the effect of creating more forbidding hierarchies between those in their first year of service versus their second.[2] As we saw in chapter 1, the latter became known colloquially as *dedy*, or "grandfathers." The increasingly brutal hazing system of *dedovshchina*, or "rule by the grandfathers," has grown since the 1970s to become a notoriously cruel hallmark of service in the late Soviet and post-Soviet militaries. By the time researchers began looking into the phenomenon in the 1980s, young men in the Soviet Union as a whole viewed military service as a particularly sadistic punishment.[3] This growing crisis in the military after 1967 has understandably occupied researchers, but it has left the period from 1945 to 1967 largely ignored by social and cultural historians of Soviet military affairs. As discussed in chapter 1, service was a much more benign experience in that period in between the horrors of the Second World War and the *dedovshchina* crisis that took hold in the 1970s, which suggests that young men's aversion to service, and authorities' concern about that rejection, was more influenced by culture than fear.

Yuri Gagarin's death in March 1968 offers a second reason for ending this book in the mid-1960s. The heroic military identity built for Gagarin and the other cosmonauts in the initial *shestiorka*, which extended from Gagarin's flight in 1961 to the last of the world tours in 1964, contributed to the postwar process of returning martial authority to Soviet men – a link presumed to have been lost in the war. After Gagarin's death, none of the *shestiorka* cosmonauts returned to space; future cosmonaut cohorts would open a new era. These moments of rupture in the postwar Soviet timeline confirm Claire McCallum's findings that the mid-1960s featured a break in visual representations of masculinity.[4] The first two postwar decades comprised a distinct period for the cultural reassertion of martial masculinity, as the country came to grips with what the war would, or should, mean for military institutions, for the women no longer welcome in them, and for the men newly charged with rebuilding them.

In other ways, however, some of the themes explored here did not end or change in the 1960s. For example, by the mid-1960s the country faced a historic low point in the numbers of young men in the population available for army service; the destruction of the war years for Soviet families and the birth rate resulted in difficulty for many conscription offices to reach their targets. But even then, women's service was not seen as the answer. The recruitment of women did increase in certain sectors, including technical and clerical work, telephone and radio operations, medicine, and food service, but not in active training for deployment.[5] More work on how authorities continued to protect the military as a space for men through to the end of the Soviet Union (and beyond) would be welcome.

Military masculinity was in flux at the end of the Second World War in the Soviet Union. Catastrophic wartime casualties and the exceptional circumstance of women serving in combat roles combined to shatter prewar ideals about what service meant for masculine identity. A political system founded through violence and legitimized through the total mobilization efforts of the proletarian soldier could not halt military activity, even after such a devastating war. The soldier had to be reimagined and resold to a public that had just emerged from war and a younger generation suspicious of state control. In doing so, military authorities worked in tandem with cultural forces to write women out and re-establish martial identity as the premier and hegemonic form of masculinity in Soviet society. Multiple voices and narratives contributed to the processes by which postwar Soviet policymakers tried to reforge the links between military service and masculinity that the war had destroyed. Re-establishing, cultivating, maintaining, and protecting military masculinity was a continuous process that came to define postwar Soviet society and culture.

# Notes

**Introduction**

1 Andrei Sakharov, *Memoirs*, trans. Richard Lourie (New York: Alfred A. Knopf, 1990), 194.
2 Ibid., 194.
3 Yuri Slezkine, *The Jewish Century* (Princeton, NJ: Princeton University Press, 2004), 333.
4 Istvan Harggitai, *Buried Glory: Portraits of Soviet Scientists* (New York: Oxford University Press, 2013), 73.
5 Gerard J. De Groot, *The Bomb: A Life* (Cambridge, MA: Harvard University Press, 2006), 195.
6 Alexei B. Kojevnikov, *Stalin's Great Science: The Times and Adventures of Soviet Physicists* (London: Imperial College Press, 2004), 296.
7 Sakharov, *Memoirs*, 195–6.
8 For a detailed discussion of the statistical intricacies involved in calculating a plausible figure, see Michael Ellman and S. Maksudov, "Soviet Deaths in the Great Patriotic War: A Note," *Europe-Asia Studies* 46, no. 4 (1994), 671–80. The authors generally accept the findings of a 1989 committee that Gorbachev commissioned to revise previous Soviet underestimations. The committee established total deaths of between 26 and 27 million. Of these, the authors estimate that 20 million were male, and 7.8 million were military deaths (excluding partisans and resistance fighters). See also Mie Nakachi, "Replacing the Dead: The Politics of Reproduction in the Postwar Soviet Union, 1944–1955" (PhD diss., University of Chicago, 2009).
9 Alexander Werth, *Russia: The Post-War Years* (New York: Taplinger Publishing Co., 1971), 24; Michael Paul Sacks, "Women in the Industrial Labor Force," in Dorothy Atkinson, Alexander Dallin, and Gail Warshofsky

Lapidus, eds., *Women in Russia* (Stanford, CA: Stanford University Press, 1977), 190.

10 Anna Krylova, *Soviet Women in Combat: A History of Violence on the Eastern Front* (Cambridge: Cambridge University Press, 2010), 10.

11 Ibid., 153.

12 Ibid., 217.

13 Roger D. Markwick and Euridice Charon Cardona, *Soviet Women on the Frontline in the Second World War* (New York: Palgrave Macmillan, 2012), 232; Reina Pennington, "'Do Not Speak of the Services You Rendered': Women Veterans of Aviation in the Soviet Union," *Journal of Slavic Military Studies* 9, no. 1 (March 1996), 121, 125; and Barbara Alpern Engel, "The Womanly Face of War: Soviet Women Remember World War II," in Nicole Ann Dombrowski, ed., *Women and War in the Twentieth Century: Enlisted with or without Consent* (New York and London: Garland Publishing, 1999), 111. For further discussions of women in the Soviet military in the Second World War, see Reina Pennington, *Wings, Women, and War: Soviet Airwomen in World War II Combat* (Lawrence, KS: University Press of Kansas, 2002); Kazimiera J. Cottam, *Women in Air War: The Eastern Front of World War II* (Nepean, ON: New Military Publishing, 1997); and Kerstin Bischl, "Female Red Army Soldiers in World War II and Beyond," in Catherine Baker, ed., *Gender in 20th-Century Eastern Europe and the USSR* (Basingstoke: Palgrave Macmillan, 2017), 113–26.

14 Thomas Schrand, "Socialism in One Gender: Masculine Values in the Stalin Revolution," in Barbara Evans Clements, Rebecca Friedman, and Dan Healey, eds., *Russian Masculinities in History and Culture* (New York: Palgrave, 2002), 203–4.

15 On the prominence of women in postwar Soviet society, see Elena Zubkova, *Russia after the War: Hopes, Illusions, and Disappointments, 1945–1957*, trans. Hugh Ragsdale (New York: M.E. Sharpe, 1998); Mie Nakachi, "Population, Politics and Reproduction: Late Stalinism and Its Legacy," in Juliane Fürst, ed., *Late Stalinist Russia: Society between Reconstruction and Reinvention* (London and New York: Routledge, 2006), 37–66.

16 "V planetarii," *Krokodil*, 30 April 1946, 15.

17 "Na karnivale," *Krokodil*, 10 August 1957, 11.

18 Engel, "The Womanly Face of War," 112.

19 Ellen Jones, *Red Army and Society: A Sociology of the Soviet Military* (Boston: Allen and Unwin, 1985), 103.

20 Ibid.

21 Marina Yusupova, "Shifting Masculine Terrains: Russian Men in Russia and the UK" (PhD diss., University of Manchester, 2016), 70.

22 Key historical work on Soviet masculinities since the 1990s includes the essays in Clements, Friedman, and Healey, eds., *Russian Masculinities in History and Culture*; Dan Healey, *Homosexual Desire in Revolutionary Russia: The Regulation of Sexual and Gender Dissent* (Chicago: University of Chicago Press, 2001); Sergei Oushakine, ed., *Muzhe(N)stvennost'* (Moscow: Novoe literaturnoe obozrenie, 2002); Ethan Pollock, "'Real Men Go to the Bania': Postwar Soviet Masculinities and the Bathhouse," *Kritika: Explorations in Russian and Eurasian History* 11, no. 1 (Winter 2010), 47–76; Dan Healey, "Comrades, Queers and 'Oddballs': Sodomy, Masculinity and Gendered Violence in Leningrad Province of the 1950s," *Journal of the History of Sexuality* 21, no. 3 (September 2012), 496–522; Claire E. McCallum, "The Return: Postwar Masculinity and the Domestic Space in Stalinist Visual Culture, 1945–53," *Russian Review* 74, no. 1 (January 2015), 117–43; Claire E. McCallum, "Scorched by the Fire of War: Masculinity, War Wounds and Disability in Soviet Visual Culture, 1941–65," *Slavonic and East European Review* 93, no. 2 (2015), 251–85; Claire E. McCallum, *The Fate of the New Man: Representing and Reconstructing Masculinity in Soviet Visual Culture, 1945–1965* (DeKalb: Northern Illinois University Press, 2018); and Erica L. Fraser, "Soviet Masculinities and Revolution," in Catherine Baker, ed., *Gender in 20th-Century Eastern Europe and the USSR* (Basingstoke: Palgrave Macmillan, 2017), 127–40. Recent dissertations in Soviet history have also explored this topic: see Marko Dumančić, "Rescripting Stalinist Masculinity: Contesting the Male Ideal in Soviet Film and Society, 1953–1968" (PhD diss., University of North Carolina at Chapel Hill, 2010); Brandon Gray Miller, "Between Creation and Crisis: Soviet Masculinities, Consumption, and Bodies after Stalin" (PhD diss., Michigan State University, 2013); and Steven Jug, "All Stalin's Men? Soldierly Masculinities in the Soviet War Effort, 1938–1945" (PhD diss., University of Illinois at Urbana–Champaign, 2013). Literature and film scholars have also contributed important work on the subject. See Eliot Borenstein, *Men without Women: Masculinity and Revolution in Russian Fiction, 1917–1929* (Durham, NC: Duke University Press, 2000); Lilya Kaganovsky, *How the Soviet Man Was Unmade: Cultural Fantasy and Male Subjectivity under Stalin* (Pittsburgh: University of Pittsburgh Press, 2008); and John Haynes, *New Soviet Man: Gender and Masculinity in Stalinist Soviet Cinema* (New York: Manchester University Press, 2003). On the post-Soviet era, see Maya Eichler, *Militarizing Men: Gender, Conscription, and War in Post-Soviet Russia* (Stanford, CA: Stanford University Press, 2012); and Tetyana Bureychak, "Masculinity in Soviet and Post-Soviet Ukraine: Models and Their Implications," in Olena Hankivsky and Anastasiya Salnykova, eds.,

*Gender, Politics, and Society in Ukraine* (Toronto: University of Toronto Press, 2012).

23 Barbara Evans Clements, "Introduction," in Clements, Friedman, and Healey, eds., *Russian Masculinities in History and Culture*, 11.

24 One of the few, but excellent, studies of military masculinity in imperial Russia or the Soviet Union is Karen Petrone's work on memories of the First World War. See Petrone, *The Great War in Russian Memory* (Bloomington, IN: Indiana University Press, 2011); and Petrone, "Imperial and Soviet Masculine Heroes and Patriotic Cultures," in Clements, Friedman, and Healey, eds., *Russian Masculinities in History and Culture*, 172–93. Recent conference proceedings have also begun to contribute to our understanding of gender anxieties during and after the war in Eastern European countries in particular, a setting often overlooked in broader European recovery narratives, but none of the papers discuss masculinity in the postwar Soviet Union. See Maren Röger and Ruth Leiserowitz eds, *Women and Men at War: A Gender Perspective on World War II and Its Aftermath in Central and Eastern Europe* (Osnabrück: Fibre-Verlag, 2012).

25 Philippa Hetherington, "Dressing the Shop Window of Socialism: Gender and Consumption in the Soviet Union in the Era of 'Cultured Trade,' 1934–53," *Gender and History* 27, no. 2 (Aug. 2015), 418.

26 Stefan Dudink, Karen Hagemann, and John Tosh, eds., *Masculinities in Politics and War: Gendering Modern History* (Manchester, UK: Manchester University Press, 2004), xii.

27 Aaron Belkin, *Bring Me Men: Military Masculinity and the Benign Façade of American Empire, 1898–2001* (Oxford: Oxford University Press, 2012), 4.

28 For example, see the essays in Paul R. Higate, *Military Masculinities: Identity and the State* (London: Praeger, 2003). The pioneering sociological work on how masculinities are often constructed in the plural was done in the 1990s by R.W. Connell, to be discussed in more detail below. See R.W. Connell, *Masculinities*, 2nd ed. (Berkeley and Los Angeles: University of California Press, 2005).

29 Mary Louise Roberts, "Beyond 'Crisis' in Understanding Gender Transformation," *Gender and History* 28, no. 2 (Aug. 2016), 360.

30 Roberts advocates for the use of the term "gender damage" instead of "crisis," as a more precise way of describing specific outcomes. While it is an intriguing concept and convincing in Roberts' work, it does not quite fit my evidence. See Roberts, "Beyond 'Crisis,'" 362–4.

31 See especially Connell, *Masculinities*. For further discussion of Connell and hierarchies of masculinities, see chapter 4.

32 R.W. Connell and James W. Messerschmidt, "Hegemonic Masculinity: Rethinking the Concept," *Gender and Society* 19, no. 6 (December 2005), 832.
33 Some of these themes are beginning to be investigated in exciting new research. On consumerism, see Miller, "Between Creation and Crisis." On fatherhood, see McCallum, "The Return"; and McCallum, *Fate of the New Man*.
34 Demetrakis Z. Demetriou, "Connell's Concept of Hegemonic Masculinity: A Critique," *Theory and Society* 30, no. 3 (2001), 355. For a more detailed summary and analysis of these and other critiques, as well as Connell's responses to them, see Connell and Messerschmidt, "Hegemonic Masculinity."
35 See Mark Edele, *Soviet Veterans of the Second World War: A Popular Movement in an Authoritarian Society, 1941–1991* (Oxford: Oxford University Press, 2008); Juliane Fürst, *Stalin's Last Generation: Soviet Post-War Youth and the Emergence of Mature Socialism* (Oxford: Oxford University Press, 2010); Miriam Dobson, *Khrushchev's Cold Summer: Gulag Returnees, Crime, and the Fate of Reform after Stalin* (Ithaca, NY: Cornell University Press, 2009); Brian LaPierre, *Hooligans in Khrushchev's Russia: Defining, Policing, and Producing Deviance during the Thaw* (Madison, WI: University of Wisconsin Press, 2012); and Healey, "Comrades, Queers and 'Oddballs.'"
36 See Edele, *Soviet Veterans of the Second World War*; Robert Dale, *Demobilized Veterans in Late Stalinist Leningrad: Soldiers to Civilians* (London and New York: Bloomsbury Academic, 2015); McCallum, "The Return"; and McCallum, *Fate of the New Man*.
37 Quoted in Ralph T. Fisher, *Pattern for Soviet Youth: A Study of the Congresses of the Komsomol, 1918–1954* (New York: Columbia University Press, 1959), 263. On these young men, the *stiliagi*, see Mark Edele, "Strange Young Men in Stalin's Moscow: The Birth and Life of the *Stiliagi*, 1945–1953," *Jahrbücher für Geschichte Osteuropas* 50, no. 1 (2002), 37–61.
38 Fürst, *Stalin's Last Generation*, 2. See also Gleb Tsipursky, *Socialist Fun: Youth, Consumption, and State-Sponsored Popular Culture in the Cold War Soviet Union, 1945–1970* (Pittsburgh: University of Pittsburgh Press, 2017).
39 For this argument, see Eichler, *Militarizing Men*, 2–3.
40 Jeffrey Burds, "Sexual Violence in Europe in World War II, 1939–1945," *Politics and Society* 37, no. 1 (March 2009), 47.
41 One of the earliest and most comprehensive treatments of this history is Norman M. Naimark, *The Russians in Germany: A History of the Soviet Zone of Occupation, 1945–1949* (Cambridge, MA: Harvard University Press, 1995). See also Atina Grossmann, "A Question of Silence: The Rape of German Women by Soviet Occupation Soldiers," in Dombrowski, ed.,

*Women and War in the Twentieth Century*, 120–36; James W. Messerschmidt, "The Forgotten Victims of World War II: Masculinities and Rape in Berlin, 1945," *Violence against Women* 12, no. 7 (July 2006), 706–12; Regina Mühlhäuser, "Reframing Sexual Violence as a Weapon and Strategy of War: The Case of the German Wehrmacht during the War and Genocide in the Soviet Union, 1941–1944," *Journal of the History of Sexuality* 26, no. 3 (Sept. 2017), 366–401; and James Mark, "Remembering Rape: Divided Social Memory and the Red Army in Hungary, 1944–1945," *Past and Present* 188 (Aug. 2005), 133–61.

42 For this argument, see Jug, "All Stalin's Men?" 243–4.
43 Messerschmidt, "The Forgotten Victims," 709–10.
44 Bureychak, "Masculinity in Soviet and Post-Soviet Ukraine," 327.
45 Slava Gerovitch, "'New Soviet Man' Inside Machine: Human Engineering, Spacecraft Design, and the Construction of Communism," *Osiris*, 22 (2007), 136.

**Chapter 1**

1 *Krokodil*, 20 May 1954, 14.
2 For a more detailed study of military masculinity in *Krokodil*, see chapter 3.
3 Mark von Hagen, *Soldiers in the Proletarian Dictatorship: The Red Army and the Soviet Socialist State, 1917–1930* (Ithaca, NY: Cornell University Press, 1990), 334. See also Sheila Fitzpatrick, *The Cultural Front: Power and Culture in Revolutionary Russia* (Ithaca, NY: Cornell University Press, 1992), 2; and David R. Stone, *Hammer and Rifle: The Militarization of the Soviet Union, 1926–1933* (Lawrence, KS: University Press of Kansas, 2000), 9.
4 Juliane Fürst, *Stalin's Last Generation: Soviet Post-War Youth and the Emergence of Mature Socialism* (Oxford: Oxford University Press, 2010), 177.
5 See Fürst, *Stalin's Last Generation*; Mark Edele, "Strange Young Men in Stalin's Moscow: The Birth and Life of the *Stiliagi*, 1945–1953," *Jahrbücher für Geschichte Osteuropas* 50, no. 1 (2002), 37–61; and Brian LaPierre, *Hooligans in Khrushchev's Russia: Defining, Policing, and Producing Deviance during the Thaw* (Madison, WI: University of Wisconsin Press, 2012).
6 For the imperial Russian and early Bolshevik eras, see von Hagen, *Soldiers in the Proletarian Dictatorship*; Stone, *Hammer and Rifle*; and Joshua A. Sanborn, *Drafting the Russian Nation: Military Conscription, Total War, and Mass Politics, 1905–1925* (DeKalb: Northern Illinois University Press, 2003). The Second World War era has produced the most military history, and those that cover social aspects of service include Roger R. Reese, *Stalin's Reluctant Soldiers: A Social History of the Red Army, 1925–1941* (Lawrence, KS: University Press of Kansas, 1996); and David Glantz, *Colossus Reborn:*

*The Red Army at War, 1941–1943* (Lawrence, KS: University Press of Kansas, 2005). The few studies that have offered a glimpse of the immediate postwar years include Ellen Jones, *Red Army and Society: A Sociology of the Soviet Military* (Boston: Allen and Unwin, 1985); Roger R. Reese, *The Soviet Military Experience: A History of the Soviet Army, 1917–1991* (New York: Routledge, 2000); and Roger Reese, *Red Commanders: A Social History of the Soviet Army Officer Corps, 1918–1991* (Lawrence, KS: University Press of Kansas, 2005).

7 For example, see Kristin Hoganson, *Fighting for American Manhood: How Gender Politics Provoked the Spanish-American and Philippine-American Wars* (New Haven: Yale University Press, 1998).

8 See Sanborn, *Drafting the Russian Nation*; George Q. Flynn, *Conscription and Democracy: The Draft in France, Great Britain, and the United States* (Westport, CT: Greenwood Press, 2002).

9 Stone, *Hammer and Rifle*, 8.

10 Joan B. Landes, "Republican Citizenship and Heterosocial Desire: Concepts of Masculinity in Revolutionary France," in Stefan Dudink, Karen Hagemann, and John Tosh, eds., *Masculinities in Politics and War: Gendering Modern History* (Manchester, UK: Manchester University Press, 2004), 96–7.

11 Anders Ahlbäck, *Manhood and the Making of the Military: Conscription, Military Service and Masculinity in Finland, 1917–39* (New York: Routledge, 2016).

12 Jones, *Red Army and Society*, 33–4.

13 See Sanborn, *Drafting the Russian Nation*; and David Alan Rich, *The Tsar's Colonels: Professionalism, Strategy, and Subversion in Late Imperial Russia* (Cambridge, MA: Harvard University Press, 1998). On the punitive conscription of Jewish men into the tsarist army beginning in 1827, see Olga Litvak, *Conscription and the Search for Modern Russian Jewry* (Bloomington: Indiana University Press, 2006).

14 Jones, *Red Army and Society*, 33.

15 See von Hagen, *Soldiers in the Proletarian Dictatorship*; Stone, *Hammer and Rifle*; Reese, *Stalin's Reluctant Soldiers*; Reese, *Soviet Military Experience*; Reese, *Red Commanders*; and Glantz, *Colossus Reborn*.

16 Jones, *Red Army and Society*, 36–7.

17 For example, L.V. Scott implies that losing access to its reserves in the Indian Army after 1948 was one reason Britain had to continue conscription after the war. See L.V. Scott, *Conscription and the Attlee Governments: The Politics and Policy of National Service, 1945–1951* (Oxford: Clarendon Press, 1993), 28.

18 Scott, *Conscription and the Attlee Governments*, 219. Interestingly, and quite the opposite of Soviet thinking on the matter, leftist opponents of universal service in Britain argued in part that military service had a corrupting influence on youth, with an opposition MP stating in 1946 that "it is an evil thing to hand over the youth of the country to the militarist people to be trained in the army." See Scott, *Conscription and the Attlee Governments*, 139.

19 Flynn, *Conscription and Democracy*, 68. By 1958, France had 300,000 troops in Algeria, 80 per cent of whom were conscripts, and many of those who returned became increasingly active in the French antiwar movement. See Flynn, *Conscription and Democracy*, 70. This dynamic is perhaps better compared to Soviet conscripts' and veterans' experiences in Afghanistan 30 years later than to the Soviet situation in the first decade after the Second World War.

20 George Q. Flynn, "Conscription and Equity in Western Democracies, 1940–75," *Journal of Contemporary History* 33, no. 1 (January 1998), 5, 18.

21 For a detailed discussion of these issues, see Ute Frevert, *A Nation in Barracks: Modern Germany, Military Conscription and Civil Society*, trans. Andres Boreham and Daniel Brückenhaus (New York: Berg, 2004), especially chapter 5.

22 On the American role in believing and perpetuating the bluff of Soviet postwar military strength (including the belief, prevalent until the Kennedy administration disproved it, that Soviet forces did not in fact demobilize at all after the war), see Matthew A. Evangelista, "Stalin's Post-War Army Reappraised," *International Security* 7 (Winter 1982–3), 110–38.

23 Roger D. Markwick and Euridice Charon Cardona, *Soviet Women on the Frontline in the Second World War* (New York: Palgrave Macmillan, 2012), 232.

24 Reese, *Soviet Military Experience*, 149; William McCagg, *Stalin Embattled, 1943–1948* (Detroit: Wayne State University Press, 1978), 19; and V.N. Donchenko, "Demobilizatsiia sovetskoi armii i reshenie problemy kadrov v pervye poslevoennye gody," *Istoriia SSSR*, 3 (1970).

25 Reese, *Soviet Military Experience*, 140.

26 On the particular brutalities of this war of annihilation, see Mark Edele and Michael Geyer, "States of Exception: The Nazi-Soviet War as a System of Violence, 1939–1945," in Michael Geyer and Sheila Fitzpatrick, eds., *Beyond Totalitarianism: Stalinism and Nazism Compared* (Cambridge: Cambridge University Press, 2009), 345–95.

27 Catherine Merridale, *Ivan's War: Life and Death in the Red Army, 1939–1945* (New York: Picador, 2006), 3.

28 Ibid., 100–2, 136–40, 209–10.

29 Maya Eichler, *Militarizing Men: Gender, Conscription, and War in Post-Soviet Russia* (Stanford, CA: Stanford University Press, 2012), 65.
30 On *dedovshchina*, see Natalie Gross, "Youth and the Army in the USSR in the 1980s," *Soviet Studies* 42, no. 3 (July 1990), 482.
31 Jason P. Gresh, "The Realities of Russian Military Conscription," *Journal of Slavic Military Studies* 24, no. 2 (April 2011), 191.
32 Andrew L. Spivak and William Alex Pridemore, "Conscription and Reform in the Russian Army," *Problems of Post-Communism* 51, no. 6 (Nov.–Dec. 2004), 34.
33 Sam Robertshaw, "Voluntary Organizations and Society-Military Relations in Contemporary Russia," *European Security* 24, no. 2 (2015), 306.
34 William E. Odom, *The Soviet Volunteers: Modernization and Bureaucracy in a Public Mass Organization* (Princeton, NJ: Princeton University Press, 1973), 3, 24–6. The Russian name was *Obshchestva druzei oborony i aviatsionno-khimicheskogo stroitel'stva.*
35 Ibid., 28–9.
36 Ibid., 308. In May 1948 Osoaviakhim split into three groups, DOSARM, DOSAV, and DOSFLOT – defence societies for the army, air force, and navy, respectively. Because of overlap and "parallelism" in their activities, however, these groups merged after only three years. In August 1951 the Council of Ministers of the USSR issued a directive to unite DOSARM, DOSAV, and DOSFLOT into one All-Union Voluntary Society for Cooperation with the Army, Aviation, and Navy (DOSAAF USSR). See *Sovetskaia voennaia entsiklopediia*, Vol. 3 (Moscow: Voenizdat, 1976–80), 256. On Osoaviakhim's role as a civilian defence organization during the Second World War, see G.M. Egorov, "Nadezhnyi pomoshchnik Sovetskikh Vooruzhennykh Sil (k 60-letiiu DOSAAF USSR)," *Voenno-istoricheskii zhurnal*, Vol. 1 (1987): 82–7.
37 Gosudarstvennyi arkhiv Rossiiskoi Federatsii (State Archive of the Russian Federation, GARF), Fond R-9552 (DOSAAF), op. 1, d. 44, ll. 29, 45.
38 *Sovetskaia voennaia entsiklopediia*, Vol. 3, 256.
39 Odom, *The Soviet Volunteers*, 122.
40 N. Kamanin, "Reshitel'no uluchshit' rabotu DOSAAF," *Kryl'ia rodiny*, February 1954, 3.
41 DOSAAF USSR, *DOSAAF – Rodine: Stat'i i ocherki o patrioticheskoi deiatel'nosti oboronnogo Obshchestva* (Moscow: Izd. DOSAAF, 1957), 207–8.
42 M. Arkadin, "Ezhenedel'no v piatnitsu," *Za oboronu*, January 1947, 26. See note 36 regarding the organization's name changes in 1948 and 1951. The society's official journal similarly underwent name changes: until July 1948 it was called *Za oboronu* (For Defence). In August 1948, after the society

had split from Osoaviakhim into DOSARM, DOSAV, and DOSFLOT, the (same) journal began publishing as *Voennye znaniia* (Military Knowledge).
43 See note 42.
44 "Slavnye sovetskie patriotki," *Voennye znaniia*, March 1951, 1.
45 GARF, Fond R-9552, op. 1, d. 44, l. 53. Emphasis mine.
46 GARF, Fond R-9552, op. 1, d. 44, l. 33.
47 GARF, Fond R-9552, op. 1, d. 44, l. 37.
48 GARF, Fond R-9552, op. 1, d. 43, l. 4.
49 V. Chumakov, "Nabolevshii vopros," *Voennye znaniia*, July 1954, 12.
50 V.I. Kuznetsov, "Novoe dobrovol'noe obshchestvo sovetskikh patriotov," *Za oboronu*, July 1948, 1.
51 "Voennye znaniia – v massy!" *Voennye znaniia*, August 1948, 1.
52 Georgii Mdivani, "Dolg i muzhestvo," *Voennye znaniia*, July 1950, 8.
53 GARF, Fond R-9552, op. 1, d. 44, l. 52.
54 M. Lebedinskii, "Parashiutist E. Naumenko pozorit zvanie Sovetskogo sportsmena," *Kryl'ia rodiny*, January 1954, 22.
55 "Parashiutist E. Naumenko pozorit zvanie Sovetskogo sportsmena" *Kryl'ia rodiny*, July 1954, 24.
56 Deborah A. Field, *Private Life and Communist Morality in Khrushchev's Russia* (New York: Peter Lang, 2007), 9. See also chapter 5.
57 "V bor'be za pervenstvo po voleibolu," *Sovetskii voin*, 10 June 1948, 21.
58 Reese, *Soviet Military Experience*, 138.
59 RGASPI, Fond M-1, op. 47, d. 309, l. 13.
60 RGASPI, Fond M-1, op. 47, d. 376, l. 35.
61 Fürst, *Stalin's Last Generation*, 16.
62 RGASPI, Fond M-1, op. 47, d. 271, l. 10.
63 RGASPI, Fond M-1, op. 47, d. 271, l. 10.
64 RGASPI, Fond M-1, op. 47, d. 376, l. 1, 26.
65 On Tajikistan: RGASPI, Fond M-1, op. 47, d. 376, l. 26. On Bashkiria: RGASPI, Fond M-1, op. 47, d. 406, l. 21. On Turkmenistan: RGASPI, Fond M-1, op. 47, d. 432, l. 9.
66 RGASPI, Fond M-1, op. 47, d. 376, l. 2.
67 RGASPI, Fond M-1, op. 47, d. 406, l. 23.
68 RGASPI, Fond M-1, op. 47, d. 432, l. 9.
69 RGASPI, Fond M-1, op. 47, d. 376, l. 2.
70 RGASPI, Fond M-1, op. 47, d. 432, l. 3.
71 RGASPI, Fond M-1, op. 47, d. 271, l. 3.
72 RGASPI, Fond M-1, op. 47, d. 329, l. 3.
73 RGASPI, Fond M-1, op. 47, d. 329, l. 3.
74 RGASPI, Fond M-1, op. 47, d. 329, l. 5.

75 In 1916, for example, imperial Russian authorities faced a serious revolt in Central Asia sparked by conscription laws, when attempts to increase troop strength during the war led the tsarist government to end exemptions for Kazakh and Kyrgyz men. See Sanborn, *Drafting the Russian Nation*, 35. After the revolution, the Bolsheviks viewed compulsory military service in Central Asia as a "means to legitimize Soviet power, promote fluency in the Russian language, integrate indigenous populations into a transborder political entity, promote social mobility, and shape local economies." See Erica Marat, *The Military and the State in Central Asia: From Red Army to Independence* (New York: Routledge, 2010), 14.
76 RGASPI, Fond M-1, op. 47, d. 376, l. 5.
77 RGASPI, Fond M-1, op. 47, d. 376, ll. 5–6
78 RGASPI, Fond M-1, op. 47, d. 376, l. 5.
79 RGASPI, Fond M-1, op. 47, d. 376, l. 6.
80 RGASPI, Fond M-1, op. 47, d. 376, ll. 8–9.
81 RGASPI, Fond M-1, op. 47, d. 329, l. 13.
82 RGASPI, Fond M-1, op. 47, d. 329, l. 14.
83 RGASPI, Fond M-1, op. 47, d. 329, ll. 21–2.
84 While histories of women in the Caucasus and Soviet Central Asia have proliferated recently, we need more work on masculinities in these regions. For one new study in this direction, see Brandon Gray Miller, "The New Soviet *Narkoman*: Drugs and Youth in Post-Stalinist Russia," *Region: Regional Studies of Russia, Eastern Europe, and Central Asia* 4, no. 1 (2015), 45–69.
85 RGASPI, Fond M-1, op. 47, d. 376, l. 31.
86 Sanborn, *Drafting the Russian Nation*, 24.
87 Harriet Fast Scott and William F. Scott, *The Armed Forces of the USSR* (Boulder, CO: Westview Press, 1984), 335.
88 Sanborn, *Drafting the Russian Nation*, 23.
89 Nina Tumarkin, *The Living and the Dead: The Rise and Fall of the Cult of World War II in Russia* (New York: Basic Books, 1994), 104; and Merridale, *Ivan's War*, 362.
90 Juliane Fürst, "Introduction: To Drop or Not to Drop?" in Juliane Fürst and Josie McLellan, eds., *Dropping Out of Socialism: The Creation of Alternative Spheres in the Soviet Bloc* (New York: Lexington Books, 2017), 3.
91 In reviewing all issues of *Za oboronu* and *Voennye znaniia* from 1945 to 1965, I have found that conscription as both a word and a concept does not appear until January 1954.
92 V. Ryl'nikov, "Kliatva na vernost' rodine," *Voennye znaniia*, January 1954, 5.
93 A. Arsen'ev, "Vernost' voinskomu dolgu," *Voennye znaniia*, March 1954, 2.

94 Josephine Woll, *The Cranes Are Flying: The Film Companion* (London and New York: I.B. Tauris, 2003), 28.
95 William T. Lee and Richard F. Staar, *Soviet Military Policy since World War II* (Stanford University Press, 1986), 15–16. On the Soviet revolution in military affairs from 1953 to 1960, see also Harriet Fast Scott, "Soviet Military Doctrine in the Nuclear Age, 1945–85," in Willard C. Frank Jr. and Philip S. Gillette, eds., *Soviet Military Doctrine from Lenin to Gorbachev, 1915–1991* (Westport, CT: Greenwood Press, 1992), 177.
96 Not all these numbers were reached. In particular, the January 1960 effort was suspended because of the Berlin crisis. See Matthew Evangelista, "'Why Keep Such an Army?' Khrushchev's Troop Reductions," *Cold War International History Project*, Working Paper no. 19 (Dec. 1997), 5.
97 N.S. Khrushchev, *Khrushchev Remembers*, trans. Strobe Talbott (Boston: Little, Brown & Co., 1970), 516.
98 Col. P. Popov, "Nastoichivo izuchat' voennoe delo," *Kryl'ia rodiny*, February 1957, 6.
99 On the military's concerns about career options as well as social welfare for officers demobilized in Khrushchev's cuts, see Evangelista, "Why Keep Such an Army?" 9–13.
100 RGASPI, Fond M-1, op. 47, d. 405, l. 8.
101 RGASPI, Fond M-1, op. 47, d. 405, l. 1, 17.
102 RGASPI, Fond M-1, op. 47, d. 415, ll. 8–12.
103 RGASPI, Fond M-1, op. 3, d. 1041, ll. 16–17.
104 RGASPI, Fond M-1, op. 3, d. 1041, ll. 16–17.
105 RGASPI, Fond M-1, op. 3, d. 1041, l. 16.
106 RGASPI, Fond M-1, op. 3, d. 1041, l. 17.
107 Jones, *Red Army and Society*, 32.
108 Fürst, *Stalin's Last Generation*, 168.

**Chapter 2**

1 Gosudarstvennyi arkhiv Rossiiskoi Federatsii (State Archive of the Russian Federation, GARF), Fond R-9552 (DOSAAF), op. 17, d. 43, l. 21.
2 GARF, Fond R-9552, op. 17, d. 43, l. 22.
3 GARF, Fond R-9552, op. 17, d. 43, l. 41.
4 GARF, Fond R-9552, op. 17, d. 43, ll. 19–20.
5 Serhy Yekelchyk, "The Civic Duty to Hate: Stalinist Citizenship as Political Practice and Civic Emotion (Kiev, 1943–53)," *Kritika: Explorations in Russian and Eurasian History* 7, no. 3 (Summer 2006), 556.

6 GARF, Fond R-9552, op. 17, d. 43, l. 21.
7 GARF, Fond R-9552, op. 17, d. 43, ll. 21–3.
8 Rossiiskii gosudarstvennyi arkhiv sotsial'no-politicheskoi istorii (Russian State Archive of Socio-Political History, RGASPI), Fond M-1 (Komsomol Archive), op. 47, d. 432, l. 4. On hooliganism, see Brian LaPierre, *Hooligans in Khrushchev's Russia: Defining, Policing, and Producing Deviance during the Thaw* (Madison, WI: University of Wisconsin Press, 2012).
9 GARF, Fond R-9552, op. 17, d. 43, l. 41.
10 Sergei Okhliabinin, *Povsednevnaia zhizn': Russkoi armii vo vremena Suvorovskykh voin* (Moscow: Molodaia gvardiia, 2004), 7.
11 *KPSS o Vooruzhennykh silakh sovetskogo soiuza: Dokumenty 1917–1981* (Moscow: Voennoe izdatel'stvo, 1981), 334–5. There was also an option for students to complete eight years at a general secondary school and then move to a Suvorov school for the final two years, although this was not part of the 1943 decree. See Ellen Jones, *Red Army and Society: A Sociology of the Soviet Military* (Boston: Allen and Unwin, 1985), 86–7.
12 RGASPI, Fond M-1, op. 47, d. 184, ll. 42–3.
13 Jones, *Red Army and Society*, 86.
14 RGASPI, Fond M-1, op. 47, d. 184, l. 42.
15 RGASPI, Fond M-1, op. 47, d. 185, l. 40.
16 RGASPI, Fond M-1, op. 47, d. 184, ll. 42–3.
17 Okhliabinin, *Povsednevnaia zhizn'*, 7.
18 Jones, *Red Army and Society*, 85.
19 See Jones, *Red Army and Society*, especially chapter 6.
20 Elena Zubkova, *Russia after the War: Hopes, Illusions, and Disappointments, 1945–1957*, trans. Hugh Ragsdale (New York: M.E. Sharpe, 1998), 21.
21 Lisa Kirschenbaum, *Small Comrades: Revolutionizing Childhood in Soviet Russia, 1917–1932* (New York: Routledge, 2001), 54.
22 RGASPI, Fond M-1, op. 47, d. 185, l. 53.
23 RGASPI, Fond M-1, op. 47, d. 185, ll. 39–40.
24 RGASPI, Fond M-1, op. 47, d. 185, l. 40. The 1943 decree establishing the schools promised that the government would pay all expenses for Suvorov students. Either this provision had changed by 1945, or administrative documents wanted to portray mothers as eager to ensure their sons got in. See *KPSS o Vooruzhennykh silakh*, 335.
25 RGASPI, Fond M-1, op. 47, d. 185, l. 126.
26 RGASPI, Fond M-1, op. 47, d. 185, l. 126.
27 RGASPI, Fond M-1, op. 47, d. 185, l. 126.
28 RGASPI, Fond M-1, op. 47, d. 185, l. 126.

29 RGASPI, Fond M-1, op. 47, d. 185, ll. 128–9.
30 RGASPI, Fond M-1, op. 47, d. 185, l. 130.
31 RGASPI, Fond M-1, op. 47, d. 185, l. 128.
32 RGASPI, Fond M-1, op. 47, d. 185, l. 128.
33 RGASPI, Fond M-1, op. 47, d. 185, l. 128. It is unclear from the document whether the multiple quotations attributed to Student Kh. were from the same person or not, but due to differences in tone and content in the answers, I am inclined to think they were from different students with the same name.
34 E. Thomas Ewing, "The Repudiation of Single-Sex Education: Boys' Schools in the Soviet Union, 1943–1954," *American Educational Research Journal* 43, no. 4 (Winter 2006), 622.
35 Ibid., 626.
36 Ibid., 627.
37 Anna Krylova, *Soviet Women in Combat: A History of Violence on the Eastern Front* (Cambridge: Cambridge University Press, 2010), 217.
38 E. Thomas Ewing, *Separate Schools: Gender, Policy, and Practice in Postwar Soviet Education* (DeKalb: Northern Illinois University Press, 2010), 147–8 and chapter 4 overall, "The Problem of Order – Boys' Schools in Crisis."
39 On the pre-Petrine origins of the practice, see Horace W. Dewey, "Political *poruka* in Muscovite Rus'," *Russian Review* 46, no. 2 (April 1987), 117–33. On its use by the nineteenth-century peasantry, see Jeffrey Burds, *Peasant Dreams and Market Politics: Labor Migration and the Russian Village, 1861–1905* (Pittsburgh: University of Pittsburgh Press, 1998). On Soviet collective surveillance, see Oleg Kharkhordin, *The Collective and the Individual in Russia: A Study of Practices* (Berkeley: University of California Press, 1999), 110–17.
40 RGASPI, Fond M-1, op. 47, d. 185, l. 148.
41 RGASPI, Fond M-1, op. 47, d. 185, l. 149.
42 RGASPI, Fond M-1, op. 47, d. 185, l. 150.
43 See Dan Healey, *Homosexual Desire in Revolutionary Russia: The Regulation of Sexual and Gender Dissent* (Chicago: University of Chicago Press, 2001), and Dan Healey, "Comrades, Queers and 'Oddballs': Sodomy, Masculinity and Gendered Violence in Leningrad Province of the 1950s," *Journal of the History of Sexuality* 21, no. 3 (Sept. 2012), 496–522.
44 RGASPI, Fond M-1, op. 47, d. 185, l. 140.
45 *Krokodil*, 30 December 1951, 3.
46 *Krokodil*, 20 February 1953, 2.
47 GARF, Fond R-9552, op. 1, d. 44, l. 60.
48 "Voennye znaniia – v massy!," 1.

49 RGASPI, Fond M-1, op. 47, d. 185, l. 52.
50 RGASPI, Fond M-1, op. 47, d. 185, l. 152.
51 RGASPI, Fond M-1, op. 47, d. 185, l. 53–4.
52 RGASPI, Fond M-1, op. 47, d. 185, l. 56.
53 E. Mikhalenkov, "Moral'nyi oblik Sovetskogo aviatsionnogo sportsmena: Byt' gotovym k oborone sotsialisticheskogo otechestva," *Kryl'ia rodiny*, March 1954, 2.
54 See Serguei Alex. Oushakine, "Vidimost' muzhestvennosti," *Znamia*, Vol. 2 (1999), 131–44; and Marina Yusupova, "Shifting Masculine Terrains: Russian Men in Russia and the UK" (PhD diss., University of Manchester, 2016), 80.
55 GARF, Fond R-9552, op. 1, d. 64, l. 10.
56 B. Aminov, "Komsomol'tsy – aktivisty Dosaafa," *Kryl'ia rodiny*, April 1952, 7
57 "Chto meshaet razvitiiu massovogo parashiutizma: pis'mo v redaktsiiu," *Kryl'ia rodiny*, May 1954, 9.
58 RGASPI, Fond M-1, op. 47, d. 185, l. 157.
59 RGASPI, Fond M-1, op. 47, d. 185, ll. 43–5.
60 "Za vysokuiu distsiplinu v aviatsionnykh klubakh," *Kryl'ia rodiny*, December 1955, 1. Other references to lack of preparation and disciplinary infractions among DOSAAF instructors in this publication include "Na strazhe mira," *Kryl'ia rodiny*, February 1952, 2; and "Chto prodolzhaet meshat' razvitiiu planerizma: Pis'mo v redaktsiiu uchastnikov XIX Vsesoiuznykh planernykh sorevnovanii," *Kryl'ia rodiny*, September 1953, 3.
61 RGASPI, Fond M-1, op. 47, d. 185, l. 52.
62 Mark von Hagen, *Soldiers in the Proletarian Dictatorship: The Red Army and the Soviet Socialist State, 1917–1930* (Ithaca, NY: Cornell University Press, 1990), 331.
63 Mark T. Hooker, *The Military Uses of Literature: Fiction and the Armed Forces in the Soviet Union* (Westport, CT: Praeger, 1996), 75.
64 RGASPI, Fond M-1, op. 47, d. 309, l. 3.
65 See Catriona Kelly, "'Thank You for the Wonderful Book': Soviet Child Readers and the Management of Children's Reading, 1950–75," *Kritika: Explorations in Russian and Eurasian History* 6, no. 4 (Fall 2005), 740.
66 Juliane Fürst, *Stalin's Last Generation: Soviet Post-War Youth and the Emergence of Mature Socialism* (Oxford: Oxford University Press, 2010), 142.
67 Ibid.
68 Denise J. Youngblood, *Russian War Films: On the Cinema Front, 1914–2005* (Lawrence, KS: University Press of Kansas, 2007), 90–1. On ways of analysing Polevoi's story through the lens of disability and the portrayals

of war wounds, see Elena Iarskaia-Smirnova and Pavel Romanov, "Heroes and Spongers: The Iconography of Disability in Soviet Posters and Film," in Michael Rassell and Elena Iarskaia-Smirnova, eds., *Disability in Eastern Europe and the Former Soviet Union: History, Policy and Everyday Life* (New York: Routledge, 2014), 77; Sarah D. Phillips, "'There Are No Invalids in the USSR!': A Missing Soviet Chapter in the New Disability History," *Disability Studies Quarterly* 29, no. 3 (2009); and Lilya Kaganovsky, *How the Soviet Man Was Unmade: Cultural Fantasy and Male Subjectivity under Stalin* (Pittsburgh: University of Pittsburgh Press, 2008), especially chapter 5.

69 Josephine Woll, *Real Images: Soviet Cinema and the Thaw* (New York: I.B. Tauris, 2000), 72–3.

70 Marina Balina, "Prose after Stalin," in Evgeny Dobrenko and Marina Balina, eds., *The Cambridge Companion to Twentieth-Century Russian Literature* (Cambridge: Cambridge University Press, 2011), 156; and Hooker, *Military Uses of Literature*, 9.

71 Hooker, *Military Uses of Literature*, 8.

72 Ibid., 9.

73 Ibid., 10–11.

74 Ibid., 11.

75 *Maxim Perepelitsa* (Maxim Perepelitsa, 1955), Dir. Anatolii Granik.

76 Ibid.

77 Nicholas Galichenko, *Glasnost – Soviet Cinema Responds* (Austin: University of Texas Press, 1991), 32.

78 *The Soldier Ivan Brovkin* (Soldat Ivan Brovkin, 1955). Dir. Ivan Lukinskii.

79 Woll, *Real Images*, 15.

80 "Neudachnyi fil'm: Pisem o *Maxim Perepelitsa*," *Krasnaia zvezda*, 5 February 1956, 3.

81 Woll, *Real Images*, 14–15.

82 *Maxim Perepelitsa*.

83 Ibid. The lyric in Russian is: "*Soldaty, v put', v put', v put'! A dlia tebia, rodnaia, est' pochta polevaia.*"

84 *Soldier Ivan Brovkin*.

85 Mikhail Andronov, "Devuch'ia liricheskaia," *Kryl'ia rodiny*, March 1956, 25.

86 Galina Brailovskaia, "Synu," *Kryl'ia rodiny*, April 1956, 16.

87 Natal'ia Makarenko, "Ia – letchika zhena," *Kryl'ia rodiny*, July 1957, 7.

88 On women's aviation before the war, see Karen Petrone, *Life Has Become More Joyous, Comrades: Celebrations in the Time of Stalin* (Bloomington, IN: Indiana University Press, 2000). Petrone's arguments are discussed in more detail in chapter 5.

89 Thomas G. Schrand, "Socialism in One Gender: Masculine Values in the Stalin Revolution," in Barbara Evans Clements, Rebecca Friedman, and Dan Healey, eds., *Russian Masculinities in History and Culture* (New York: Palgrave, 2002), 196. See also Eric Naiman, *Sex in Public: The Incarnation of Early Soviet Ideology* (Princeton, NJ: Princeton University Press, 1997).
90 V. Leonov, "Rasskazy o voinskoi sluzhbe: Sovetskoe voiskovoe tovarishchestvo," *Voennye znaniia*, October 1950, 8.

**Chapter 3**

1 *Krokodil*, 10 July 1963, 16.
2 Serguei Alex. Oushakine, "Laughter under Socialism: Exposing the Ocular in Soviet Jocularity," *Slavic Review* 70, no. 2 (Summer 2011), 249.
3 On this view, see Janet G. Tucker, "Introduction: Parody, Satire and Intertextuality in Russian Literature," in Janet G. Tucker, ed., *Against the Grain: Parody, Satire, and Intertextuality in Russian Literature* (Bloomington, IN: Slavica, 2002), 16.
4 For example, see the interview excerpts with Soviet cartoonists throughout Frank Althaus and Mark Sutcliffe, eds., *Drawing the Curtain: The Cold War in Cartoons* (London: Fontanka, 2012).
5 Victoria E. Bonnell, *Iconography of Power: Soviet Political Posters under Lenin and Stalin* (Berkeley and Los Angeles: University of California Press, 1997), 3; Chonghoon Lee, "Visual Stalinism from the Perspective of Heroisation: Posters, Paintings, and Illustrations in the 1930s," *Totalitarian Movements and Political Religions* 8, nos. 3–4 (Sept.–Dec. 2007), 503–4. On the role of posters from the Civil War era in particular, see Stephen White, *The Bolshevik Poster* (New Haven: Yale University Press, 1988).
6 For a Cold War–era view of Soviet cartoons in *Pravda* and *Izvestiia* solely as sources of propaganda, see Michael M. Milenkovitch, *The View from Red Square: A Critique of Cartoons from Pravda and Izvestiia, 1947–1964* (New York: Hobbs, Dorman and Co., 1966).
7 Rodger Swearingen, *What's So Funny, Comrade?* (New York: Praeger, 1961), 3; Vladimir Kazanevsky, "The History of the Cartoon in the USSR," *Humor* 8, no. 2 (1995), 168–9.
8 William Nelson, ed., *Out of the Crocodile's Mouth: Russian Cartoons about the United States from "Krokodil," Moscow's Humor Magazine* (Washington, DC: Public Affairs Press, 1949), 8.
9 Sheila Fitzpatrick, *Everyday Stalinism: Ordinary Life in Extraordinary Times: Soviet Russia in the 1930s* (Oxford: Oxford University Press, 2000), 29.

10 Michael Mulkay, *On Humor: Its Nature and Its Place in Modern Society* (Cambridge: Polity Press, 1988), 1, 217.
11 Emil Draitser, *Making War, Not Love: Gender and Sexuality in Russian Humor* (New York: St. Martin's Press, 1999), 5. On Cold War political cartoons in other contexts, see Belinda Carstens-Wickham, "Gender in Cartoons of German Unification," *Journal of Women's History* 10, no. 1 (Spring 1998), 127–56; Jonathan A. Becker, "The Disappearing Enemy: The Image of the United States in Soviet Political Cartoons," *Journalism and Mass Communication Quarterly* 73, no. 3 (Autumn 1996), 609–19; and Randall L. Bytwerk, "The Dolt Laughs: Satirical Publications under Hitler and Honecker," *Journalism Quarterly* 69, no. 4 (Winter 1992), 1029–38. On the varied uses of ethnic caricatures in East European history, see Dagnosław Demski and Kamila Baraniecka-Olszewska, eds., *Images of the Other in Ethnic Caricatures of Central and Eastern Europe* (Biblioteka Etnografi i Polskiej, no. 59. Warsaw: Institute of Archaeology and Ethnology, Polish Academy of Sciences, 2010).
12 See Stephen M. Norris, "The Sharp Weapon of Soviet Laughter: Boris Efimov and Visual Humor," *Russian Literature* 74, nos. 1–2 (July 2013), 31–62; and Althaus and Sutcliffe, eds., *Drawing the Curtain*.
13 For a detailed discussion of these issues, see Deborah A. Field, *Private Life and Communist Morality in Khrushchev's Russia* (New York: Peter Lang, 2007); and Igor S. Kon, *The Sexual Revolution in Russia: From the Age of the Czars to Today*, trans. James Riordan (New York: The Free Press, 1995), especially chapter 5, "Sexophobia in Action." For an engaging personal account of these issues, see Cathy Young, *Growing Up in Moscow: Memories of a Soviet Girlhood* (New York: Ticknor and Fields, 1989).
14 Kon, *The Sexual Revolution in Russia*, 80.
15 Ibid., 70.
16 On painting, see Susan E. Reid, "Masters of the Earth: Gender and Destalinization in Soviet Reformist Painting of the Khrushchev Thaw," *Gender and History* 11, no. 2 (July 1999), 277.
17 Dan Healey, "From Stalinist Pariahs to Subjects of 'Managed Democracy': Queers in Moscow 1945 to the Present," in Matt Cook and Jennifer V. Evans, eds., *Queer Cities, Queer Cultures: Europe since 1945* (New York: Bloomsbury, 2014), 95–6.
18 Mulkay, *On Humor*, 122.
19 Gershon Legman, quoted in Draitser, *Making War, Not Love*, 203.
20 Draitser, *Making War, Not Love*, 14.
21 *Krokodil*, 30 July 1945, 1.
22 *Krokodil*, 30 April 1948, 7.

23 *Krokodil*, 30 December 1949, 9.
24 *Krokodil*, 20 March 1950, 5.
25 *Krokodil*, 10 July 1961, 9.
26 Steven J. Brady, "The U.S. Congress and German-American Relations," in Detlef Junker, ed., *The United States and Germany in the Era of the Cold War, Vol. 1* (Cambridge: Cambridge University Press, 2004), 136.
27 *Krokodil*, 20 August 1953, 2. Literally, "You are starting the dance on the wrong foot," the caption was a reference to a common Russian phrase.
28 *Krokodil*, 30 March 1946, 12.
29 *Krokodil*, 30 May 1951, 5.
30 *Krokodil*, 10 April 1963, 16.
31 *Krokodil*, 10 June 1950, 9.
32 *Krokodil*, 20 October 1953, 16.
33 *Krokodil*, 30 December 1958, 16.
34 *Krokodil*, 30 December 1949, 8.
35 From the minutes of the Third Conference of the Cominform: "The brutality with which staunch fighters for Communism are being exterminated in Yugoslavia is comparable only to the atrocities of the Hitlerite fascists or of the butchers Tsaldaris in Greece and Franco in Spain." See Fondazione Giangiacomo Feltrinelli, ed., *The Cominform: Minutes of the Three Conferences, 1947/1948/1949, Volume 24* (Milan: Feltrinelli Editore, 1994), 841.
36 *Krokodil*, 30 December 1950, 9.
37 *Krokodil*, 10 February 1946, 3.
38 Elizabeth A. Wood, "Prostitution Unbound: Representations of Sexual and Political Anxieties in Postrevolutionary Russia," in Jane T. Costlow, Stephanie Sandler, and Judith Vowles, eds,. *Sexuality and the Body in Russian Culture* (Stanford, CA: Stanford University Press, 1998), 126.
39 Jacqueline Tavernier-Courbin, "Humor Is a Serious Matter," *Thalia: Studies in Literary Humor* 8, no. 2 (Fall/Winter 1985), 16.
40 Dan Healey, *Homosexual Desire in Revolutionary Russia: The Regulation of Sexual and Gender Dissent* (Chicago: University of Chicago Press, 2001), 182.
41 Bonnell, *Iconography of Power*, 197.
42 Ibid., 263.
43 Polly Jones, "Reimagining the Enemy: Soviet Images of the West after the Second World War," in Althaus and Sutcliffe, eds., *Drawing the Curtain*, 24.
44 Reid, "Masters of the Earth," 284.
45 For further discussion of Marianne's image, see Maurice Agulhon, *Marianne into Battle: Republican Imagery and Symbolism in France, 1789–1880*, trans. Janet Lloyd (Cambridge: Cambridge University Press, 1981).

46 *Krokodil*, 30 October 1949, 3.
47 Lynn Visson, quoted in Draitser, *Making War, Not Love*, 84.
48 *Krokodil*, 20 January 1955, 1.
49 *Krokodil*, 30 January 1958, 1.
50 Wendy C. Nielsen, *Women Warriors in Romantic Drama* (Newark: University of Delaware Press, 2013), 136–7.
51 *Krokodil*, 10 February 1963, 12.
52 *Krokodil*, 20 June 1949, 5. "There's many a slip 'twixt cup and lip" is an approximate English translation of the proverb, "*I vidit oko, tol'ko zub neimët.*" One might also translate *mir* as either "world" or "peace" in the context of this poem.
53 *Krokodil*, 20 February 1951, 1.
54 Bonnell, *Iconography of Power*, 41.
55 *Krokodil*, 20 October 1952, 1.
56 See Lucy Candib and Richard Schmitt, "About Losing It: The Fear of Impotence," in Larry May, Robert Strikwerda, and Patrick D. Hopkins, eds., *Rethinking Masculinity: Philosophical Explorations in Light of Feminism*, 2nd ed. (London: Rowman and Littlefield, 1996).
57 *Krokodil*, 20 August 1949, 1.
58 Eric Hobsbawm, "Man and Woman in Socialist Iconography," *History Workshop Journal* 6, no. 1 (October 1978), 125–6. Women did continue to appear in a limited capacity after this time, but Hobsbawm notes that men always represented industrial labour, the most important role in socialism.
59 Toby Clark, "The 'New Man's' Body: A Motif in Early Soviet Culture," in Matthew Cullerne Bown and Brandon Taylor, eds., *Art of the Soviets: Painting, Sculpture, and Architecture in a One-Party State, 1917–1992* (Manchester, UK: Manchester University Press, 1993), 46.
60 *Krokodil*, 10 July 1954, 3.
61 On policymakers' concerns about wartime conditions affecting the health of conscription-age men from the end of the war through much of the 1950s, see chapter 1. On the discrepancy between healthy men in visual imagery and persistent health conditions in early Soviet reality, see Clark, "The 'New Man's' Body," 46.
62 For detailed discussions of this variety of interpretations and forms, see Lilya Kaganovsky, *How the Soviet Man Was Unmade: Cultural Fantasy and Male Subjectivity under Stalin* (Pittsburgh: University of Pittsburgh Press, 2008); Michael Rassell and Elena Iarskaia-Smirnova, eds., *Disability in Eastern Europe and the Former Soviet Union: History, Policy and Everyday Life* (New York: Routledge, 2014); Anna Krylova, "'Healers of Wounded Souls': The Crisis of Private Life in Soviet Literature, 1944–1946," *Journal of Modern*

*History* 73, no. 2 (June 2001), 307–31; and Claire E. McCallum, "Scorched by the Fire of War: Masculinity, War Wounds and Disability in Soviet Visual Culture, 1941–65," *Slavonic and East European Review* 93, no. 2 (2015), 251–85.

63 McCallum, "Scorched by the Fire of War," 284–5.

64 Carstens-Wickham, "Gender in Cartoons of German Unification," 128.

65 Kazanevsky, "The History of the Cartoon in the USSR," 168.

**Chapter 4**

1 Andrei Sakharov, *Memoirs*, trans. Richard Lourie (New York: Alfred A. Knopf, 1990), 194.

2 E.L. Feinberg, "Sud'ba rossiiskogo intelligenta," in A.F. Andreev, ed., *Kapitsa, Tamm, Semenov: V ocherkakh i pis'makh* (Moscow: Izd. Vagrius, 1998), 242–3.

3 The Prometheus metaphor is not uncommon in nuclear science. For a further exploration of this imagery, see Kai Bird and Martin J. Sherwin, *American Prometheus: The Triumph and Tragedy of J. Robert Oppenheimer* (New York: Vintage Books, 2006).

4 M.A. Markov and A.N. Gorbunov, eds., *Vospominaniia o V. I. Vekslere* (Moscow: Nauka, 1987), 252.

5 Paul R. Josephson, *Red Atom: Russia's Nuclear Power Program from Stalin to Today* (Pittsburgh: University of Pittsburgh Press, 2005), 2–3.

6 On personal narratives empowering historically disenfranchised subjects, see Mary Jo Maynes, Jennifer L. Pierce, and Barbara Laslett, *Telling Stories: The Use of Personal Narratives in the Social Sciences and History* (Ithaca, NY: Cornell University Press, 2008), 1–2. On the term "ego-documents," see Mary Fulbrook and Ulinka Rublack, "In Relation: The 'Social Self' and Ego-Documents," *German History* 28, no. 3 (2010), 264. Terminology can be slippery for this genre of documents overall, however. Despite the fact that Sakharov labelled his text as "memoirs" while Ginzburg called his an "autobiography," for example, I have chosen to group them together under the defining principle that in each narrative, "the author is also the main character." See Sigurður Gylfi Magnússon, "Gender: A Useful Category in the Analysis of Ego-Documents?" *Scandinavian Journal of History* 38, no. 2 (2013), 203.

7 Peter Middleton, *The Inward Gaze: Masculinity and Subjectivity in Modern Culture* (London: Routledge, 1992), 12.

8 David Holloway, *Stalin and the Bomb: The Soviet Union and Atomic Energy, 1939–1956* (New Haven and London: Yale University Press, 1994), 196–7;

Alexei B. Kojevnikov, *Stalin's Great Science: The Times and Adventures of Soviet Physicists* (London: Imperial College Press, 2004), 152–3; Veniamin Tsukerman and Zinaida Azarkh, *Arzamas-16 – Soviet Scientists in the Nuclear Age: A Memoir*, trans. Timothy Sergay (Nottingham: Bramcote Press, 1999), ix–x. In 1996, the town reclaimed its historic name, Sarov.

9 Maynes et al., *Telling Stories*, 12.

10 See Jochen Hellbeck, *Revolution on My Mind: Writing a Diary under Stalin* (Cambridge, MA: Harvard University Press, 2006); and Igal Halfin, *Terror in My Soul: Communist Autobiographies on Trial* (Cambridge, MA: Harvard University Press, 2003).

11 Ethan Pollock, *Stalin and the Soviet Science Wars* (Princeton, NJ: Princeton University Press, 2006), 85.

12 David Holloway, "How the Bomb Saved Soviet Physics," *The Bulletin of the Atomic Scientists* 50, no. 6 (1994), 46.

13 Paul R. Josephson, "Atomic-Powered Communism: Nuclear Culture in the Postwar USSR," *Slavic Review* 55, no. 2 (1996), 304. For a fascinating comparative account of Soviet and American communities that formed around nuclear production sites, see Kate Brown, *Plutopia: Nuclear Families, Atomic Cities, and the Great Soviet and American Plutonium Disasters* (Oxford: Oxford University Press, 2013).

14 Much of Khrushchev-era science was dominated by the persecution of geneticists for attempting to denounce Communist Party favourite Trofim Lysenko, who insisted that ideology could be transmitted genetically. See David Joravsky, *The Lysenko Affair* (Cambridge, MA: Harvard University Press, 1970); Valerii N. Soifer, *Lysenko and the Tragedy of Soviet Science*, trans. Leo Gruliow and Rebecca Gruliow (New Brunswick, NJ: Rutgers University Press, 1994); Nikolai Krementsov, *Stalinist Science* (Princeton, NJ: Princeton University Press, 1997); and Peter Kneen, "Physics, Genetics and the Zhdanovshchina," *Europe-Asia Studies* 50, no. 7 (Nov. 1998), 1183–202.

15 See Asif Siddiqi, "Scientists and Specialists in the Gulag: Life and Death in Stalin's *Sharashka*," *Kritika: Explorations in Russian and Eurasian History* 16, no. 3 (Summer 2015), 557–88; Asif Siddiqi, "The Sharashka Phenomenon," *Russian History Blog*, 10 March 2011, http://russianhistoryblog.org/2011/03/the-sharashka-phenomenon; and Kojevnikov, *Stalin's Great Science*, 156. In literature and memoirs, Alexander Solzhenitsyn's *The First Circle* famously chronicled this phenomenon; other survivor stories include L.L. Kerber, *Tupolev* (St. Petersburg: Politekhnika, 1999); Dimitri Panin, *The Notebooks of Sologdin* (London: Hutchinson, 1976); and Aleksandr Aleksandrovich Baev, *Ocherki. Perepiska. Vospominaniia* (Moscow: Nauka, 1998).

16 Holloway, "How the Bomb Saved Soviet Physics," 48.
17 R.W. Connell, *Masculinities*, 2nd ed. (Berkeley and Los Angeles: University of California Press, 2005), 78–9.
18 Sakharov, *Memoirs*, 42.
19 Ibid., 69. Emphasis in the original.
20 Vitaly L. Ginzburg, *On Superconductivity and Superfluidity: A Scientific Autobiography* (Berlin and Heidelberg: Springer-Verlag, 2009), 144.
21 Sakharov, *Memoirs*, 119. While Arzamas was not a *sharashka*, it was a closed city and curtailed freedom of movement for its inhabitants. For a deep reading of life in the closed cities of Ozersk and its counterpart of Richland, Washington, in the United States, both secret centres of plutonium production, see Brown, *Plutopia*.
22 Iu.B. Khariton, B.V. Adamskii, Iu.A. Romanov, et al., "Glazami fizikov Arzamasa-16," in Andreev, *Kapitsa, Tamm, Semenov*, 312–13.
23 Sakharov, *Memoirs*, 96.
24 Roald Z. Sagdeev, *The Making of a Soviet Scientist: My Adventures in Nuclear Fusion and Space from Stalin to Star Wars* (New York: John Wiley and Sons, 1994), 55. Jay Bergman also uses the word "conscription" to describe physicists' lack of choice in conducting research for the military. See Jay Bergman, *Meeting the Demands of Reason: The Life and Thought of Andrei Sakharov* (Ithaca, NY: Cornell University Press, 2009), 36.
25 Sagdeev, *The Making of a Soviet Scientist*, 55.
26 Yuri Orlov, *Opasnye mysli: memuary iz russkoi zhizni* (Moscow: Argumenty i fakty, 1992), 93.
27 *Krokodil*, 28 February 1953, 3.
28 Ginzburg, *On Superconductivity and Superfluidity*, 155.
29 Markov and Gorbunov, eds., *Vospominaniia o V. I. Vekslere*, 252.
30 Sakharov, *Memoirs*, 194–5.
31 Richard S. Esbenshade, "Remembering to Forget: Memory, History, and National Identity in Postwar East-Central Europe," *Representations* 49 (1995), 73, 77.
32 Bird and Sherwin, *American Prometheus*, 350.
33 Connell, *Masculinities*, 106.
34 The term "complicit masculinity" is Connell's. She further defines the patriarchal dividend as "the advantage to men as a group of maintaining an unequal gender order." See Raewyn Connell, *Gender*, 2nd ed. (Cambridge: Polity Press, 2009), 142.
35 Sakharov's second marriage to activist Elena Bonner lasted from 1972 until his death in 1989. She wrote her own fascinating memoir of their dissident

activities: *Alone Together: The Story of Elena Bonner and Andrei Sakharov's Internal Exile in the Soviet Union* (New York: Vintage Books, 1988).

36 This is not to indict Sakharov for calling his wife in a text the name by which he knew her in life; nevertheless, to my knowledge, he used diminutive names in the memoir only with Klavdiia Alekseevna and with his second wife, Bonner (whom he called Lusia), as well as with some of the women with whom he worked. The men in his narrative were almost always called by their surnames.

37 Sakharov, *Memoirs*, 58.

38 Ibid., 134.

39 Orlov, *Opasnye mysli*, 105.

40 Ibid., 133. Orlov also referred to Ira only by the diminutive form of her name.

41 Ibid., 143–4.

42 Sagdeev, *The Making of a Soviet Scientist*, 79–80.

43 Marrying women defined only by their association to the narrator's physicist colleagues was not confined to the Soviet side of the Cold War or to these particular narratives: in their biography of J. Robert Oppenheimer, Bird and Sherwin title a chapter on Oppenheimer's future wife after an alleged quote: "I'm Going to Marry a Friend of Yours, Steve." Bird and Sherwin, *American Prometheus*, 153.

44 Sagdeev, *The Making of a Soviet Scientist*, 81.

45 Sakharov, *Memoirs*, 109. Sakharov refers to Arzamas-16 in his memoirs as "the Installation" [*Ob"ekt*], as all its residents generally did. For the rest of his life, Sakharov apparently never used the words "Arzamas-16" or even "Sarov," the town's historic name (and the one it started to use again in 1996). See Gennady Gorelik and Antonina W. Bouis, *The World of Andrei Sakharov: A Russian Physicist's Path to Freedom* (Oxford: Oxford University Press, 2005), 149.

46 Nikolay M. Yanev, "In Memory of N.A. Dmitriev," *Pliska Studia Mathematica* 24 (2015), 13–20, http://www.math.bas.bg/pliska/Pliska-24/Pliska-24-2015-013-020.pdf.

47 Alexander Vucinich, *Empire of Knowledge: The Academy of Sciences of the USSR (1917–1970)* (Berkeley and Los Angeles: University of California Press, 1984), 293.

48 Jill M. Bystydzienski and Sharon R. Bird, "Introduction," in Bystydzienski and Bird, eds., *Removing Barriers: Women in Academic Science, Technology, Engineering, and Mathematics* (Bloomington: Indiana University Press, 2006), 6.

49 Sakharov, *Memoirs*, 112. In the English version of the text, "boys" was placed in quotation marks, although not in the Russian version

(*mal'chiki*). See Andrei Sakharov, *Vospominaniia* (Moscow: Izdatel'stvo imeni Chekhova, 1990), 152. In both, however, Sakharov's usage of a term denoting a junior form of masculinity is interesting (and rare). While "girls" (*devushki*) was a common word in discussing women, "boys" was not common for adult men.

50 Sagdeev, *The Making of a Soviet Scientist*, 51.

51 Orlov, *Opasnye mysli*, 98.

52 Vitalii I. Gol'danskii, *Essays of a Soviet Scientist: A Revealing Portrait of a Life in Science and Politics* (Woodbury, NY: American Institute of Physics, 1997), 76.

53 Gorelik, *The World of Andrei Sakharov*, 155. It seems that the Cold War gave rise to a transnational dismissal of women's scientific contributions. One is reminded here of *Hidden Figures*, Margot Lee Shetterly's 2016 book, later made into a successful film, that shone a long overdue spotlight on the contributions of African American mathematicians and engineers Katherine Johnson, Dorothy Vaughan, and Mary Jackson to the American space program.

54 Sakharov, *Memoirs*, 118.

55 A.A. Abrikosov, "Recollections of L.D. Landau," in I.M. Khalatnikov, ed., *Landau, the Physicist and the Man: Recollections of L.D. Landau*, trans. J.B. Sykes (Oxford: Pergamon Press, 1989), 32–3.

56 Sagdeev, *The Making of a Soviet Scientist*, 46–7.

57 Ibid., 109.

58 Gorelik, *The World of Andrei Sakharov*, 168.

59 Ibid., 91.

60 Michael Roper reported similar results from interviewing British corporate men about their rising careers in the 1950s: "They conjured vivid descriptions of the men who had influenced their careers for better or worse, but were strangely unforthcoming about the personalities of their wives." See Michael Roper, *Masculinity and the British Organization Man since 1945* (Oxford: Oxford University Press, 1994), 164–5.

61 Orlov, *Opasnye mysli*, 95.

62 Khariton et al., "Glazami fizikov Arzamasa-16," 307.

63 Gol'danskii, *Essays of a Soviet Scientist*, 80.

64 Ibid. This incident and the poetry contest above took place in the late 1940s, not at Arzamas but at the Institute of Chemical Physics in Moscow, where Gol'danskii, Zel'dovich, and other memoirists worked until being moved to Arzamas for more intensive weapons research.

65 V.E. Zakharov, "My Reminiscences about Ya.B. Zeldovich," in R.A. Sunyaev, ed., *Zeldovich: Reminiscences* (London: Chapman and Hall, 2004), 203.

66 Sakharov, *Memoirs*, 121.
67 Ibid., 121–2.
68 Ibid., 132.
69 On workplace harassment in the 1920s, a time when the new Bolshevik ideology of emancipation and equality for women should have been most influential, see Diane P. Koenker, "Men against Women on the Shop Floor in Early Soviet Russia: Gender and Class in the Socialist Workplace," *American Historical Review* 100, no. 5 (Dec. 1995), 1438–64.
70 Josephson, *Red Atom*, 4.
71 See Sonja D. Schmid, "Celebrating Tomorrow Today: The Peaceful Atom on Display in the Soviet Union," *Social Studies of Science* 36, no. 3 (2006), 331–65.
72 *Krokodil*, 10 July 1954, 3.
73 Zakharov, "My Reminiscences about Ya.B. Zeldovich," 202.
74 Susan Costanzo, "The 1959 *Liriki-Fiziki* Debate: Going Public with the Private?" in Lewis H. Siegelbaum, ed., *Borders of Socialism: Private Spheres of Soviet Russia* (New York: Palgrave Macmillan, 2006), 251.
75 Vladislav Zubok, *Zhivago's Children: The Last Russian Intelligentsia* (Cambridge, MA: Harvard University Press, 2009), 140.
76 V.P. Vizgin, "Fenomen 'kul'ta atoma' v SSSR (1950–1960-e gg.)," in V.P. Vizgin, ed., *Istoriia sovetskogo atomnogo proekta: Dokumenty, vospominaniia, issledovaniia* (St. Petersburg: Institut istorii estestvoznaniia i tekhniki, 2002), 424.
77 Paul R. Josephson, *Lenin's Laureate: Zhores Alferov's Life in Communist Science* (Cambridge, MA: MIT Press, 2010), 196.
78 *Krokodil*, 30 December 1955, 4.
79 Vizgin, "Fenomen 'kul'ta atoma' v SSSR," 467–8.
80 A. Agranovskii, "Deviat' normal'nogo dnei," *Izvestiia*, 7 March 1962, 6.
81 E. Gabrilovich, "Neskol'ko dnei," *Literaturnaia gazeta*, 27 February 1962, 3.
82 V. Orlov, "Atomy i liudi," *Pravda*, 20 March 1962, 4.
83 Marko Dumančić, "De-Stalinizing Soviet Science: Rethinking the Moral Implications of Scientific Progress in Khrushchev-Era Film," *Studies in Russian and Soviet Cinema* 6, no. 1 (2012), 82.
84 Vizgin, "Fenomen 'kul'ta atoma' v SSSR," 471.
85 Josephine Woll, *Real Images: Soviet Cinema and the Thaw* (New York: St. Martin's Press, 2000), 128.
86 Sakharov, *Memoirs*, 97.
87 Feinberg, "Sud'ba rossiiskogo intelligenta," 243.
88 Ibid.
89 Sakharov, *Memoirs*, 170.

90 Ibid., 181. Although he does not mention it, one wonders whether Sakharov, writing into the 1980s, might not have been influenced here by J. Robert Oppenheimer's iconic quotation after witnessing the Alamogordo nuclear test in July 1945: "I am become death, the shatterer of worlds." For a fascinating analysis of the performativity value of those words, see Charles Thorpe, *Oppenheimer: The Tragic Intellect* (Chicago: University of Chicago Press, 2006), 160–2.
91 Woll, *Real Images*, 128.
92 Hellbeck, *Revolution on My Mind*, 10.
93 See Halfin, *Terror in My Soul*.
94 See Leona Toker, *Return from the Archipelago: Narratives of Gulag Survivors* (Bloomington: Indiana University Press, 2000).
95 Although not all Gulag survivors wrote as dissidents, one might place Alexander Solzhenitsyn's *The Gulag Archipelago* or Irina Ratushinskaya's *Grey Is the Color of Hope* into this category, as well as Sakharov's *Memoirs*. See Beth Holmgren, ed., *The Russian Memoir: History and Literature* (Chicago: Northwestern University Press, 2003), xxiv.
96 On the *glasnost'* era, see Irina Paperno, "Personal Accounts of the Soviet Experience," *Kritika: Explorations in Russian and Eurasian History* 3, no. 4 (Fall 2002), 577. On the post-Soviet period, see Irina Paperno, *Stories of the Soviet Experience: Memoirs, Diaries, Dreams* (Ithaca, NY: Cornell University Press, 2009), 2; and Holmgren, *The Russian Memoir*, xxxi. Scholars of Eastern Europe and the Soviet Union have also extensively studied such writing as sites of nostalgia. See Svetlana Boym, *The Future of Nostalgia* (New York: Basic Books, 2001); and Maria Todorova and Zsuzsa Gille, eds., *Post-Communist Nostalgia* (New York: Berghahn Books, 2010). One can identify several genres of postsocialist personal narratives (for the Soviet Union as well as Eastern Europe), including the political memoir, the memoir of everyday life, and the conversation or interview genre, in which the remembered stories are filtered through another layer of narrative. See Dmitrii Shepilov, *The Kremlin's Scholar: A Memoir of Soviet Politics under Stalin and Khrushchev*, ed. Stephen V. Bittner, trans. Anthony Austin (New Haven: Yale University Press, 2007); Slavenka Drakulić, *How We Survived Communism and Even Laughed* (New York: Harper Collins, 1993); V.M. Molotov, *Molotov Remembers: Inside Kremlin Politics: Conversations with Felix Chuev*, ed. Albert Resis (Chicago: Ivan R. Dee, 1993); and Donald J. Raleigh, ed., *Russia's Sputnik Generation: Soviet Baby Boomers Talk about Their Lives* (Bloomington: Indiana University Press, 2006).
97 Sakharov, *Memoirs*, xix–xx. Physicists other than Sakharov similarly cite the particular Cold War moment in which they worked as key to their

desire to write about their lives, including on the American side. See Edward Teller with Judith Shoolery, *Memoirs: A Twentieth Century Journey in Science and Politics* (Cambridge: Perseus Publishing, 2001), 2. For other well-known American physicists' memoirs, see Herbert F. York, *Arms and the Physicist* (Woodbury, NY: American Institute of Physics Press, 1995); and Peter Martel, *Memories of a Hayseed Physicist* (New York: Strategic Book Publishing, 2008).

98 Sagdeev, *The Making of a Soviet Scientist*, v.

99 Ginzburg, *On Superconductivity and Superfluidity*, 143.

100 Ibid., 139.

101 Orlov also drew heavily on the word and concept of the "danger" of Soviet life-writing in his personal narrative about Arzamas-16, entitled *Opasnye mysli* (Dangerous Thoughts). In English, his memoir was published as *Dangerous Thoughts: Memoirs of a Russian Life* (New York: William Morrow, 1991).

102 Maynes et al., *Telling Stories*, 1–2.

103 Ibid., x. See also *Aspasia* 7 (2013), Special Issue: Women's Autobiographical Writing and Correspondence; Toby W. Clyman and Judith Vowles, eds., *Russia through Women's Eyes: Autobiographies from Tsarist Russia* (New Haven: Yale University Press, 1999); Marianne Liljestrom, Arja Rosenholm, and Irina Savkina, eds., *Models of Self: Russian Women's Autobiographical Texts* (Helsinki: Kikimora Publications, 2000); and Catriona Kelly, *A History of Russian Women's Writing* (Oxford: Oxford University Press, 1994).

104 See Fay Ajzenberg-Selove, *A Matter of Choices: Memoirs of a Female Physicist* (New Brunswick, NJ: Rutgers University Press, 1994); Joan Freeman, *A Passion for Physics: The Story of a Woman Physicist* (New York: Taylor & Francis, 1991); Ruth H. Howes and Caroline L. Herzenberg, *Their Day in the Sun: Women of the Manhattan Project* (Philadelphia: Temple University Press, 1999); and Ann Hibner Koblitz, *A Convergence of Lives: Sofia Kovalevskaia – Scientist, Writer, Revolutionary* (New Brunswick, NJ: Rutgers University Press, 1993).

**Chapter 5**

1 Lev Danilkin, *Iurii Gagarin* (Moscow: Molodaia gvardiia, 2011), 355.

2 Ibid., 352.

3 Ibid., 355.

4 Andrew L. Jenks, *The Cosmonaut Who Couldn't Stop Smiling: The Life and Legend of Yuri Gagarin* (DeKalb, IL: Northern Illinois University Press, 2012), 6.

5 Andrew Jenks and Lev Danilkin have led scholars in asking new questions about Gagarin's legacy. See Jenks, *Cosmonaut Who Couldn't Stop Smiling*, and Danilkin, *Iurii Gagarin*. There have been several other studies of the Soviet space program published recently, including Slava Gerovitch, *Voices of the Soviet Space Program: Cosmonauts, Soldiers, and Engineers Who Took the USSR into Space* (New York: Palgrave Macmillan, 2014); Asif Siddiqi, *The Red Rockets' Glare: Spaceflight and the Soviet Imagination, 1857–1957* (Cambridge: Cambridge University Press, 2010); James T. Andrews and Asif A. Siddiqi, eds., *Into the Cosmos: Space Exploration and Soviet Culture* (Pittsburgh: University of Pittsburgh Press, 2011); and Eva Maurer et al., eds., *Soviet Space Culture: Cosmic Enthusiasm in Socialist Societies* (New York: Palgrave Macmillan, 2011).

6 After this cohort, the Soviet manned space program experienced several setbacks that led to less frequent flights until 1967. The Group of Six was also defined by their spacecraft, the *Vostok*, which flew these six missions before the improved *Voskhod* line forced the cancellation of *Vostok* missions 7 to 13. For an excellent comprehensive account of the Soviet space program, see Asif A. Siddiqi, *Challenge to Apollo: The Soviet Union and the Space Race, 1945–1974* (Washington, DC: NASA History Division, 2000).

7 Slava Gerovitch, "'Why Are We Telling Lies?' The Creation of Soviet Space History Myths," *Russian Review* 70, no. 3 (July 2011), 466.

8 Stefan Brandt, "Astronautic Subjects: Postmodern Identity and the Embodiment of Space in American Science Fiction," *Gender Forum* 16 (2006), 15. http://genderforum.org/wp-content/uploads/2017/05/200616_GenderRoomoursII.pdf.

9 Evgenii Riabchikov, "Volia k pobede," *Aviatsiia i kosmonavtika*, no. 4 (1962), 19. Quoted in Slava Gerovitch, "'New Soviet Man' Inside Machine: Human Engineering, Spacecraft Design, and the Construction of Communism," *Osiris*, 22 (2007), 136.

10 Danilkin, *Iurii Gagarin*, 7.

11 On the early Soviet era, see Rolf Hellebust, *Flesh to Metal: Soviet Literature and the Alchemy of Revolution* (Ithaca, NY: Cornell University Press, 2003); and Eric Naiman, *Sex in Public: The Incarnation of Early Soviet Ideology* (Princeton, NJ: Princeton University Press, 1997). Naiman discusses early Soviet utopian visions of immortality and sex-free reproduction, by which extreme revolutionaries sought to use science to overcome human limitations.

12 *Krokodil*, 10 November 1957, 2.

13 *Krokodil*, 20 October 1957, 2.

14 *Sem'ia i shkola*, January 1960, 24.

15 See Lynne Viola, *Peasant Rebels under Stalin: Collectivization and the Culture of Peasant Resistance* (Oxford: Oxford University Press, 1996); and Victoria

E. Bonnell, *Iconography of Power: Soviet Political Posters under Lenin and Stalin* (Berkeley and Los Angeles: University of California Press, 1997).

16 *Krokodil*, 20 November 1957, 1.

17 Between *Sputnik* and Gagarin's flight, the Soviet space program conducted many other experiments to see whether living creatures could survive in space. For a detailed discussion of the now-famous, and tragic, plight of the Soviet space dogs, see Amy Nelson, "Cold War Celebrity and the Courageous Canine Scout: The Life and Times of the Soviet Space Dogs," in Andrews and Siddiqi, eds., *Into the Cosmos*, 133–55.

18 John Glenn and Nick Taylor, *John Glenn: A Memoir* (New York: Bantam Books, 1999), 237.

19 Asif A. Siddiqi, "Cosmic Contradictions: Popular Enthusiasm and Secrecy in the Soviet Space Program," in Andrews and Siddiqi, eds,. *Into the Cosmos*, 49. On Baikonur as a fake launch site, 57. On specific elements of the program needing to be kept secret, 67–8.

20 On arctic explorers, see John McCannon, "Positive Heroes at the Pole: Celebrity Status, Socialist-Realist Ideals and the Soviet Myth of the Arctic, 1932–39," *Russian Review* 56, no. 3 (July 1997), 346–65.

21 Gerovitch, "'New Soviet Man' Inside Machine," 136.

22 Ibid., 141. In his memoirs, John Glenn emphasized his own need to pilot his capsule manually for much of his flight when he encountered trouble with the automatic controls, perhaps in a continuing post–Cold War jab at the Soviets' automation. See Glenn and Taylor, *John Glenn*, 265–6, 272.

23 For a full discussion of manned vs. unmanned flight and the debate's symbolism in describing broader agency for Soviet actors within the regime, see Gerovitch, "'New Soviet Man' Inside Machine."

24 Rossiiskii gosudarstvennyi arkhiv nauchno-tekhnicheskoi dokumentatsii (Russian State Archive of Scientific-Technical Documentation, RGANTD), Fond 31, op. 6, d. 340, l. 3.

25 See Mie Nakachi, "Population, Politics and Reproduction: Late Stalinism and Its Legacy," in Juliane Fürst, ed., *Late Stalinist Russia: Society between Reconstruction and Reinvention* (London and New York: Routledge, 2006), 37–66.

26 Rudolf Schlesinger, ed., *The Family in the USSR: Documents and Readings* (London: Routledge and Kegan Paul, 1949), 368, 372.

27 Ibid., 403.

28 Helene Carlbäck, "Lone Mothers and Fatherless Children: Public Discourse on Marriage and Family Law," in Melanie Ilič and Jeremy Smith, eds., *Soviet State and Society under Nikita Khrushchev* (London and New York: Routledge, 2009), 87.

29 On service evasion, see chapter 2. On government concerns about unmarried men and absentee fathers after the war, see Nakachi, "Population, Politics and Reproduction."
30 Deborah A. Field, *Private Life and Communist Morality in Khrushchev's Russia* (New York: Peter Lang, 2007), 9.
31 Ibid.
32 Jenks, *Cosmonaut Who Couldn't Stop Smiling*, 208.
33 Ibid.
34 *Krokodil*, 20 May 1961, 12.
35 Victoria Smolkin-Rothrock, "Cosmic Enlightenment: Scientific Atheism and the Soviet Conquest of Space," in Andrews and Siddiqi, eds., *Into the Cosmos*, 163.
36 Matthew H. Hersch, review of *Into That Silent Era: Trailblazers of the Space Era, 1961–1965*, by Francis French et al., *Journal of American Culture* 30, no. 4 (December 2007), 455. For a detailed discussion of masculinity and American space culture, see Dario Llinares, *The Astronaut: Cultural Mythology and Idealised Masculinity* (Newcastle upon Tyne: Cambridge Scholars Publishing, 2011).
37 Glenn and Taylor, *John Glenn*, 220–1.
38 N.P. Kamanin, *Skrytyi kosmos: Kosmicheskie dnevniki Generala Kamanina (kn. pervaia, 1960–1963 gg).* (Moscow: Infortekst IF, 1995), 58–9.
39 Iaroslav Golovanov, *Zametki vashego sovremennika, tom 1, 1953–1970* (Moscow: Dobroe slovo, 2001), knizhka 16. Available online at: http://epizodsspace.airbase.ru/bibl/golovanov/gol-zap/1/kn1-1.html.
40 N. Kamanin, *Pervyi grazhdanin vselennoi* (Moscow: Molodaia gvardiia, 1962), 106. For further analysis of the ways Gagarin consistently breached boundaries between "truth" and "lies," see Jenks, *Cosmonaut Who Couldn't Stop Smiling*, chapter 8: "Sacred Lies, Profane Truths," and Gerovitch, "'Why Are We Telling Lies?'"
41 Kamanin, *Skrytyi kosmos (kn. 1)*, 66.
42 Golovanov, *Zametki vashego sovremennika*, knizhka 16.
43 Claire E. McCallum, "The Return: Postwar Masculinity and the Domestic Space in Stalinist Visual Culture, 1945–53," *Russian Review* 74 (January 2015), 142; and Claire E. McCallum, *The Fate of the New Man: Representing and Reconstructing Masculinity in Soviet Visual Culture, 1945–1965* (DeKalb: Northern Illinois University Press, 2018), 170–2.
44 On the Khrushchev government's preoccupation with "hooliganism" and policing youth behaviour, see Brian LaPierre, *Hooligans in Khrushchev's Russia: Defining, Policing, and Producing Deviance during the Thaw* (Madison, WI: University of Wisconsin Press, 2012).

45 Kamanin, *Skrytyi kosmos (kn. 1)*, 94.
46 Ibid., 99–100.
47 Bart Hendrickx, "The Kamanin Diaries, 1960–1963," *Journal of the British Interplanetary Society* 50 (1997), 39.
48 Kamanin, *Skrytyi kosmos (kn. 1)*, 57–8, 82.
49 Ibid., 81.
50 Ibid., 58.
51 Quoted in Hendrickx, "The Kamanin Diaries," 40.
52 O. Apenchenko and V. Peskov, "Reportazh iz doma pervogo kosmonavta," *Komsomol'skaia pravda* (14 April 1961), 2. Their second daughter was born a month before Gagarin's flight.
53 *Sem'ia i shkola*, June 1961, 4.
54 *Rabotnitsa*, May 1961, 4.
55 "Beseda N.S. Khrushcheva po telefonu s kosmonavtom G.S. Titovym," *Pravda*, 7 August 1961, 1.
56 RGANTD, *Iu. A. Gagarin vo vremia otdykha v Sochi*, No. 120. The film in undated, but judging by the baby's age, it seems to have been made in late 1961 or early 1962.
57 Apenchenko and Peskov, "Reportazh iz doma pervogo kosmonavta," 2.
58 N.P. Kamanin, *Skrytyi kosmos: Kosmicheskie dnevniki Generala Kamanina (kn. vtoraia: 1964–66 gg.)* (Moscow: Infortekst IF, 1997), 42–3.
59 See Sue Bridger, "The Cold War and the Cosmos: Valentina Tereshkova and the First Woman's Space Flight," in Melanie Ilič, Susan E. Reid, and Lynne Attwood, eds., *Women in the Khrushchev Era* (New York: Palgrave Macmillan, 2004), 222–37; Cathleen Lewis, "The Red Stuff: A History of the Public and Material Culture of Early Human Spaceflight in the USSR" (PhD diss., George Washington University, 2008); and Roshanna P. Sylvester, "She Orbits over the Sex Barrier: Soviet Girls and the Tereshkova Moment," in Andrews and Siddiqi, eds., *Into the Cosmos*, 195–212.
60 Kamanin, *Skrytyi kosmos (kn. 1)*, 62.
61 Bridger, "The Cold War and the Cosmos," 226.
62 See Reina Pennington, *Wings, Women, and War: Soviet Airwomen in World War II Combat* (Lawrence: University Press of Kansas, 2002); Kazimiera J. Cottam, *Women in Air War: The Eastern Front of World War II* (Nepean, ON: New Military Publishing, 1997); and Karen Petrone, *Life Has Become More Joyous, Comrades: Celebrations in the Time of Stalin* (Bloomington, IN: Indiana University Press, 2000)
63 Petrone, *Life Has Become More Joyous*, 74.
64 Sylvester, "She Orbits over the Sex Barrier." See also Sylvester's research notes online: "Russian Space History – Dreams in Orbit," *Russian History*

*Blog*, 9 December 2013, http://russianhistoryblog.org/2013/12/russian-space-history-dreams-in-orbit-3/, and "'Even Though I Am a Girl …': John Glenn's Fan Mail and Sexism in the Early Space Program," *The Conversation*, 12 December 2016, https://theconversation.com/even-though-i-am-a-girl-john-glenns-fan-mail-and-sexism-in-the-early-space-program-70252.

65 Petrone, *Life Has Become More Joyous*, 71.

66 Ibid., 74.

67 Lewis, "The Red Stuff," 144.

68 Margaret A. Weitekamp, "The 'Astronautrix' and the 'Magnificent Male': Jerrie Cobb's Quest to Be the First Woman in America's Manned Space Program," in Avital H. Bloch and Lauri Umansky, eds., *Impossible to Hold: Women and Culture in the 1960s* (New York: New York University Press, 2005), 9–28.

69 RGANTD, *Sovetskoe kosmovidenie*, No. 967. Director: M. Volodarskii. Undated.

70 P.R. Popovich, *Ispitaniia kosmosom i zemlei* (Kiev: Izd-vo "Molod'," 1982), 134.

71 Kamanin, *Skrytyi kosmos (kn. 1)*, 101; Glenn and Taylor, *John Glenn*, 288.

72 *Ogonek*, June 1963, 32–3.

73 Bridger, "The Cold War and the Cosmos," 227–8.

74 N. Kamanin, "Introduction," in Valentina Nikolaeva-Tereshkova, *Vselennaia – otkrytyi okean! Rasskaz letchika-kosmonavta SSSR* (Moscow: Izd-vo "Pravda," 1964), 4.

75 *Ogonek*, June 1963, 4–5.

76 *Krokodil*, 30 June 1963, 1.

77 Ibid., 3.

78 Ibid., 2.

79 Ibid.

80 My research confirms what Roshanna Sylvester has found, in that the press (and Khrushchev himself) almost always referred to Tereshkova as "Valya," while using the full names or surnames of the male cosmonauts. See Sylvester, "She Orbits over the Sex Barrier," 195, 209.

81 T. Dad'iants, "Parizhanki o russkoi Vale," *Ogonek*, 18 June 1963, 30.

82 Anke Hilbrenner, "Soviet Women in Sports in the Brezhnev Years: The Female Body and Soviet Modernism," in Nikolaus Katzer et al., eds., *Euphoria and Exhaustion: Modern Sport in Soviet Culture and Society* (Frankfurt and New York: Campus Verlag, 2010), 301.

83 There is some debate about the origins of the quotation. Kamanin notes that in Tereshkova's book, *Vselennaia – otkrytyi okean! Rasskaz*

*letchika-kosmonavta SSSR*, it is attributed to her former flight instructor in Yaroslavl', but that the nickname was more likely given to her at the training centre only a few months before her flight. See Kamanin, *Skrytyi kosmos (kn. 2)*, 29.

84 Jenks, *Cosmonaut Who Couldn't Stop Smiling*, 187–8.

85 Valentina Ponomareva, *Zhenskoe litso kosmosa* (Moscow: Gelios, 20020, 58.

86 Ibid., 57.

87 Kamanin, *Skrytyi kosmos (kn. 1)*, 158.

88 See Bernice Madison, "Social Services for Women: Problems and Priorities," in Dorothy Atkinson, Alexander Dallin, and Gail Warshofsky Lapidus, eds., *Women in Russia* (Stanford: Stanford University Press, 1977), 310; and Ekaterina Alexandrova, "Why Soviet Women Want to Get Married," in Tatiana Mamonova, ed., *Women in Russia: Feminist Writings from the Soviet Union* (Boston: Beacon Press, 1984), 39. Mamonova's anecdotal evidence indicates that it was much more socially acceptable to be divorced than never married.

89 Ponomareva, *Zhenskoe litso kosmosa*, 288–9.

90 Kamanin, *Skrytyi kosmos (kn. 2)*, 29–30. Although it was not entirely the norm, a married woman hyphenating her surname in the Soviet Union would not have appeared unusual – certainly not as much as in the United States in 1964.

91 Popovich, *Ispitaniia kosmosom i zemlei*, 126.

92 Kamanin, *Skrytyi kosmos (kn. 2)*, 29–30.

93 Jenks, *Cosmonaut Who Couldn't Stop Smiling*, 189. On her rank, see Bridger, "The Cold War and the Cosmos," 229.

94 *Sem'ia i shkola*, November 1963, 24.

95 *Krokodil*, 30 December 1963, 2.

96 *Rabotnitsa*, July 1965, 1. The same photograph evidently made the rounds of the international press as well, as it also appeared in a *Times* (London) picture gallery on 4 May 1965, 10.

97 Liubov Denisova, *Rural Women in the Soviet Union and Post-Soviet Russia*, trans. Irina Mukhina (London and New York: Routledge, 2010), 24–5.

98 Kamanin kept detailed diaries of the tour stops. See Kamanin, *Skrytyi kosmos (knigi 1 & 2)*.

99 RGANTD, Fond 173, op. 1, d. 27.

100 See David Caute, *The Dancer Defects: The Struggle for Cultural Supremacy during the Cold War* (Oxford: Oxford University Press, 2005). On Cold War–era tourism abroad by ordinary Soviet citizens, see Anne E. Gorsuch, *All This Is Your World: Soviet Tourism at Home and Abroad after Stalin* (Oxford: Oxford University Press, 2011).

101 *Komsomol'skaia pravda*, 15 April 1961, 1; and 4 June 1961, 1.
102 Sergei Khrushchev, "Yesteryear, Yuri Gagarin's Seven Years of Glory," *Moscow News*, No. 15 (2001), 6.
103 Golovanov, *Zametki vashego sovremennika*, knizhka 16.
104 Siddiqi, "Cosmic Contradictions," 55.
105 Bridger, "The Cold War and the Cosmos," 224.
106 On Gagarin's "bromance" appeal, see Jenks, *Cosmonaut Who Couldn't Stop Smiling*, 210.
107 RGANTD, Fond 31, op. 6, d. 349, ll. 58–9.
108 N.N. Denisov, *Na orbitakh mira i druzhby (iz zapisnoi knizhki korrespondenta "Pravdy")* (Moscow: Izd-vo "Znanie," 1963), 43.
109 "Major Gagarin's Visit to Ghana Hailed," *Evening News* (Accra), 5 February 1962, 3.
110 On the book exchange, see Denisov, *Na orbitakh mira i druzhby*, 44–5. On the ghostwriting of cosmonaut autobiographies, see Gerovitch, "'Why Are We Telling Lies?'" 466.
111 "Yuri Gagarin (World's First Spaceman) Hails Ghana's Example in National Construction," *The Ghanaian Times*, 5 February 1962, 2.
112 RGANTD, Fond 31, op. 6, d. 349, l. 46.
113 RGANTD, Fond 31, op. 6, d. 349, l. 54.
114 Kamanin, *Skrytyi kosmos (kn. 2)*, 28.
115 Kamanin, *Skrytyi kosmos (kn. 1)*, 75.
116 On the queen's and Kennedy's travels to India in the early 1960s, see Antoinette Burton, *The Postcolonial Careers of Santha Rama Rau* (Durham, NC: Duke University Press, 2007), 92–4.
117 "Hapless Hunting," *Time*, 10 March 1961.
118 Kamanin, *Skrytyi kosmos (kn. 2)*, 42.
119 "Woman Cosmonaut at the Palace," *The Times* (London), 6 February 1964, 12. On her doctor's orders, see Kamanin, *Skrytyi kosmos (kn. 2)*, 8.
120 "Space Woman Visits Commons," *The Times* (London), 8 February 1964, 6.
121 "Woman Cosmonaut Goes Home," *The Times* (London), 11 February 1964, 7.
122 Denisov, *Na orbitakh mira i druzhby*, 44–5.
123 Ibid., 45.
124 Ibid., 45–7.
125 RGANTD, Fond 31, op. 6, d. 340, l. 14. *Pravda* correspondent Denisov also tells this story. See Denisov, *Na orbitakh mira i druzhby*, 42.
126 Quoted in Scott W. Palmer, *Dictatorship of the Air: Aviation Culture and the Fate of Modern Russia* (Cambridge: Cambridge University Press, 2006), 4.
127 Denisov, *Na orbitakh mira i druzhby*, 20.

128 "Vas zhdet vozdushnyi okean," *Komsomol'skaia pravda*, 9 July 1961. *Sputnik* was launched on 4 October 1957.
129 On the persistence of Gagarin's positive image in postsocialist Russian culture, see Alexei Yurchak, "Gagarin and the Rave Kids: Transforming Power, Identity, and Aesthetics in Post-Soviet Nightlife," in Adele Marie Barker, ed., *Consuming Russia: Popular Culture, Sex, and Society since Gorbachev* (Durham, NC: Duke University Press, 1999), 94.
130 Jenks, *Cosmonaut Who Couldn't Stop Smiling*, 245. For more on Gagarin's death and the cult of celebrity that has grown around it from 1968 through to the present day, see Jenks, *Cosmonaut Who Couldn't Stop Smiling*, especially chapters 8 and 9.

## Conclusion

1 For examples, see Lilya Kaganovsky, *How the Soviet Man Was Unmade: Cultural Fantasy and Male Subjectivity under Stalin* (Pittsburgh: University of Pittsburgh Press, 2008); Anna Krylova, "'Healers of Wounded Souls': The Crisis of Private Life in Soviet Literature, 1944–46," *Journal of Modern History* 73 (June 2001), 307–31; and Frances Bernstein, "Rehabilitation Staged: How Soviet Doctors 'Cured' Disability in the Second World War," in Susan Burch and Michael Rembis, eds., *Disability Histories* (Urbana: University of Illinois Press, 2014), 218–36.
2 Maya Eichler, *Militarizing Men: Gender, Conscription, and War in Post-Soviet Russia* (Stanford: Stanford University Press, 2012), 65.
3 Natalie Gross, "Youth and the Army in the USSR in the 1980s," *Soviet Studies* 42, no. 3 (July 1990), 482.
4 Claire E. McCallum, *The Fate of the New Man: Representing and Reconstructing Masculinity in Soviet Visual Culture, 1945–1965* (DeKalb: Northern Illinois University Press, 2018), 197.
5 Ellen Jones, *Red Army and Society: A Sociology of the Soviet Military* (Boston: Allen and Unwin, 1985), 101.

# Bibliography


## Archival Sources

### Gosudarstvennyi arkhiv Rossiiskoi Federatsii (GARF), Moscow

Fond R-9552 (DOSAAF fond)
Materials related to training instructors in mass organization work in republic, krai, and oblast' DOSAAF organizations
Opis' 1, dela 43 and 44.
Materials related to the administration of military training and military sport
Opis' 1, dela 64 and 120.
Materials related to the editorial staff and conferences of the journal, Voennye znaniia
Opis; 17, delo 43.

### Rossiiskii gosudarstvennyi arkhiv sotsial'no-politicheskoi istorii (RGASPI: Komsomol branch), Moscow

Fond M-1 (Komsomol Archive)
Materials related to literacy among pre-conscription and conscription-age youth
Opis' 3, delo 797
Materials related to strengthening mass-defence and armed forces preparatory work among Komsomol members
Opis' 3, delo 903
Opis' 47, dela 182, 309, 329, 395, 405, 406, 461, and 479
Materials related to perceived deficiencies in mass defence training among Komsomol organizations in non-Russian republics
Opis' 3, delo 1041

Opis' 47, delo 309, 376, 432, 461, 462
Material related to Komsomol work with specialized military academies, including the Suvorov academies
Opis' 47, dela 184, 185, 271, 415, 448

**Rossiiskii gosudarstvennyi arkhiv nauchno-tekhnicheskoi dokumentatsii (RGANTD), Moscow**

Personal files of A.A. Zvorykin, photographer on cosmonaut tours
Fond 173, opis' 1, dela 27, 29, 30, 32, 43, 47, 48, and 58
Personal files of Nikolai Aleksandrovich Varvarov, journalist on cosmonaut tours
Fond 31, opis' 6, dela 331, 340, and 349.
Films from the RGANTD archive are listed with other films in the separate category below.

**Films**

**RGANTD footage, likely aired on television. Citations include the full information available in RGANTD files.**

*Dve materi.* No. 270 (1979).
*Iu. A. Gagarin vo vremia otdykha v Sochi.* No. 120. Undated.
*Kosmonavty pervogo otriada na otdykhe.* No. 1012. Undated.
*Pervyi reis k zvezdam.* Undated.
Pokhorony letchika-kosmonavta SSSR Gagarina Iu.A. i polkovnika VVS Serepina V. No. 797 (30 March 1968).
*Sovetskoe kosmovidenie.* No. 967. Dir. M. Volodarskii. Undated.

**Films with wide theatrical release**

*Maxim Perepelitsa.* (Maxim Perepelitsa, 1955). Dir. Anatolii Granik.
*Nine Days in One Year* (Deviat' dnei odnogo goda, 1962). Dir. Mikhail Romm.
*The Cranes Are Flying* (Letiat zhuravli, 1957). Dir. Mikhail Kalatozov.
*The Soldier Ivan Brovkin* (Soldat Ivan Brovkin, 1955). Dir. Ivan Lukinskii.

**Newspapers**

*Evening News* (Accra, Ghana)
*Izvestiia*
*Komsomol'skaia pravda*

*Krasnaia zvezda*
*Literaturnaia gazeta*
*Pravda*
*The Ghanaian Times*
*The Times* (London)

## Magazines and Journals

*Krokodil*
*Kryl'ia rodiny*
*Ogonek*
*Rabotnitsa*
*Sem'ia i shkola*
*Sovetskii voin*
*Voennye znaniia*
*Za oboronu*
*Time* (US)

## Published Primary Sources

### *Memoirs, Diaries, and Reminiscences*

*When available, I consulted the Russian and English versions of a text. In those cases, both are listed.*

Ajzenberg-Selove, Fay. *A Matter of Choices: Memoirs of a Female Physicist*. New Brunswick, NJ: Rutgers University Press, 1994.

Aleksandrov, A.P., ed. *Akademik A.I. Alikhanov: Vospominaniia, pis'ma, dokumenty*. Leningrad: Nauka, 1989.

Andreev, A.F., ed, *Kapitsa, Tamm, Semenov: V ocherkakh i pis'makh*. Moscow: Izd. Vagrius, 1998.

Berg, Raisa. *Acquired Traits: Memoirs of a Geneticist from the Soviet Union*. Trans. David Lowe. New York: Viking, 1988.

Bonner, Elena. *Alone Together: The Story of Elena Bonner and Andrei Sakharov's Internal Exile in the Soviet Union*. New York: Vintage Books, 1988.

Denisov, N.N. *Na orbitakh mira i druzhby (Iz zapisnoi knizhki korrespondenta "Pravdy")*. Moscow: Izd-vo "Znanie," 1963.

Drakulić, Slavenka. *How We Survived Communism and Even Laughed*. New York: Harper Collins, 1993.

Fermi, Laura. *Atoms in the Family: My Life with Enrico Fermi*. Chicago: University of Chicago Press, 1954.

Gagarin, Iurii. *Doroga v kosmos: Rasskaz letchika-kosmonavta SSSR*. Moscow: Gosudarstvennoe izd-vo detskoi literatury, 1963.

– *Est' plamia: Stat'i, rechi, pis'ma, inter'viu*. Moscow: Molodaia gvardiia, 1968.

Gagarina, A.T. *Slovo o syne*. Moscow: Molodaia gvardiia, 1986.

Ginzburg, Vitaly L. *On Superconductivity and Superfluidity: A Scientific Autobiography*. Berlin and Heidelberg: Springer-Verlag, 2009.

Ginzburg, V.L. *O sverkhprovodimosti i o sverkhtekuchesti. Avtobiografiia* (Moscow: Izdatel'stvo Fiziko-matematicheskoi literatury, 2006.

Glenn, John, and Nick Taylor. *John Glenn: A Memoir*. New York: Bantam Books, 1999.

Gol'danskii, Vitalii I. *Essays of a Soviet Scientist: A Revealing Portrait of a Life in Science and Politics*. Woodbury, NY: American Institute of Physics, 1997.

Golovanov, Iaroslav. *Zametki vashego sovremennika, tom 1, 1953–1970*. Moscow: Dobroe slovo, 2001. http://epizodsspace.airbase.ru/bibl/golovanov/gol-zap/1/kn1-1.html.

Kamanin, N.P. *Pervyi grazhdanin vselennoi*. Moscow: Molodaia gvardiia, 1962.

– *Skrytyi kosmos: Kosmicheskie dnevniki Generala Kamanina (kn. pervaia: 1960–63 gg)*. Moscow: Infortekst IF, 1995.

– *Skrytyi kosmos: Kosmicheskie dnevniki Generala Kamanina (kn. vtoraia: 1964–66 gg)*. Moscow: Infortekst IF, 1997.

Khalatnikov, I.M., ed. *Landau, the Physicist and the Man: Recollections of L.D. Landau*. Trans. J.B. Sykes. Oxford: Pergamon Press, 1989.

Khrushchev, N.S. *Khrushchev Remembers*. Boston: Little Brown and Co., 1970.

Kochina, Pelageia Ia. *Nauka, Liudi, Gody: Vospominaniia i vystupleniia*. Moscow: Nauka, 1988.

Markov, M.A., and A.N. Gorbunov, eds. *Vospominaniia o V.I. Vekslere*. Moscow: Nauka, 1987.

Martel, Peter. *Memories of a Hayseed Physicist*. New York: Strategic Book Publishing, 2008.

Nikolaeva-Tereshkova, Valentina. *Vselennaia – Otkrytyi okean! Rasskaz letchika-kosmonavta SSSR*. Moscow: Izd-vo "Pravda," 1964.

Orlov, Yuri. *Dangerous Thoughts: Memoirs of a Russian Life*. New York: William Morrow, 1991.

Orlov, Iurii. *Opasnye mysli: Memuary iz russkoi zhizni*. Moscow: Argumenty i fakty, 1992.

Ponomareva, Valentina. *Zhenskoe litso kosmosa*. Moscow: Gelios, 2002.

Popovich, P.R. *Ispitaniia kosmosom i zemlei*. Kiev: Izd-vo "Molod'," 1982.

Sagdeev, Roald Z. *The Making of a Soviet Scientist: My Adventures in Nuclear Fusion and Space from Stalin to Star Wars*. New York: John Wiley & Sons, 1994.

Sakharov, Andrei. *Memoirs*. Trans. Richard Lourie. New York: Alfred A. Knopf, 1990.

– *Vospominaniia*. Moscow: Izdatel'stvo imeni Chekhova, 1990.

Sunyaev, R.A., ed. *Zeldovich: Reminiscences*. London: Chapman and Hall, 2004.

Teller, Edward, and Judith Shoolery. *Memoirs: A Twentieth Century Journey in Science and Politics*. Cambridge: Perseus Publishing, 2001.

Tsukerman, Veniamin, and Zinaida Azarkh. *Arzamas-16 – Soviet Scientists in the Nuclear Age: A Memoir*. Trans. Timothy Sergay. Nottingham: Bramcote Press, 1999.

Yanev, Nikolay M. "In Memory of N.A. Dmitriev." *Pliska Studia Mathematica* 24 (2015): 13–20. http://www.math.bas.bg/pliska/Pliska-24/Pliska-24-2015-013-020.pdf.

York, Herbert F. *Arms and the Physicist*. Woodbury, NY: American Institute of Physics Press, 1995.

### *Document Collections*

*KPSS o Vooruzhennykh silakh sovetskogo soiuza: Dokumenty 1917–1981*. Moscow: Voennoe izdatel'stvo, 1981.

Riabev, L.D., ed. *Atomnyi proekt SSSR: Dokumenty i materialy. Tom I: 1938–1945*. Moscow: Nauka-Fizmatlit, 1998.

– *Atomnyi proekt SSSR: Dokumenty i materialy. Tom II: Atomnaia bomba, 1945–1954*. Moscow and Sarov: Nauka-Fizmatlit, 1999.

Schlesinger, Rudolf, ed. *The Family in the USSR: Documents and Readings*. London: Routledge & Kegan Paul Ltd., 1949.

## **Secondary Sources**

*When one chapter in an edited collection was consulted, it is listed separately. When more than one chapter in an edited collection was consulted, only the collection overall is listed.*

Agulhon, Maurice. *Marianne into Battle: Republican Imagery and Symbolism in France, 1789–1880*. Trans. Janet Lloyd. Cambridge: Cambridge University Press, 1981.

Ahlbäck, Anders. *Manhood and the Making of the Military: Conscription, Military Service and Masculinity in Finland, 1917–39*. New York: Routledge, 2016.

Althaus, Frank, and Mark Sutcliffe, eds. *Drawing the Curtain: The Cold War in Cartoons*. London: Fontanka, 2012.

*Aspasia: The International Yearbook of Central, Eastern, and Southeastern European Women's and Gender History* 7 (2013), Special Issue: Women's Autobiographical Writing and Correspondence.

Atkinson, Dorothy, Alexander Dallin, and Gail Warshofsky Lapidus, eds. *Women in Russia*. Stanford: Stanford University Press, 1977.

Baker, Catherine, ed. *Gender in 20th-Century Eastern Europe and the USSR*. Basingstoke, UK: Palgrave Macmillan, 2017.

Becker, Jonathan A. "The Disappearing Enemy: The Image of the United States in Soviet Political Cartoons." *Journalism and Mass Communication Quarterly* 73, no. 3 (Autumn 1996): 609–19.

Belanovskii, S.A., and S.N. Marzeeva. *Dedovshchina v armii: Sbornik sotsiologicheskikh dokumentov*. Moscow: In-t narodnokhoziaistvennogo prognozirovaniia, 1991.

Belkin, Aaron. *Bring Me Men: Military Masculinity and the Benign Façade of American Empire, 1898–2001*. Oxford: Oxford University Press, 2012.

Bergman, Jay. *Meeting the Demands of Reason: The Life and Thought of Andrei Sakharov*. Ithaca, NY: Cornell University Press, 2009.

Berman, Harold J., and Miroslav Kerner. *Soviet Military Law and Administration*. Cambridge, MA: Harvard University Press, 1955.

Bernstein, Frances. "Rehabilitation Staged: How Soviet Doctors 'Cured' Disability in the Second World War." In *Disability Histories*, ed. Susan Burch and Michael Rembis. Urbana: University of Illinois Press, 2014.

Bird, Kai, and Martin J. Sherwin. *American Prometheus: The Triumph and Tragedy of J. Robert Oppenheimer*. New York: Vintage Books, 2006.

Bonnell, Victoria. *Iconography of Power: Soviet Political Posters under Lenin and Stalin*. Berkeley: University of California Press, 1997.

Borenstein, Eliot. *Men without Women: Masculinity and Revolution in Russian Fiction, 1917–1929*. Durham, NC: Duke University Press, 2000.

Bourke, Joanna. *Dismembering the Male: Men's Bodies, Britain, and the Great War*. Chicago: University of Chicago Press, 1996.

Bown, Matthew Cullerne, and Brandon Taylor, eds. *Art of the Soviets: Painting, Sculpture, and Architecture in a One-Party State, 1917–1992*. Manchester, UK: Manchester University Press, 1993.

Boym, Svetlana. *The Future of Nostalgia*. New York: Basic Books, 2001.

Brandt, Stefan. "Astronautic Subjects: Postmodern Identity and the Embodiment of Space in American Science Fiction." *Gender Forum* 16 (2006): 3-32. http://genderforum.org/wp-content/uploads/2017/05/200616_GenderRoomoursII.pdf.

Braudy, Leo. *From Chivalry to Terrorism: War and the Changing Nature of Masculinity*. New York: Alfred A. Knopf, 2003.

Bridger, Sue. "The Cold War and the Cosmos: Valentina Tereshkova and the First Woman's Space Flight." In *Women in the Khrushchev Era*, ed. Melanie Ilič, Susan E. Reid, and Lynne Attwood. Houndsmills, UK: Palgrave Macmillan, 2004.

Brown, Kate. *Plutopia: Nuclear Families, Atomic Cities, and the Great Soviet and American Plutonium Disasters*. Oxford: Oxford University Press, 2013.

Burds, Jeffrey. *Peasant Dreams and Market Politics: Labor Migration and the Russian Village, 1861–1905*. Pittsburgh: University of Pittsburgh Press, 1998.

– "Sexual Violence in Europe in World War II, 1939–1945." *Politics and Society* 37, no. 1 (March 2009): 35–74.

Bureychak, Tetyana. "Masculinity in Soviet and Post-Soviet Ukraine: Models and Their Implications." In *Gender, Politics, and Society in Ukraine*, ed. Olena Hankivsky and Anastasiya Salnykova. Toronto: University of Toronto Press, 2012.

Burton, Antoinette. *The Postcolonial Careers of Santha Rama Rau*. Durham: Duke University Press, 2007.

Bystydzienski, Jill M., and Sharon R. Bird, eds. *Removing Barriers: Women in Academic Science, Technology, Engineering, and Mathematics*. Bloomington: Indiana University Press, 2006.

Bytwerk, Randall L. "The Dolt Laughs: Satirical Publications under Hitler and Honecker." *Journalism Quarterly* 69, no. 4 (Winter 1992): 1029–38.

Carstens-Wickham, Belinda. "Gender in Cartoons of German Unification." *Journal of Women's History* 10, no. 1 (Spring 1998): 127–56.

Caute, David. *The Dancer Defects: The Struggle for Cultural Supremacy during the Cold War*. Oxford University Press, 2003.

Chow, Rey. "Larry Feign, Ethnographer of a 'Lifestyle': Political Cartoons from Hong Kong." *Boundary* 24, no. 2 (Summer 1997): 21–45.

Clements, Barbara Evans. *Bolshevik Women*. Cambridge: Cambridge University Press, 1997.

Clements, Barbara Evans, Rebecca Friedman, and Dan Healey, eds. *Russian Masculinities in History and Culture*. New York: Palgrave, 2002.

Clyman, Toby W., and Judith Vowles, eds. *Russia through Women's Eyes: Autobiographies from Tsarist Russia*. New Haven: Yale University Press, 1999.

Cohn, Carol. "Wars, Wimps, and Women: Talking Gender and Thinking War." In *Gendering War Talk*, ed. Miriam Cooke and Angela Woollacott. Princeton, NJ: Princeton University Press, 1993.

Colton, Timothy J. *Commissars, Commanders, and Civilian Authority: The Structure of Soviet Military Politics*. Cambridge, MA: Harvard University Press, 1979.

Connell, R.W. *Masculinities*. Berkeley: University of California Press, 1995.

– *The Men and the Boys*. Berkeley: University of California Press, 2001.

Connell, R.W., and James W. Messerschmidt. "Hegemonic Masculinity: Rethinking the Concept." *Gender and Society* 19, no. 6 (December 2005): 829–59.

Connell, Raewyn. *Gender.* 2nd ed. Cambridge: Polity Press, 2009.

Costanzo, Susan. "The 1959 *Liriki-Fiziki* Debate: Going Public with the Private?" In *Borders of Socialism: Private Spheres of Soviet Russia,* ed. Lewis H. Siegelbaum. New York: Palgrave Macmillan, 2006.

Costlow, Jane T., Stephanie Sandler, and Judith Vowles, eds. *Sexuality and the Body in Russian Culture.* Stanford: Stanford University Press, 1993.

Cottam, Kazimiera J. *Women in Air War: The Eastern Front of World War II.* Nepean, ON: New Military Publishing, 1997.

Cuordileone, K.A. *Manhood and American Political Culture in the Cold War.* New York: Routledge, 2005.

Dale, Robert. *Demobilized Veterans in Late Stalinist Leningrad: Soldiers to Civilians.* London and New York: Bloomsbury Academic, 2015.

Danilkin, Lev. *Iurii Gagarin.* Moscow: Molodaia gvardiia, 2011.

Dawson, Graham. *Soldier Heroes: British Adventure, Empire and the Imagining of Masculinities.* New York: Routledge, 1994.

Dean, Robert. *Imperial Brotherhood: Gender and the Making of Cold War Foreign Policy.* Amherst: University of Massachusetts Press, 2001.

De Groot, Gerard J. *The Bomb: A Life.* Cambridge, MA: Harvard University Press, 2006.

Demetriou, Demetrakis Z. "Connell's Concept of Hegemonic Masculinity: A Critique." *Theory and Society* 30, no. 3 (2001): 337–61.

Demski, Dagnosław, and Kamila Baraniecka-Olszewska, eds. *Images of the Other in Ethnic Caricatures of Central and Eastern Europe.* Biblioteka Etnografi i Polskiej, no. 59. Warsaw: Institute of Archaeology and Ethnology, Polish Academy of Sciences, 2010.

Denisova, Liubov. *Rural Women in the Soviet Union and Post-Soviet Russia.* Trans. Irina Mukhina. London and New York: Routledge, 2010.

Dewey, Horace W. "Political *poruka* in Muscovite Rus'." *Russian Review* 46, no. 2 (April 1987): 117–33.

Diamond, Diane, Michael S. Kimmel, and Kirby Schroeder, "'What's This about a Few Good Men?' Negotiating Gender in Military Education." In *Masculinities at School,* ed. Nancy Lesko. London: Sage Publications, 2000.

Dobrenko, Evgeny, and Marina Balina, eds. *The Cambridge Companion to Twentieth-Century Russian Literature.* Cambridge: Cambridge University Press, 2011.

Dobson, Miriam. *Khrushchev's Cold Summer: Gulag Returnees, Crime, and the Fate of Reform after Stalin.* Ithaca, NY: Cornell University Press, 2009.

– "Building Peace, Fearing the Apocalypse? Nuclear Danger in Soviet Cold War Culture." In *Understanding the Imaginary War: Culture, Thought and Nuclear Conflict, 1945–90*, ed. Matthew Grant and Benjamin Ziemann. Manchester, UK: Manchester University Press, 2016.

Dombrowski, Nicole Ann, ed. *Women and War in the Twentieth Century: Enlisted with or without Consent*. New York and London: Garland Publishing, 1999.

Donchenko, V.N. "Demobilizatsiia sovetskoi armii i reshenie problemy kadrov v pervye poslevoennye gody." *Istoriia SSSR*, 3 (1970).

Draitser, Emil. *Making War, Not Love: Gender and Sexuality in Russian Humor*. New York: St. Martin's Press, 1999.

Dudink, Stefan, Karen Hagemann, and John Tosh, eds. *Masculinities in Politics and War: Gendering Modern History*. Manchester, UK: Manchester University Press, 2004.

Dumančić, Marko. "Rescripting Stalinist Masculinity: Contesting the Male Ideal in Soviet Film and Society, 1953–1968." PhD diss., University of North Carolina at Chapel Hill, 2010.

– "De-Stalinizing Soviet Science: Rethinking the Moral Implications of Scientific Progress in Khrushchev-Era Film." *Studies in Russian and Soviet Cinema* 6, no. 1 (2012): 75–92.

Edele, Mark. "Strange Young Men in Stalin's Moscow: The Birth and Life of the *Stiliagi*, 1945–1953." *Jahrbücher für Geschichte Osteuropas* 50, no. 1 (2002): 37–61.

– *Soviet Veterans of the Second World War: A Popular Movement in an Authoritarian Society, 1941–1991*. Oxford: Oxford University Press, 2008.

Edele, Mark, and Michael Geyer. "States of Exception: The Nazi-Soviet War as a System of Violence, 1939–1945." In *Beyond Totalitarianism: Stalinism and Nazism Compared*, ed. Michael Geyer and Sheila Fitzpatrick. Cambridge: Cambridge University Press, 2009.

Egorov, G.M. "Nadezhnyi pomoshchnik Sovetskikh Vooruzhennykh Sil (k 60-letiiu DOSAAF USSR)." *Voenno-istoricheskii zhurnal* 1 (1987): 82–7.

Eichler, Maya. *Militarizing Men: Gender, Conscription, and War in Post-Soviet Russia*. Stanford: Stanford University Press, 2012.

Ellman, Michael, and S. Maksudov. "Soviet Deaths in the Great Patriotic War: A Note." *Europe-Asia Studies* 46, no. 4 (1994): 671–80.

Enloe, Cynthia. *The Morning After: Sexual Politics at the End of the Cold War*. Berkeley: University of California Press, 1993.

Esbenshade, Richard S. "Remembering to Forget: Memory, History, and National Identity in Postwar East-Central Europe." *Representations* 49 (Winter 1995): 72–97.

Evangelista, Matthew A. "Stalin's Post-War Army Reappraised." *International Security* 7 (Winter 1982–3): 110–38.

– "'Why Keep Such an Army?' Khrushchev's Troop Reductions." *Cold War International History Project*, Working Paper no. 19 (Dec. 1997): 1–43.

Ewing, E. Thomas. "The Repudiation of Single-Sex Education: Boys' Schools in the Soviet Union, 1943–1954." *American Educational Research Journal* 43, no. 4 (Winter 2006): 621–50.

– *Separate Schools: Gender, Policy, and Practice in Postwar Soviet Education*. DeKalb: Northern Illinois University Press, 2010.

Field, Deborah A. *Private Life and Communist Morality in Khrushchev's Russia*. New York: Peter Lang, 2007.

Fisher, Ralph T. *Pattern for Soviet Youth: A Study of the Congresses of the Komsomol, 1918–1954*. New York: Columbia University Press, 1959.

Fitzpatrick, Sheila. *The Cultural Front: Power and Culture in Revolutionary Russia*. Ithaca, NY: Cornell University Press, 1992.

– *Everyday Stalinism: Ordinary Life in Extraordinary Times: Soviet Russia in the 1930s*. Oxford: Oxford University Press, 2000.

Flynn, George Q. "Conscription and Equity in Western Democracies, 1940–75." *Journal of Contemporary History* 33, no. 1 (Jan. 1998): 5–20.

– *Conscription and Democracy: The Draft in France, Great Britain, and the United States*. Westport, CT: Greenwood Press, 2002.

Freeman, Joan. *A Passion for Physics: The Story of a Woman Physicist*. New York: Taylor & Francis, 1991.

Frevert, Ute. *A Nation in Barracks: Modern Germany, Military Conscription and Civil Society*. Trans. Andres Boreham and Daniel Brückenhaus. New York: Berg, 2004.

Fulbrook, Mary, and Ulinka Rublack. "In Relation: The 'Social Self' and Ego-Documents." *German History* 28, no. 3 (2010): 263–72.

Fürst, Juliane, ed. *Late Stalinist Russia: Society between Reconstruction and Reinvention*. New York: Routledge, 2006.

– *Stalin's Last Generation: Soviet Post-War Youth and the Emergence of Mature Socialism*. Oxford: Oxford University Press, 2010.

Fürst, Juliane, and Josie McLellan, eds. *Dropping Out of Socialism: The Creation of Alternative Spheres in the Soviet Bloc*. New York: Lexington Books, 2017.

Galichenko, Nicholas. *Glasnost – Soviet Cinema Responds*. Austin: University of Texas Press, 1991.

Gerovitch, Slava. "'New Soviet Man' Inside Machine: Human Engineering, Spacecraft Design, and the Construction of Communism." *Osiris* 22 (2007): 135–57.

– "'Why Are We Telling Lies?' The Creation of Soviet Space History Myths." *Russian Review* 70, no. 3 (July 2011): 460–84.

– *Voices of the Soviet Space Program: Cosmonauts, Soldiers, and Engineers Who Took the USSR into Space.* New York: Palgrave Macmillan, 2014.

Glantz, David M. *Stumbling Colossus: The Red Army on the Eve of World War.* Lawrence: University Press of Kansas, 1998.

– *Colossus Reborn: The Red Army at War, 1941–1943.* Lawrence: University Press of Kansas, 2005.

Gobarev, Victor. "Khrushchev and the Military: Historical and Psychological Analyses." *Journal of Slavic Military Studies* 11, no. 3 (Sept. 1998): 128–44.

Goldman, Wendy Z. *Women, the State and Revolution: Soviet Family Policy and Social Life, 1917–1936.* Cambridge: Cambridge University Press, 1993.

Gorelik, Gennady, and Antonina W. Bouis. *The World of Andrei Sakharov: A Russian Physicist's Path to Freedom.* Oxford: Oxford University Press, 2005.

Gorsuch, Anne E. *All This Is Your World: Soviet Tourism at Home and Abroad after Stalin.* Oxford: Oxford University Press, 2011.

Graham, Loren R. *Science in Russia and the Soviet Union: A Short History.* Cambridge: Cambridge University Press, 1993.

Gresh, Jason P. "The Realities of Russian Military Conscription." *Journal of Slavic Military Studies* 24, no. 2 (April 2011): 185–216.

Gross, Natalie. "Youth and the Army in the USSR in the 1980s." *Soviet Studies* 42, no. 3 (July 1990): 481–98.

Halfin, Igal. *Terror in My Soul: Communist Autobiographies on Trial.* Cambridge, MA: Harvard University Press, 2003.

Harggitai, Istvan. *Buried Glory: Portraits of Soviet Scientists.* New York: Oxford University Press, 2013.

Haynes, John. *New Soviet Man: Gender and Masculinity in Stalinist Soviet Cinema.* Manchester, UK: Manchester University Press, 2003.

Healey, Dan. *Homosexual Desire in Revolutionary Russia: The Regulation of Sexual and Gender Dissent.* Chicago: University of Chicago Press, 2001.

– "Comrades, Queers and 'Oddballs': Sodomy, Masculinity and Gendered Violence in Leningrad Province of the 1950s." *Journal of the History of Sexuality* 21, no. 3 (Sept. 2012): 496–522.

– "From Stalinist Pariahs to Subjects of 'Managed Democracy': Queers in Moscow 1945 to the Present." In *Queer Cities, Queer Cultures: Europe since 1945*, ed. Matt Cook and Jennifer V. Evans. New York: Bloomsbury, 2014.

Hellbeck, Jochen. *Revolution on My Mind: Writing a Diary under Stalin.* Cambridge, MA: Harvard University Press, 2006.

Hellebust, Rolf. *Flesh to Metal: Soviet Literature and the Alchemy of Revolution*. Ithaca, NY: Cornell University Press, 2003.

Hendrickx, Bart. "The Kamanin Diaries, 1960–1963." *Journal of the British Interplanetary Society* 50 (1997): 33–40.

– "The Kamanin Diaries, 1964–1966." *Journal of the British Interplanetary Society* 51 (1998): 413–40.

Hersch, Matthew H. "Review: Francis French et al., *Into That Silent Era: Trailblazers of the Space Era, 1961–1965*." *Journal of American Culture* 30, no. 4 (Dec. 2007): 455.

Hetherington, Philippa. "Dressing the Shop Window of Socialism: Gender and Consumption in the Soviet Union in the Era of 'Cultured Trade', 1934–53." *Gender and History* 27, no. 2 (Aug. 2015): 417–45.

Higate, Paul R. *Military Masculinities: Identity and the State*. Westport, CT: Praeger, 2003.

Higham, Robin, and Frederick W. Kagan, eds. *The Military History of the Soviet Union*. New York: Palgrave, 2002.

Higonnet, Margaret Randolph, et al., eds. *Behind the Lines: Gender and the Two World Wars*. New Haven: Yale University Press, 1987.

Hilbrenner, Anke. "Soviet Women in Sports in the Brezhnev Years: The Female Body and Soviet Modernism." In *Euphoria and Exhaustion: Modern Sport in Soviet Culture and Society*, ed. Nikolaus Katzer et al. Frankfurt and New York: Campus Verlag, 2010.

Hobsbawm, Eric. "Man and Woman in Socialist Iconography." *History Workshop Journal* 6, no. 1 (Oct. 1978): 121–38.

Hoganson, Kristin L. *Fighting for American Manhood: How Gender Politics Provoked the Spanish-American and Philippine-American Wars*. New Haven: Yale University Press, 1998.

Holloway, David. "How the Bomb Saved Soviet Physics." *The Bulletin of the Atomic Scientists* 50, no. 6 (Nov.–Dec. 1994): 46–55.

– *Stalin and the Bomb: The Soviet Union and Atomic Energy, 1939–1956*. New Haven: Yale University Press, 1994.

Holmgren, Beth, ed. *The Russian Memoir: History and Literature*. Chicago: Northwestern University Press, 2003.

Hooker, Mark T. *The Military Uses of Literature: Fiction and the Armed Forces in the Soviet Union*. Westport, CT: Praeger, 1996.

Howes, Ruth H., and Caroline L. Herzenberg. *Their Day in the Sun: Women of the Manhattan Project*. Philadelphia: Temple University Press, 1999.

Hunt, Lynn. *The Family Romance of the French Revolution*. Berkeley: University of California Press, 1993.

Ilič, Melanie, and Jeremy Smith, eds. *Soviet State and Society under Nikita Khrushchev*. New York: Routledge, 2009.

Jenks, Andrew L. *The Cosmonaut Who Couldn't Stop Smiling: The Life and Legend of Yuri Gagarin*. DeKalb: Northern Illinois University Press, 2012.

Jones, Ellen. *Red Army and Society: A Sociology of the Soviet Military*. Boston: Allen & Unwin, 1985.

Jones, Polly. *Myth, Memory, Trauma: Rethinking the Stalinist Past in the Soviet Union, 1953–70*. New Haven: Yale University Press, 2013.

Joravsky, David. *The Lysenko Affair*. Cambridge, MA: Harvard University Press, 1970.

Josephson, Paul R. "Atomic-Powered Communism: Nuclear Culture in the Postwar USSR." *Slavic Review* 55, no. 2 (Summer 1996): 297–324.

– *New Atlantis Revisited: Akademgorodok, the Siberian City of Science*. Princeton, NJ: Princeton University Press, 1997.

– *Red Atom: Russia's Nuclear Power Program from Stalin to Today*. Pittsburgh: University of Pittsburgh Press, 2005.

– *Lenin's Laureate: Zhores Alferov's Life in Communist Science*. Cambridge, MA: MIT Press, 2010.

Jug, Steven. "All Stalin's Men? Soldierly Masculinities in the Soviet War Effort, 1938–1945." PhD diss., University of Illinois at Urbana–Champaign, 2013.

Junker, Detlef, ed. *The United States and Germany in the Era of the Cold War, Vol. 1*. Cambridge: Cambridge University Press, 2004.

Kaganovsky, Lilya. *How the Soviet Man Was Unmade: Cultural Fantasy and Male Subjectivity under Stalin*. Pittsburgh: University of Pittsburgh Press, 2008.

Karlinsky, Simon. "Russia's Gay Literature and Culture: The Impact of the October Revolution." In *Hidden from History: Reclaiming the Gay and Lesbian Past*, ed. Martin Bauml Duberman, Martha Vicinus, and George Chauncey Jr. New York: New American Library, 1989.

Kazanevsky, Vladimir. "The History of the Cartoon in the USSR." *Humor* 8, no. 2 (1995): 167–76.

Kelly, Catriona. *A History of Russian Women's Writing*. Oxford: Oxford University Press, 1994.

– "'Thank You for the Wonderful Book': Soviet Child Readers and the Management of Children's Reading, 1950–75." *Kritika: Explorations in Russian and Eurasian History* 6, no. 4 (Fall 2005): 717–53.

Kharkhordin, Oleg. *The Collective and the Individual in Russia: A Study of Practices*. Berkeley: University of California Press, 1999.

Khrushchev, Sergei. "Yesteryear, Yuri Gagarin's Seven Years of Glory." *Moscow News*, 15 (2001): 6.

Kimmel, Michael S. "Masculinity as Homophobia: Fear, Shame and Silence in the Construction of Gender Identity." In *Feminism and Masculinities*, ed. Peter Murphy. Oxford: Oxford University Press, 2004.

Kirschenbaum, Lisa. *Small Comrades: Revolutionizing Childhood in Soviet Russia, 1917–1932*. New York: Routledge, 2001.

Kneen, Peter. "Physics, Genetics and the Zhdanovshchina." *Europe-Asia Studies* 50, no. 7 (Nov. 1998): 1183–202.

Koblitz, Ann Hibner. *A Convergence of Lives: Sofia Kovalevskaia – Scientist, Writer, Revolutionary*. New Brunswick, NJ: Rutgers University Press, 1993.

Koenker, Diane P. "Men against Women on the Shop Floor in Early Soviet Russia: Gender and Class in the Socialist Workplace." *American Historical Review* 100, no. 5 (Dec. 1995): 1438–64.

Kojevnikov, Alexei B. *Stalin's Great Science: The Times and Adventures of Soviet Physicists*. London: Imperial College Press, 2004.

Kolkowicz, Roman. *The Soviet Military and the Communist Party*. Princeton, NJ: Princeton University Press, 1967.

Kon, Igor S. *The Sexual Revolution in Russia: From the Age of the Czars to Today*. Trans. James Riordan. New York: The Free Press, 1995.

Krementsov, Nikolai. *Stalinist Science*. Princeton, NJ: Princeton University Press, 1997.

Krylova, Anna. "'Healers of Wounded Souls': The Crisis of Private Life in Soviet Literature, 1944–1946," *Journal of Modern History* 73, no. 2 (June 2001): 307–31.

– *Soviet Women in Combat: A History of Violence on the Eastern Front*. Cambridge: Cambridge University Press, 2010.

LaPierre, Brian. *Hooligans in Khrushchev's Russia: Defining, Policing, and Producing Deviance during the Thaw*. Madison: University of Wisconsin Press, 2012.

Lathrop, Gregory L. "Soviet Civil-Military Relations: Integration on the Mass Level." PhD diss., University of Notre Dame, 1979.

Lee, Chonghoon. "Visual Stalinism from the Perspective of Heroisation: Posters, Paintings, and Illustrations in the 1930s." *Totalitarian Movements and Political Religions* 8, nos. 3–4 (Sept.–Dec. 2007): 503–21.

Lee, William T., and Richard F. Staar. *Soviet Military Policy since World War II*. Stanford: Stanford University Press, 1986.

Lewis, Cathleen. "The Red Stuff: A History of the Public and Material Culture of Early Human Spaceflight in the USSR." PhD diss., George Washington University, 2008.

Liljestrom, Marianne, Arja Rosenholm, and Irina Savkina, eds. *Models of Self: Russian Women's Autobiographical Texts*. Helsinki: Kikimora Publications, 2000.

Litvak, Olga. *Conscription and the Search for Modern Russian Jewry*. Bloomington: Indiana University Press, 2006.

Llinares, Dario. *The Astronaut: Cultural Mythology and Idealised Masculinity*. Newcastle upon Tyne: Cambridge Scholars Publishing, 2011.

Magnússon, Sigurður Gylfi. "Gender: A Useful Category in the Analysis of Ego-Documents?" *Scandinavian Journal of History* 38, no. 2 (2013): 202–22.

Mamonova, Tatiana, ed. *Women in Russia: Feminist Writings from the Soviet Union*. Boston: Beacon Press, 1984.

Marat, Erica. *The Military and the State in Central Asia: From Red Army to Independence*. New York: Routledge, 2010.

Mark, James. "Remembering Rape: Divided Social Memory and the Red Army in Hungary, 1944–1945." *Past and Present* 188 (Aug. 2005): 133–61.

Markwick, Roger D., and Euridice Charon Cardona. *Soviet Women on the Frontline in the Second World War*. New York: Palgrave Macmillan, 2012.

Maurer, Eva, et al., eds., *Soviet Space Culture: Cosmic Enthusiasm in Socialist Societies*. New York: Palgrave Macmillan, 2011.

May, Larry, Robert Strikwerda, and Patrick D. Hopkins, eds. *Rethinking Masculinity: Philosophical Explorations in Light of Feminism*. 2nd ed. London: Rowman and Littlefield, 1996.

Maynes, Mary Jo, Jennifer L. Pierce, and Barbara Laslett. *Telling Stories: The Use of Personal Narratives in the Social Sciences and History*. Ithaca, NY: Cornell University Press, 2008.

McCagg, William O. *Stalin Embattled: 1943–1948*. Detroit: Wayne State University Press, 1978.

McCallum, Claire E. "The Return: Postwar Masculinity and the Domestic Space in Stalinist Visual Culture, 1945–53." *Russian Review* 74, no. 1 (Jan. 2015): 117–43.

– "Scorched by the Fire of War: Masculinity, War Wounds and Disability in Soviet Visual Culture, 1941–65." *Slavonic and East European Review* 93, no. 2 (2015): 251–85.

– *The Fate of the New Man: Representing and Reconstructing Masculinity in Soviet Visual Culture, 1945–1965*. DeKalb: Northern Illinois University Press, 2018.

McCannon, John. "Positive Heroes at the Pole: Celebrity Status, Socialist-Realist Ideals and the Soviet Myth of the Arctic, 1932–39." *Russian Review* 56, no. 3 (July 1997): 346–65.

Medvedev, Zhores A. *Soviet Science*. New York: W.W. Norton & Company, 1978.

Merridale, Catherine. *Ivan's War: Life and Death in the Red Army, 1939–1945.* New York: Picador, 2006.

Messerschmidt, James W. "The Forgotten Victims of World War II: Masculinities and Rape in Berlin, 1945." *Violence Against Women* 12, no. 7 (July 2006): 706–12.

Middleton, Peter. *The Inward Gaze: Masculinity and Subjectivity in Modern Culture.* London: Routledge, 1992.

Milenkovitch, Michael M. *The View from Red Square: A Critique of Cartoons from Pravda and Izvestiia, 1947–1964.* New York: Hobbs, Dorman and Co., 1966.

Miller, Brandon Gray. "Between Creation and Crisis: Soviet Masculinities, Consumption, and Bodies after Stalin." PhD diss., Michigan State University, 2013.

– "The New Soviet *Narkoman*: Drugs and Youth in Post-Stalinist Russia." *Region: Regional Studies of Russia, Eastern Europe, and Central Asia* 4, no. 1 (2015): 45–69.

Molotov, V.M. *Molotov Remembers: Inside Kremlin Politics. Conversations with Felix Chuev.* Ed. Albert Resis. Chicago: Ivan R. Dee, 1993.

Morgan, David H.J. "Theater of War: Combat, the Military, and Masculinities." In *Theorizing Masculinities*, ed. Harry Brod and Michael Kaufman. Thousand Oaks, CA: Sage Publications, 1994.

Mosse, George L. *The Image of Man: The Creation of Modern Masculinity.* Oxford: Oxford University Press, 1996.

Muehlenbeck, Philip E., ed. *Gender, Sexuality, and the Cold War: A Global Perspective.* Nashville: Vanderbilt University Press, 2017.

Mühlhäuser, Regina. "Reframing Sexual Violence as a Weapon and Strategy of War: The Case of the German Wehrmacht during the War and Genocide in the Soviet Union, 1941–1944." *Journal of the History of Sexuality* 26, no. 3 (Sept. 2017): 366–401.

Mulkay, Michael. *On Humor: Its Nature and Its Place in Modern Society.* Cambridge: Polity Press, 1988.

Nadelson, Theodore. *Trained to Kill: Soldiers at War.* Baltimore: Johns Hopkins University Press, 2005.

Naiman, Eric. *Sex in Public: The Incarnation of Early Soviet Ideology.* Princeton, NJ: Princeton University Press, 1997.

Naimark, Norman M. *The Russians in Germany: A History of the Soviet Zone of Occupation, 1945–1949.* Cambridge, MA: Harvard University Press, 1995.

Nakachi, Mie. "Replacing the Dead: The Politics of Reproduction in the Postwar Soviet Union, 1944–1955." PhD diss., University of Chicago, 2009.

Nelson, William, ed. *Out of the Crocodile's Mouth: Russian Cartoons about the United States from "Krokodil," Moscow's Humor Magazine.* Washington, DC: Public Affairs Press, 1949.

Nichols, Thomas M. *The Sacred Cause: Civil-Military Conflict over Soviet National Security, 1917–1992*. Ithaca, NY: Cornell University Press, 1993.

Nielsen, Wendy C. *Women Warriors in Romantic Drama*. Newark: University of Delaware Press, 2013.

Norris, Stephen M. "The Sharp Weapon of Soviet Laughter: Boris Efimov and Visual Humor." *Russian Literature* 74, nos. 1–2 (July 2013): 31–62.

Nye, Robert. *Masculinity and Male Codes of Honor in Modern France*. New York: Oxford University Press, 1993.

– "Western Masculinities in War and Peace." *American Historical Review* 112, no. 2 (April 2007): 417–38.

Odom, William E. *The Soviet Volunteers: Modernization and Bureaucracy in a Public Mass Organization*. Princeton, NJ: Princeton University Press, 1973.

– *The Collapse of the Soviet Military*. New Haven: Yale University Press, 1998.

Okhliabinin, Sergei. *Povsednevnaia zhizn': Russkoi armii vo vremena Suvorovskykh voin*. Moscow: Molodaia gvardiia, 2004.

Oushakine, Serguei Alex. "Vidimost' muzhestvennosti." *Znamia* 2 (1999): 131–44.

–, ed. *Muzhe(N)stvennost'*. Moscow: Novoe literaturnoe obozrenie, 2002.

– "Laughter under Socialism: Exposing the Ocular in Soviet Jocularity." *Slavic Review* 70, no. 2 (Summer 2011): 247–55.

Palmer, Scott W. *Dictatorship of the Air: Aviation Culture and the Fate of Modern Russia*. Cambridge: Cambridge University Press, 2006.

Paperno, Irina. "Personal Accounts of the Soviet Experience." *Kritika: Explorations in Russian and Eurasian History* 3, no. 4 (Fall 2002): 577–610.

– *Stories of the Soviet Experience: Memoirs, Diaries, Dreams*. Ithaca, NY: Cornell University Press, 2009.

Pennington, Reina. "'Do Not Speak of the Services You Rendered': Women Veterans of Aviation in the Soviet Union." *Journal of Slavic Military Studies* 9, no. 1 (March 1996): 120–51.

– *Wings, Women, and War: Soviet Airwomen in World War II Combat*. Lawrence: University of Kansas Press, 2002.

Petrone, Karen. *Life Has Become More Joyous, Comrades: Celebrations in the Time of Stalin*. Bloomington: Indiana University Press, 2000.

– *The Great War in Russian Memory*. Bloomington: Indiana University Press, 2011.

Phillips, Sarah D. "'There Are No Invalids in the USSR!': A Missing Soviet Chapter in the New Disability History." *Disability Studies Quarterly* 29, no. 3 (2009).

Pipes, Richard. "Militarism and the Soviet State." *Daedalus* 109, no. 4 (Fall 1980): 1–12.

Pollock, Ethan. *Stalin and the Soviet Science Wars*. Princeton, NJ: Princeton University Press, 2006.

– "'Real Men Go to the Bania': Postwar Soviet Masculinities and the Bathhouse." *Kritika: Explorations in Russian and Eurasian History* 11, no.1 (Winter 2010): 47–76.

Raleigh, Donald J., ed. *Russia's Sputnik Generation: Soviet Baby Boomers Talk about Their Lives.* Bloomington: Indiana University Press, 2006.

Rassell, Michael, and Elena Iarskaia-Smirnova, eds. *Disability in Eastern Europe and the Former Soviet Union: History, Policy and Everyday Life.* New York: Routledge, 2014.

Reese, Roger R. *Stalin's Reluctant Soldiers: A Social History of the Red Army, 1925–1941.* Lawrence: University Press of Kansas, 1996.

– *The Soviet Military Experience: A History of the Soviet Army, 1917–1991.* New York: Routledge, 2000.

– *Red Commanders: A Social History of the Soviet Army Officer Corps, 1918–1991.* Lawrence: University Press of Kansas, 2005.

Reid, Susan E. "Masters of the Earth: Gender and Destalinisation in Soviet Reformist Painting of the Khrushchev Thaw." *Gender and History* 11, no. 2 (July 1999): 276–312.

Rich, David Alan. *The Tsar's Colonels: Professionalism, Strategy, and Subversion in Late Imperial Russia.* Cambridge, MA: Harvard University Press, 1998.

Roberts, Mary Louise. *Civilization without Sexes: Reconstructing Gender in Postwar France, 1917–1927.* Chicago: University of Chicago Press, 1994.

– *What Soldiers Do: Sex and the American GI in World War II France.* Chicago: University of Chicago Press, 2013.

– "Beyond 'Crisis' in Understanding Gender Transformation." *Gender and History* 28, no. 2 (Aug. 2016): 358–66.

Robertshaw, Sam. "Voluntary Organizations and Society-Military Relations in Contemporary Russia." *European Security* 24, no. 2 (2015): 304–18.

Röger, Maren, and Ruth Leiserowitz, eds. *Women and Men at War: A Gender Perspective on World War II and Its Aftermath in Central and Eastern Europe.* Osnabrück: Fibre-Verlag, 2012.

Roper, Michael. *Masculinity and the British Organization Man since 1945.* Oxford: Oxford University Press, 1994.

Roper, Michael, and John Tosh, eds. *Manful Assertions: Masculinities in Britain since 1800.* New York: Routledge, 1991.

Rosenblum, Nancy L. "Romantic Militarism." *Journal of the History of Ideas* 43, no. 2 (April–June 1982): 249–68.

Sanborn, Joshua A. *Drafting the Russian Nation: Military Conscription, Total War, and Mass Politics, 1905–1925.* DeKalb: Northern Illinois University Press, 2003.

Schmid, Sonja D. "Celebrating Tomorrow Today: The Peaceful Atom on Display in the Soviet Union." *Social Studies of Science* 36, no. 3 (2006): 331–65.

Scott, Harriet Fast. "Soviet Military Doctrine in the Nuclear Age, 1945–85." In *Soviet Military Doctrine from Lenin to Gorbachev, 1915–1991*, ed. Willard C. Frank Jr. and Philip S. Gillette. Westport, CT: Greenwood Press, 1992.

Scott, Harriet Fast, and William F. Scott. *The Armed Forces of the USSR*. Boulder, CO: Westview Press, 1984.

Scott, Joan W. "Gender: A Useful Category of Historical Analysis." *American Historical Review* 91, no. 5 (Dec. 1986): 1053–75.

– "Unanswered Questions." *American Historical Review* 113 no. 5 (Dec. 2008): 1422–9.

Scott, L.V. *Conscription and the Attlee Governments: The Politics and Policy of National Service, 1945–1951*. Oxford: Oxford University Press, 1993.

Shepilov, Dmitrii. *The Kremlin's Scholar: A Memoir of Soviet Politics under Stalin and Khrushchev*. Ed. Stephen V. Bittner. Trans. Anthony Austin. New Haven: Yale University Press, 2007.

Siddiqi, Asif. *Challenge to Apollo: The Soviet Union and the Space Race, 1945–1974*. Washington, DC: NASA History Division, 2000.

– *The Red Rockets' Glare: Spaceflight and the Soviet Imagination, 1857–1957*. Cambridge: Cambridge University Press, 2010.

– "The Sharashka Phenomenon." *Russian History Blog*, 10 March 2011. http://russianhistoryblog.org/2011/03/the-sharashka-phenomenon.

– "Scientists and Specialists in the Gulag: Life and Death in Stalin's *Sharashka*." *Kritika: Explorations in Russian and Eurasian History* 16, no. 3 (Summer 2015): 557–88.

Siddiqi, Asif A., and James T. Andrews, eds. *Into the Cosmos: Space Exploration and Soviet Culture*. Pittsburgh: University of Pittsburgh Press, 2011.

Slezkine, Yuri. *The Jewish Century*. Princeton, NJ: Princeton University Press, 2004.

Snyder, R. Claire. *Citizen-Soldiers and Manly Warriors: Military Service and Gender in the Civic Republican Tradition*. Oxford: Rowman & Littlefield, 1999.

Soifer, Valerii N. *Lysenko and the Tragedy of Soviet Science*. Trans. Leo Gruliow and Rebecca Gruliow. New Brunswick, NJ: Rutgers University Press, 1994.

*Sovetskaia voennaia entsiklopediia*. Vol. 3. Moscow: Voenizdat, 1976–1980.

Spackman, Barbara. *Fascist Virilities: Rhetoric, Ideology, and Social Fantasy in Italy*. Minneapolis: University of Minnesota Press, 1996.

Spivak, Andrew L., and William Alex Pridemore. "Conscription and Reform in the Russian Army." *Problems of Post-Communism* 51, no. 6 (Nov.–Dec. 2004): 33–43.

Steans, Jill. *Gender and International Relations: An Introduction*. New Brunswick, NJ: Rutgers University Press, 1998.

Stites, Richard. *The Women's Liberation Movement in Russia: Feminism, Nihilism, and Bolshevism, 1860–1930*. Princeton, NJ: Princeton University Press, 1991.

Stone, David. *Hammer and Rifle: The Militarization of the Soviet Union, 1926–1933*. Lawrence: University Press of Kansas, 2000.

Swearingen, Rodger. *What's So Funny, Comrade?* New York: Praeger, 1961.

Swider, Raymond J. *Soviet Military Reform in the Twentieth Century: Three Case Studies*. New York: Greenwood Press, 1992.

Sylvester, Roshanna. "Russian Space History – Dreams in Orbit." *Russian History Blog*, 9 Dec. 2013. http://russianhistoryblog.org/2013/12/russian-space-history-dreams-in-orbit-3/.

– "'Even Though I Am a Girl …': John Glenn's Fan Mail and Sexism in the Early Space Program." *The Conversation*, 12 Dec. 2016. https://theconversation.com/even-though-i-am-a-girl-john-glenns-fan-mail-and-sexism-in-the-early-space-program-70252.

Tavernier-Courbin, Jacqueline. "Humor Is a Serious Matter." *Thalia: Studies in Literary Humor* 8, no. 2 (Fall/Winter 1985): 13–20.

Theweleit, Klaus. *Male Fantasies*. Trans. Stephen Conway. Minneapolis: University of Minnesota Press, 1987.

Thorpe, Charles. *Oppenheimer: The Tragic Intellect*. Chicago: University of Chicago Press, 2006.

Todorova, Maria, and Zsuzsa Gille, eds. *Post-Communist Nostalgia*. New York: Berghahn Books, 2010.

Toker, Leona. *Return from the Archipelago: Narratives of Gulag Survivors*. Bloomington: Indiana University Press, 2000.

Tsipursky, Gleb. *Socialist Fun: Youth, Consumption, and State-Sponsored Popular Culture in the Cold War Soviet Union, 1945–1970*. Pittsburgh: University of Pittsburgh Press, 2017.

Tucker, Janet G., ed. *Against the Grain: Parody, Satire, and Intertextuality in Russian Literature*. Bloomington: Slavica, 2002.

Tumarkin, Nina. *The Living and the Dead: The Rise and Fall of the Cult of World War II in Russia*. New York: Basic Books, 1994.

Varga-Harris, Christine. *Stories of House and Home: Soviet Apartment Life during the Khrushchev Years*. Ithaca, NY: Cornell University Press, 2015.

Viola, Lynne. *Peasant Rebels under Stalin: Collectivization and the Culture of Peasant Resistance*. Oxford: Oxford University Press, 1996.

Vizgin, V.P. "Fenomen 'kul'ta atoma' v SSSR (1950–1960-e gg.)." In *Istoriia sovetskogo atomnogo proekta: Dokumenty, vospominaniia, issledovaniia*, ed. V.P. Vizgin. St. Petersburg: Institut istorii estestvoznaniia i tekhniki, 2002.

Von Hagen, Mark. *Soldiers in the Proletarian Dictatorship: The Red Army and the Soviet Socialist State, 1917–1930*. Ithaca, NY: Cornell University Press, 1990.

Vucinich, Alexander. *Empire of Knowledge: The Academy of Sciences of the USSR, 1917–1970*. Berkeley: University of California Press, 1984.

Waters, Elizabeth. "The Female Form in Soviet Political Iconography, 1917–32." In *Russia's Women: Accommodation, Resistance, Transformation*, ed. Barbara Evans Clements, Barbara Alpern Engel, and Christine D. Worobec. Berkeley: University of California Press, 1991.

Weiner, Amir. *Making Sense of War: The Second World War and the Fate of the Bolshevik Revolution*. Princeton, NJ: Princeton University Press, 2001.

Weitekamp, Margaret A. "The 'Astronautrix' and the 'Magnificent Male': Jerrie Cobb's Quest to Be the First Woman in America's Manned Space Program." In *Impossible to Hold: Women and Culture in the 1960s*, ed. Avital H. Bloch and Lauri Umansky. New York: New York University Press, 2005.

Werth, Alexander. *Russia: The Post-War Years*. New York: Taplinger, 1971.

White, Stephen. *The Bolshevik Poster*. New Haven: Yale University Press, 1988.

Woll, Josephine. *Real Images: Soviet Cinema and the Thaw*. New York: I.B. Tauris, 2000.

– *The Cranes Are Flying: The Film Companion*. London and New York: I.B. Tauris, 2003.

Wood, Elizabeth A. *The Baba and the Comrade: Gender and Politics in Revolutionary Russia*. Bloomington: Indiana University Press, 1997.

Yekelchyk, Serhy. "The Civic Duty to Hate: Stalinist Citizenship as Political Practice and Civic Emotion (Kiev, 1943–53)." *Kritika: Explorations in Russian and Eurasian History* 7, no. 3 (Summer 2006): 529–56.

Youngblood, Denise. *Russian War Films: On the Cinema Front, 1914–2005*. Lawrence: University Press of Kansas, 2007.

Yurchak, Alexei. "Gagarin and the Rave Kids: Transforming Power, Identity, and Aesthetics in Post-Soviet Nightlife." In *Consuming Russia: Popular Culture, Sex, and Society since Gorbachev*, ed. Adele Marie Barker. Durham, NC: Duke University Press, 1999.

Yusupova, Marina. "Shifting Masculine Terrains: Russian Men in Russia and the UK." PhD diss., University of Manchester, 2016.

Zubkova, Elena. *Russia after the War: Hopes, Illusions, and Disappointments, 1945–1957*. Trans. Hugh Ragsdale. New York: M.E. Sharpe, 1998.

Zubok, Vladislav. *Zhivago's Children: The Last Russian Intelligentsia*. Cambridge, MA: Harvard University Press, 2009.

# Index